INCARNATING GRACE

Incarnating Grace

A THEOLOGY OF HEALING FROM SEXUAL TRAUMA

Julia Feder

FORDHAM UNIVERSITY PRESS   NEW YORK 2024

Portions of Chapters 2 and 3 were originally published as "The Body and Posttraumatic Healing: A Teresian Approach," *Journal of Moral Theology* 9, no. 1 (January 2020): 75–97.

Copyright © 2024 Fordham University Press

All rights reserved. No part of this publication may be reproduced, stored in a retrieval system, or transmitted in any form or by any means—electronic, mechanical, photocopy, recording, or any other—except for brief quotations in printed reviews, without the prior permission of the publisher.

Fordham University Press has no responsibility for the persistence or accuracy of URLs for external or third-party Internet websites referred to in this publication and does not guarantee that any content on such websites is, or will remain, accurate or appropriate.

Fordham University Press also publishes its books in a variety of electronic formats. Some content that appears in print may not be available in electronic books.

Visit us online at www.fordhampress.com.

Library of Congress Cataloging-in-Publication Data available online at https://catalog.loc.gov.

Printed in the United States of America
26 25 24   5 4 3 2 1
First edition

*To my mother, my first theology teacher,
and my children, for whom I hope*

Contents

FOREWORD BY DONNA FREITAS   ix

Introduction: Saving Grace   1

1. Salvation as Mystical-Political Healing   7
2. Teresa of Avila: A Saint for Survivors   27
3. Teresa's Embodied Anthropology   49
4. The Survivor as *Imago Dei*: Created for Friendship   69
5. Edward Schillebeeckx's Theology of Suffering   90
6. The Story of Jesus and the Mystical-Political Shape of Salvation   103
7. Courage in the Work of Posttraumatic Healing   122
8. Recovery and Hope   152

Conclusion: A Theology of Healing   165

ACKNOWLEDGMENTS   181

NOTES   183

INDEX   235

Foreword
Donna Freitas

In graduate school, I became obsessed with medieval women mystics, particularly Teresa of Avila. I wrote my dissertation on mystical theology as feminist liberation theology, and I wondered if reading women mystics through the lens of liberation theology might be transformative, not only for suffering, but toward the end of human flourishing.

While I was doing this work, I was also living through one of the greatest violations of consent I would ever experience, via one of my graduate professors. This left me searching for hope and healing among the mystics for so many reasons, both theological and personal—for our world today, for women, for the vulnerable among us, but also on my own behalf, as I sought a way through and out of this particular darkness.

Julia Feder is also searching for hope and healing among the mystics.

The area of sexual assault, trauma, and healing—especially within the context of theology and spirituality—is a domain that many scholars still hesitate to enter. Yet, in Feder's *Incarnating Grace*, she draws on the writings of Teresa of Avila and Edward Schillebeeckx in order to step into this much-needed, oft-ignored space. In the aftermath of sexual violence, we often work to heal the body and the mind but forget the soul; the trauma done to our relationship with God. How someone who suffers this kind of violence against their person may enter a long, *Dark Night of the Soul* from which they never emerge. In the pages that follow, Feder not only does *not* forget, she seeks for us a way out of the dark night. She boldly stands at the heart of this struggle to make sense of something that, as Feder writes, is always "senseless." She assures us that she has not forgotten our souls. She shares with us why this topic, to her, is also personal.

"Healing from sexual trauma is a mystical-political practice," Feder writes. "That is to say, it is a process (often lifelong) that involves the reparation of one's relationship with God and one's relationships with one's communities."

Feder's eye on Teresa and Schillebeeckx is always critical, showing us where these thinkers may empower us toward healing and where their ideas may prove problematic to sexual assault and misconduct. In other words, we are in good, careful hands with Feder. In the vein of the political, a quiet resistance on Feder's part is evident here—but it is also clear. She is speaking to that which is so often silenced by asking these profound voices from the past to minister to us in the now.

As a woman, a survivor, and a scholar of religion and theology today, Feder's writing, and work is an exciting leap forward in a space where so many of us hesitate to tread; yet which is also one of the places in theology we most need to go. How lucky for scholars and students, searching for resources that expand beyond the psychology of trauma and healing, that Feder has so carefully considered those subjects central to so many of us—our relationships with God, prayer, and spirituality—and the specific challenges sexual trauma poses to our hearts and souls.

If only Feder's wonderful *Incarnating Grace* had been available when I was a graduate student. This book would have been one of the most important of my education. I wonder how my life—and my lens for seeing abuse and confronting it—might have been different if I'd had Feder's voice and words to accompany my scholarly journey through the mystics, and especially my attempts to heal on a personal level.

Would I have felt less alone?

I believe the answer is *yes*.

INCARNATING GRACE

Introduction
Saving Grace

Over the past seven years, I have introduced nearly one thousand freshmen to the history and theology of the Christian tradition. When I began teaching, I assumed that my students, the majority of whom happened to be pre-health majors, would be most engaged in the portion of the course that analyzes the relationship between faith and science. But I quickly discovered that my students are much more interested in the more basic, less abstract—and, inevitably, more personal—human questions about suffering: Why have I experienced suffering? If I pray enough, will God protect me from suffering? Does God want us to suffer? Can suffering bring us closer to God?

Sometimes I show my students a crafted bookmark that belonged to my mother in the early 1960s. I found it lodged between the pages of an old prayer book that she had passed down to me. The bookmark is a small rectangle of cream paper with a red foil backing. A cutout picture of Jesus pointing to his heart is pasted in the corner and underneath, in gold script, reads, "Do not fear suffering for by enduring it you can increase My glory and repair the sins of the world." This sentiment still feels familiar to my students, who were raised in Christian households, fifty years later.

When I think about my mother who held this bookmark as she prayed in a church pew in South Philadelphia, while at the same time was being sexually abused in her own home, I know that the Christian tradition has failed terribly. It has failed her, and so many other survivors who somehow received the message that traumatic suffering is a vehicle for God's saving grace. Violence does not add to God's glory. It is only the posttraumatic healing process that is salvific.

Acts of sexual violence are horrific. Those who have experienced sexual violence firsthand often suffer from its enduring effects daily. Many who have encountered sexual violence secondhand, through a personal relationship with a victim-survivor or simply in (often benevolent) warnings that perpetrators could be lurking "anywhere," live with the anxiety of protecting themselves and their loved ones. Sexual violence disorients the seer and rings in the ear of the hearer.

Those who experience the horror of sexual violence (either directly or indirectly) know that violent sexual acts defy the natural order. The sexual violation of the bodies of children and teens threatens a basic human instinct to protect and nurture youth, and the coercion of adults against their will into sexual acts distorts (what can feel like) the natural beauty and easy joy of sexual coupling. The feeling of "unnaturalness" that accompanies sexual violence is what, in part, contemporary Christian thinkers mean when they talk about extreme suffering as "senseless."[1] The suffering of sexual violence serves no higher purpose or greater human value. This kind of suffering defies all ways of making sense of the world as good and orderly.

And yet, it would not be accurate to describe acts of sexual violence as against the natural order, if this claim is that they are exceptional or rare. More than half of women and almost one in three men in the United States describe themselves as having experienced sexual violence involving physical contact at some time in their lives.[2] And sexual exploitation need not involve physical contact to be profoundly damaging to the victim. The case of Daniel Kenney, a Jesuit priest and high school teacher who coerced more than fifteen students and other minors in his care to disrobe, sometimes in the context of the sacrament of confession, is a case in point.[3] Though Kenney did not touch his victims, survivors report enduring shame. One survivor, Erik, recounts:

> "It's just going to sit there in a box and pop out like every year or so,
> and I'll never get rid of it. I ignore it and forget about it for a while.
> But it's always (there). It's like this monster in my basement."[4]

What we once thought of as uncommon,[5] we now know to be quite ordinary. Sexual violence is a salient feature of our common life together. It is widespread in our schools, our churches, and our homes.

In the Christian tradition, "salvation" is the restoration of wholeness. Because sexual violence profoundly threatens human wholeness, posttraumatic healing is a matter of human salvation. Posttraumatic healing restores the relationships that have been damaged by sexual violence—the relationships that the survivor has with herself, with others, with the institutions in which she is embedded, and with God.

Healing from sexual trauma is a mystical-political practice. That is to say, it is a process (often lifelong) that involves the reparation of one's relationship with God and one's relationships with one's communities. This mystical-political practice is both incarnational and eschatological.

By "incarnational," I mean that posttraumatic healing is fully enfleshed and human. It is embodied and contextual, conditioned by history and circumstance, and—by virtue of God's full embrace of human life and circumstance in the person of Jesus Christ—pregnant with God.

By "eschatological," I mean that it is partial and incomplete, requiring assistance from God and insufficient on its own terms, yet not desperately or depressingly so. In the Christian tradition, the incomplete and failing state of things is not the final word. And because the Christian story is a story of the persistence of relationships in the face of violence, this tradition contains rich resources to animate the mystical-political shape of posttraumatic healing.

Before laying out these resources in Chapters 3 through 8, I will describe the breadth of traumatic wounding and the shape of traumatic recovery as articulated by psychologists. I argue, however, that the fullness of posttraumatic healing requires reserves deeper than that which can be articulated by the secular field of psychology alone. Healing requires hope, solidly grounded in the genuine expectation that transformation is possible through God's creative work and our free, creative, and courageous cooperation. Hope sustains survivors and their allies in imagining the impossible. Hope gives them the energy that they need to persevere in the long and slow work of personal, interpersonal, and socio-political recovery.

Throughout this book, I will prioritize survivors' stories of traumatic wounding and healing. While this gives us the benefit of hearing from survivors in their own words, it may also be overwhelming to read the details of another's abuse. To warn the reader of the presence of potentially disturbing details, I have set all survivors' stories off in block, indented quotations. I hope that this will provide the reader with options: to skip over potentially disturbing details or to engage more deeply, depending on the reader's intellectual, psychological, and spiritual needs.

In Chapter 2, I will introduce the reader to Teresa of Avila, the sixteenth-century Spanish mystic who critiqued her society's obsession with honor and class distinction and had a spiritual vision of the embodied human person as the *Imago Dei* and friend of God. Laying out a biographical sketch of the Carmelite saint that highlights her political and social context allows us to understand Teresa as one who offers the survivor not only a mystical vision of posttraumatic healing, but also a vision of social and political posttraumatic healing: a transformation of her culture's patriarchal exchange of women's bodies as objects, into networked communities of female friendship and mutual care. Teresa can, thus, offer us a generative starting point for a mystical-political theology of posttraumatic healing.

Chapters 3 and 4 set out Teresa's theological insights, which are most helpful for constructing a posttraumatic theology of healing; the human person as embodied, created in the image of God, and oriented toward friendship. Teresa's understanding of the human person as the *Imago Dei* clearly names the human person as possessive of an inherent beauty that, on the one hand, should be preserved and held sacred through precious care, yet, on the other, cannot be destroyed by maltreatment. Because the human person is fully embodied, and union with God represents the fullness of bodily integration (rather than transcendence of the body), care for bodies (one's own and vulnerable others') is integral to sacred fidelity to God.

However, Teresa can suggest, at times, that experiences of suffering present opportunities to serve God. She risks suggesting that God desires human suffering. In the context of sexual violence, no suggestion could be more damaging to survivors. Rape is senseless suffering—never desired by God or productive of any good in the human person. God does not desire any person to suffer rape in order to "learn a lesson," avoid a greater suffering, or grow closer to God. Rape is pointless evil. Teresa's thought needs the correction of contemporary theologians who have thought carefully about the absurdity of evil.

The reader will notice that the idea that sexual violence is senseless suffering is a refrain repeated in every chapter of this text. The notion of "senseless suffering" is a technical term that comes from Edward Schillebeeckx, a twentieth-century Catholic Flemish priest and theologian. I will turn explicitly to his thought in Chapters 5 and 6. Schillebeeckx can remind us that if God is worthy of worship, then God does not will human suffering and does not use suffering as a tool to bring about salvation. God is not disclosed in the crosses of our experiences, but rather beside our crosses as an indignant witness. God is neither behind abuse, animating it; nor above abuse, indifferent to it. Instead, God is closely present to the victim-survivor, making the absence of human goodness known to her.

In Chapters 7 and 8, I will turn to two Christian virtues that can animate posttraumatic healing—courage and hope. In Chapter 7, I offer a reflection on courage in the work of posttraumatic recovery. Because of the long, comprehensive, and arduous nature of posttraumatic healing, many trauma psychologists have noted the importance of courage in the work of posttraumatic recovery. Secular trauma theorists recognize that healing relies, in part, upon courageous action taken by survivors, empowered by a hope for the future, to pursue healing. Continued suffering is a component of the healthy process of healing. In the context of sexual violence, courage is a commitment to healing, however long, comprehensive, and arduous this process might become. Jesus models this kind of courage, not as a willing suffering servant, but as one who resists the violence of the Roman Empire and assigns his own meaning to his life and work.

In Chapter 8, I argue that Christian hope can provide a language to empower courageous activity undertaken toward healing that authentically expects something new but is also grounded in a realistic understanding of human capacities. The language of Christian eschatological hope is able to hold in tension what we can accomplish (with God), and an awareness that the fullness of healing has still not yet arrived. A Christian eschatological vision expands the grounds for human hope beyond the limits of human achievement, such that we can affirm the fragmentary and partial achievements of personal, interpersonal, and socio-political healing as mediations of God's promise of salvation without restricting our imaginative vision merely to what appears possible through human ends. This allows us to lift up small successes as participation in bringing about God's desire for the world—for example, extending statutes of limitations for prosecuting sexual abuse crimes against minors—while still holding onto far-flung visions of a world in which rape is unthinkable and prosecution guidelines are unnecessary.

I conclude with a reflection on my hope that Christians can stop talking about traumatic suffering as a vehicle for God's saving grace. Instead, God's grace is operative in, and through, the process of healing from everything that wounds us. These processes are at once mystical and political since they draw us closer to God and they transform our collective lives. We have yet to experience the fullness of posttraumatic healing—full freedom from the grip of rape culture. We wait for this transformation in hope. And while we wait, we mourn, we protest, and we imagine a new future with courage.

1
Salvation as Mystical-Political Healing

In order to develop a posttraumatic theology of healing, we will first need to examine how sexual trauma wounds us at all levels of human life—the personal, the material, the interpersonal, the social-political, and the spiritual. Because it is often difficult to notice the ways in which sexual violence formally structures our shared lives, we will devote special attention to an analysis of rape culture. Recovery from sexual violence requires the establishment of safety, remembrance and mourning, and reconnection with community. The breadth and depth of all that is in need of healing requires reserves deeper, and more comprehensive, than can be articulated by the secular field of psychology alone. Posttraumatic healing is a mystical-political practice which is both eschatological and incarnational. It is "eschatological" insofar as there is much healing within our human reach, but the fullness of comprehensive healing still runs out ahead of us. And it is "incarnational" insofar as recovery never erases pain, but instead transforms it into new life. An incarnational account of healing relies on a transformational model of resurrection.

Sexual Trauma

Trauma is, broadly speaking, the state of being overwhelmed, physically as well as psychologically, by an external threat of annihilation or total destruction. The effects of traumatic violence are far-reaching: both the psyche and the body are negatively affected by the act of violence. Traumatic wounding can damage the wholeness of the human person on multiple levels: materially-personally, interpersonally, socially, and spiritually.

On the personal-material level, traumatic violence can block the victim's attention to the present and the new. Because the traumatized individual is giving her attention to the past traumatic event, she encounters difficulties when responding to new perceptions that are *unrelated* to the original traumatic event. If the new perception does have some relationship to the original traumatic memory, such as a similar smell or sound, the new perception can trigger the past traumatic memory, and the victim's response to this new event is a replayed reaction to the old event.[1]

Traumatic triggers can easily overwhelm survivors so that they become accustomed to "life happening *to* them,"[2] rather than exercising their own agency in organizing their world (even in the most mundane matters, such as keeping to a schedule or securing a job). This lack of agency in everyday life mirrors the lack of a sense of agency in the original traumatic encounter(s).[3] The original traumatic event, as an experience of helplessness, endures in continued experiences of disempowerment throughout one's posttraumatic life. Trauma survivors struggle to secure a sense of their own bodily integrity, a foundation for positive self-esteem, and a basic degree of autonomy and/or individual competence.[4]

On the interpersonal level, sexual trauma can present barriers to healthy adult relationships, especially healthy sexual relationships. Researchers have identified a correlation between sexual abuse (especially in childhood) and risky sexual behaviors later in life, such as a higher number of sexual partners and less condom use,[5] higher rates of marital separation, as well as higher rates of self-reported dissatisfaction in sexually intimate relationships.[6] In non-sexual human relationships, interpersonal challenges persist. Traumatized individuals often struggle to maintain healthy boundaries with others and to maintain a sense of their own desires as distinct (and, in some cases, conflicting) from the desires of another.[7]

On a social-political level, sexual trauma can work to dismantle trust in the fundamental structures of human-social organizations, such as the family, educational structures, or religious institutions. In her description of the torture of political prisoners, literary theorist Elaine Scarry offers an image that might also be illuminating in considering the long-term effects of domestic abuse.

> The room, both in its structure and its content, is converted into a weapon, deconverted, undone. Made to participate in the annihilation of the prisoners, made to demonstrate that everything is a weapon, the objects themselves, and with them the fact of civilization, are annihilated: there is no wall, no window, no door, no bathtub, no refrigerator, no chair, no bed.[8]

Transformed from safe objects which protect the individual from the elements, disease, and hunger, the symbols of the home become symbols of terror and violence. Because sexual abuse often occurs in the home, in the context of the family or the familiar,[9] sexual trauma can unravel the domestic realm itself. Scarry argues that this is ultimately an "unmaking of civilization" for the domestic is the "ground of all making."[10] The pain and damage of violence extends well beyond the event itself into the reality that this (these) event(s) has undone one's very sense of security in the world.

In the case of traumatized individuals, it is, perhaps truer than in any other instance, that the personal (i.e., the domestic) is the political. What happens in the family affects the social-political realm overall. Psychiatrist Judith Herman argues, "Rape and combat might thus be considered complementary social rites of initiation into the coercive violence at that foundation of adult society."[11] The habitual violation of the bodies of those who are vulnerable in society creates a sense of normalcy surrounding grave acts of injustice such that they become part of the fabric of the ordinary social order.[12]

On a spiritual-religious level, sexual trauma inevitably transforms the way its victims understand the relationship of God to created reality. After an experience of violence where individuals had once perceived the world as a safe place, they may now question their safety and the safety of those they love. Where individuals once perceived God as a protective figure, they may now perceive God as indifferent to human suffering, or perhaps even as one who is in the business of punishing unatoned sins with violence. For some, who have never experienced safety, a threatening or distant vision of God is all that might have ever been at play in their spiritual imagination.

Sexual trauma can affect religious belief in a multitude of ways, but at least one study shows that only a *small* percentage of individuals become *more* religious following sexual trauma. It is much more likely that sexual trauma generates greater secularization.[13] Because strong supportive relationships are critical to the recovery process, secularization (particularly if increased social isolation accompanies it) can create barriers to recovery. For the minority who react to sexual abuse with intensified religious practice, it tends to be a source of external engagement and distraction, rather than a tool for examining the self in a deeper fashion.[14]

Not all victims suffer from the full range of traumatic symptoms described here. The *kind* of sexual violence experienced,[15] the *context* in which traumatic violence was originally encountered,[16] and the *profile* of the victim herself (age, sex, prior mental health, genetic predisposition, etc.)[17] all influence the degree of persistent traumatic wounding. Subjective characteristics of the perception of the event, as well as others' reactions when the victim expresses what has happened to her, contribute to the degree of traumatic wounding.[18] Some researchers suggest that the risk for developing severe PTSD is better predicted, not through exposure to a focal traumatic event, as much as through cumulative exposure to trauma, including the general accrual of "cumulative stress."[19] The cumulative stress of living in a sexist, racist, or homophobic society puts women, people of color, and queer people at greater risk of developing sexual trauma in response to sexual violence. To describe this cumulative effect of negative stress endured over time, trauma theorists have developed the terms "chronic trauma" or "insidious trauma."[20] In chronically traumatic social environments, traumatic symptoms such as victim-blaming, isolation, and loss of social status are maintained through everyday experiences of discrimination and dehumanization.[21] Rather than a dramatic interruption of violence that shatters an otherwise intact worldview, insidious trauma often shapes one's worldview from birth, according to experiences of constant violence.[22] For example, philosopher Theresa Tobin argues that doctrinal misogyny in the Roman Catholic Church functions as a chronically traumatic kind of "quiet violence" that erodes one's agency beginning from birth and building momentum over the course of one's life.[23] Insidious trauma is experienced by individuals, but it is directed at whole communities or groups of people whose intrinsic identity is socially devalued (e.g., women, queer people, people of color, etc.).[24]

Rape Culture

Feminist theorists have argued that contemporary American culture, writ large, has so normalized and even encouraged sexual violence that it can be understood as a "rape culture." American rape culture, along with most cultures around the world, conditions women and other marginalized sexual identities to be vulnerable to sexual violence and cumulative traumatic stress. In rape culture, the threat of rape significantly contributes to the cultural construction of identity for those who are non-dominant. As journalist Susan Brownmiller argued in 1975, rape has functioned as a "conscious process of intimidation by which *all men* keep *all women* in a state of fear."[25] The threat of rape also functions to intimidate other socially vulnerable individuals—queer people, threatening to enforce norms of gender conformity,[26] people of color,[27] and undocumented individuals— communicating that their bodies are the property of others.[28] The threat of rape functions socially to reify hierarchies of power and submission. This has a terrorizing effect in which one does not have to be raped in order to be marked by rape.

The fear of rape organizes women and other nondominant people's lives in significant ways, determining how they live and move in their bodies on a daily basis. It coerces women and other socially nondominant individuals into dependence upon dominant men (understood as their only means for protection), ironically enforcing relationships of obligation that can then function as the grounds for violent treatment by these guardian men. As survivor and psychotherapist Audrey Savage puts it in her fictionalized dialogue between a mother and daughter:

> Daughter (Furrowing her brow): I'm not sure I understand. From what you say, it would seem that father and brother are no different than the men I need to be afraid of—the men you said I needed to protect myself against.
> Mother (Horrified): Oh, yes, they are! They are here to protect us.
> Daughter: Now I'm really confused. You say that there are men out there that will hurt me; and father and brother will protect me from those men. But then you say that father and brother have decided that I am an inferior being; and if I say differently they will hurt me. . .
> Mother: Yes. First of all, as an inferior being, you must find a man to protect you. You must always have a man to protect you. You are not safe at any time unless you have a man to protect you.
> Daughter: I must find a man to protect me and be with me at all times.
> Mother: Yes, and in order to have this man to protect you, there are certain things you must do. First, you must be beautiful. That means you must spend most of your time being sure you are beautiful. You must buy the best and most expensive clothes, clothes that will make him pay attention to you. You must keep your hair in ways that he will like. You must make up your face so it is extra pretty, and so he won't see anything about you that he might not like. And most of all, you must stay thin. Men won't like you and they won't protect you if you get fat. Do you understand all of that?[29]

The threat of rape "forms a kind of backdrop for daily, even seemingly trivial, decisions"[30] including how one might exercise, what jewelry one might wear,[31] how one might sit down[32], or who one decides to go to happy hour with after work. Journalist Shanita Hubbard describes her childhood experience of walking home from school, passing a corner where men tended to congregate, as a lesson in getting acculturated to terror.

> On this intersection, like so many others in the world, your body and your sense of safety were both up for grabs. On a good day, if you and a

girlfriend remained silent, walking past the group of "corner dudes," who were all about 15 years your senior and screaming about what they would do to your 12-year-old body, would be a short-lived experience. On other days, especially if you were walking alone, things would escalate quickly. One of the men would grab your butt and you would pretend you didn't feel it. Fighting back would make things worse: If you resisted, they would scream at you, curse at you and, in one particular case, attempt to follow you home until you ran inside a store and waited them out. But cross this intersection enough times and such things start to feel normal.[33]

With this sustained threat in the background of everyday life, when sexual violence *does* happen, it is often experienced as a *fulfilled* threat, surprising only in as much as it was a fear already imagined; one that the victim thought she had sufficiently warded off through "daily protective practices," performed like spells—such as wearing the right clothing, staying inside at the right times, refraining from taking up too much space or attention, and acting sufficiently innocent in order to gain protective allies.[34] Thus, philosopher Ann Cahill concludes, "the prevalence of rape and the threat of rape literally forms aspects of feminine bodily comportment. Rape not only happens to women; it is a fundamental moment in the production of women qua women."[35]

While all women live with the threat of rape and this threat has made their worlds "fragile," those who have, in fact, become victims of rape live with "shattered" worlds.[36] When rape is experienced, it is "an assault on the whole body-self of the victim,"[37] and one's behavior and self-understanding are radically altered. Cahill argues, "[t]o know oneself as not only rapable, but as raped, is to become a different self."[38]

Anthropologist and rape survivor Cathy Winkler argued in 1991 that rape is "social murder" since, in the act of rape, the rapist intends to control his victim in a totalizing fashion, exterminating her sense of self in relation to others, and imposing his own definition of her desires and thoughts. During her own attack, Winkler's rapist repeatedly argued that Winkler enjoyed what was happening to her. He justified his own actions by explaining that she was the one who compelled his violence. She reports:

> His first words after clubbing me with his fists were: "You made me beat you up." He reiterated this line many times throughout the attack: "It's your fault. I didn't want to hurt you."[39]

Just two years earlier, psychiatrist Leonard Shengold argued that childhood sexual abuse is "soul murder," since it is the "deliberate attempt to eradicate or compromise the separate identity of another person."[40] For trauma theorists, it is clear that sexual violence is not violence "lite." There can be no strong dichotomy between violence that results in death and traumatic sexual violence: neither is less extreme, neither is less final.

Rape is so pervasive and normalized in rape culture that, as Ann Cahill argues, "the threat of rape is a formative moment in the construction of the distinctively feminine body."[41] Consequently, "even bodies of women who have not been raped are likely to carry themselves in such a way as to express the truths and values of a rape culture."[42] The values of rape culture, including the idea that "the feminine body is not only essentially weak, but also somehow accountable for its own vulnerability,"[43] creates an impossible bind for women: all are "guilty pre-victims"[44] responsible for their own demise even before any actions are taken. As Cahill elaborates:

> If it [i.e., the feminine body] attempts something beyond its highly limited capacities, if it wanders beyond its safety zone, it—*by virtue of its own characteristics*—can expect to be hurt. The woman who experiences her body in this way does not locate the dangers presented to her body as originating from outside her body. Rather, they have as their source the fact and nature of her body itself. If that body is hurt or violated, the blame must rest on the woman's failure to sufficiently limit its movements.[45]

Thus, women's bodies themselves are perceived to be inherently dangerous, provoking violence by mistakes and miscalculations in the continual process of curtailment.[46] The values of rape culture provide the grammar that make the statements of Winkler's rapist, as described above, possible: she didn't have the right kinds of locks on her windows to prevent his forceful home entry,[47] she "like[d] it,"[48] she "made" him attack her,[49] and he wanted to take her to the hospital to receive medical attention for her injuries.[50] It is according to this framework that all sexual interactions are interpreted in rape culture: violent sexual expression is merely an extreme version of morally permissible forms of sexual expression. As theologian Marie Fortune puts it, in rape culture, "dominance and submission and power and powerlessness create the formula which sparks erotic desire in both men and women" and rape is a situation when this spark has unfortunately gotten out of hand.[51]

As Fortune notes, this logic cannot be compatible with a rich theology of creation.

> If sexual violence is part of the natural, created order, then women are created to be victims and are *by their nature* always at risk on a cosmic

as well as a mundane level. This assumption requires an understanding of God as one who is hostile and cruel to have created two classes of persons—the victims and the victimizers. Nothing in the core of Jewish or Christian beliefs can substantiate this conception of God's nature or human nature. Our Scripture does not begin with "In the beginning God created victim and victimizer and saw that it was good;" but rather, "In the beginning God created humankind, male and female."[52]

Part of the solution must be "the erotization of equality" so that "both women and men [. . .] find erotic pleasure in approaching each other as equals, sharing both proactive and receptive sexual activity."[53] Yet, this would require a radical reconfiguration of our communities' current assumptions about sexual expression since it is likely that, in our current context(s), "[f]reely chosen, fully informed, and mutually agreed upon sexual activity with another might in fact be a rare experience."[54]

Recovery from Traumatic Sexual Violence

Psychiatrist Judith Herman describes the traumatic recovery process in three non-linear stages: the establishment of safety; remembrance and mourning; and reconnection with everyday life.[55]

Establishment of Safety

In the first stage of recovery, the survivor regains a sense of safety in her body as well as personal agency. On the most basic level, this concerns practical matters of securing a safe living situation, finding some financial security, developing a plan for self-protection, etc. On a more abstract level, this first stage of recovery involves safe experimentation with maintaining a sense of feeling in control of oneself in the midst of activities of passivity and helplessness. Trauma researchers name a variety of activities that can help the individual to experiment with different balances of security and risk: play and sports, physical challenges such as hiking or camping, art-making, or performance.[56] We can add prayer to this list, for in prayer one can practice a kind of controlled receptivity. These kinds of practices restore a sense of agency to the survivor and contribute to an overall sense of autonomy that liberates her from the destructive cycle often relived by survivors of sexual abuse—i.e., thinking that one has discovered an "omnipotent rescuer," experiencing extreme disappointment when this rescuer falls short of expectations, and then feeling retraumatized, neglected, and abused.⁵⁷ Once the individual can begin to recognize that she does not need to be rescued in a total fashion, but rather that she merely needs to be given the tools and the opportunity to establish her own safety and a *relative* sense of control (i.e., not every element in her environment needs to be controlled, some degree of lack of control is normal and healthy), recovery can progress.⁵⁸

Remembrance and Mourning

In the second stage of recovery, the survivor rehearses traumatic memories in order to integrate them into her life story, without them taking over the entire narrative of her life.⁵⁹ Direct engagement with traumatic memories is necessary for integration of these memories. Traumatic healing cannot consist of trying to forget the traumatic event and move on. Rather, healing must involve remembering the trauma and working through it with patience and diligence. This restores a sense of agency to the survivor as the director of her own life.

The work of reconstruction is difficult and requires, as Herman puts it, some "tolerance for the state of being ill."⁶⁰ It requires intense cognitive, emotional, and moral effort. Cognitively, reconstruction requires her to ask difficult questions of herself, of the meaning of suffering, and of the structure of the world. Emotionally, reconstruction requires her to endure the weight of the painful answers to these questions, or perhaps the pain of never finding definitive answers at all. And morally, reconstruction requires a commitment to seek justice (for herself and others) without a rationale for the original act of violence.⁶¹

Paradoxically, this work of building one's defenses and garnering fighting strength is not opposed to emotional vulnerability. It is precisely *in* the process of feeling and acknowledging the depths of pain caused by trauma that healing can advance. Mourning is integral to this stage of the recovery process and receptivity to pain in the process of mourning requires courage. Survivors can often resist mourning out of fear—for one can never be sure when the pain of mourning will end, if at all—or out of a desire to appear strong and defiant. Herman explains:

> She may consciously refuse to grieve as a way of denying victory to the perpetrator. In this case it is important to reframe the patient's mourning as an act of courage rather than humiliation. To the extent that the patient is unable to grieve, she is cut off from a part of herself and robbed of an important part of her healing. Reclaiming the ability to feel the full range of emotions, including grief, must be understood as an act of resistance rather than submission to the perpetrator's intent.

Only through mourning everything that she has lost can the patient discover her indestructible inner life.[62]

The victim can never receive compensation for what has been lost in the traumatic event, but she can honor what has been lost through grief.[63] It is only after, and indeed *through*, mourning that resistance to the traumatic violence is possible.

Traumatic violence alienates the victim from her community. Mourning, if shared by the community, can play a role in healing the wounds that the traumatized individual bears.[64] Restoration of the relationship between the traumatized individual and her community rests on two requirements: recognition and restitution.[65] Communal mourning functions as a public recognition of sorrow and grief.

The work of mourning is a public and communal activity of witnessing death. Mourning allows for the bearing of grief and "convert[s] silence into speech."[66] Shared mourning allows for the possibility of a good death (i.e., one that is witnessed, can "move between the body and speech," and can be articulated), rather than a bad death (i.e., one that is "unwitnessed and kinless").[67] The work of mourning ultimately extends beyond the personal to the political and social transformation of the world into the kind of place in which pain is acknowledged.

But more than grief is needed. Some form of restitution is required to "rebuild the survivor's sense of order and justice."[68] Within a legal framework, restitution is most frequently conceived as monetary compensation for medical expenses and lost earnings, but can also include a commitment to a public apology, the implementation of safer working conditions,[69] or institutional policy changes—such as the adoption of a community standard of affirmative sexual consent,[70] a zero tolerance standard for sexual assault,[71] or a multiple chaperone policy to protect minors.[72] Yet, restitution from the community to the victim is infrequently offered when the victim and the perpetrator share close social links. Herman explains:

> Traditional legal standards recognize a crime of rape only if the perpetrator uses extreme force, which far exceeds that usually needed to terrorize a woman, or if he attacks a woman who belongs to a category of restricted social access, the most notorious example of which is an attack on a white woman by a black man. The greater the degree of social relationship, the wider the latitude of permitted coercion, so that an act of forced sex committed by a stranger may be recognized as rape, while the same act committed by an acquaintance is not.

Since most rapes are in fact committed by acquaintances or intimates, most rapes are not recognized by law.[73]

It can be easy to conclude that "rape [. . .] is not prohibited; it is regulated."[74]

Reconnection

The third stage of recovery involves moving beyond a past orientation toward a future orientation; ready for the formation of new relationships and new beliefs. As one moves from the stage of remembrance and mourning to the stage of reconnection, it is not that grief ends, but rather that attention to ordinary life can begin. As Herman puts it, "[t]ime starts to move again"[75] and the traumatic event is no longer the central event in one's daily consciousness.

The work in stage three closely resembles the work of stage one—care for one's body, one's relationships, and one's environment—but now, in this stage, attention is more focused, and care is more comprehensive. Herman explains, "while in the first stage the goal was simply to secure a defensive position of basic safety, by the third stage the survivor is ready to engage more actively in the world. She can establish an agenda. She can recover some of her aspirations from the time before the trauma, or perhaps for the first time she can discover her own ambitions."[76]

As in the first stage of recovery, taking risks can be beneficial here—even risks of greater intensity. Planned encounters with danger can be helpful, such as wilderness trips or self-defense classes in which "model muggers" attack survivors and they learn how to fight back. Planned encounters can carry a risk of retraumatization, but the differences between the original traumatic event and this kind of planned exposure to danger, can be significant enough for gaining strength and reprogramming the body and psyche.[77] The goal is to teach the survivor that, as Herman writes, "[n]ot all danger is overwhelming; not all fear is terror. By voluntary, direct exposure, the survivor relearns the gradations of fear. The goal is not to obliterate fear but to learn how to live with it, and even how to use it as a source of energy and enlightenment."[78]

"Self-possession"—a sense of internal control despite unpredictable external realities—is a primary goal of this stage of recovery. This is not a naive sense of self-possession in which one operates under the illusion that one is radically independent (i.e., in need of no supporting relationships, nor requiring any cooperation with one's environment). Rather, it is a sense that one can participate in the shaping of one's world and one's future, despite a lack of total control of relational and environmental others.

Self-possession allows for the possibility of building a life beyond the traumatic event "by drawing upon those aspects of herself that she most values from the time before the trauma, from the experience of the trauma itself, and from the period of recovery [and in i]ntegrating all of these elements, she creates a new self, both ideally and in actuality."[79] This process necessarily involves acting with compassion toward one's own wounds. If one is able to imagine some sense of self-possession and agency in changing one's life for the better, one is more likely to be able to forgive oneself and act generously toward the memory of one's traumatized self.

Self-compassion prepares the victim-survivor for the possibility of engaging well with relational others. For sexual trauma victims, healthy sexual relationships can be particularly challenging. Herman recommends slowly exploring healthy sexual expression, first by oneself and then eventually with a partner.[80] In a therapeutic context, specifically, group work has been found to be particularly useful in creating the conditions for traumatic healing through social belonging. As Herman explains:

> The solidarity of a group provides the strongest antidote to traumatic experience. Trauma isolates; the group re-creates a sense of belonging. Trauma shames and stigmatizes; the group bears witness and affirms. Trauma degrades the victim; the group exhalts her. Trauma dehumanizes the victim; the group restores her humanity.[81]

Non-therapeutic, healthy interpersonal relationships, and other forms of social belonging are also healing.[82]

The work undertaken in this stage can prepare the survivor for action that transcends her own personal recovery. Survivors do not all need to become social activists, but many find meaning in engaging in a "survivor mission"— public action in pursuit of social justice. A survivor mission might involve passing on one's story to the next generation, educating others about the realities of sexual violence, or making space for recognition and restitution to future survivors.[83] Social action displays the power of the *victim*-turned-*survivor* for all to see. Social action defies, in the most extreme way possible, the aims of perpetrators of sexual violence—secrecy and shame.[84] In contributing to her own healing, the survivor heals others.[85]

Social Support

The recovery process is not an entirely linear one. For example, many victims struggling with recovery, and who are working on reconnection with daily life, may find themselves catapulted back into the stage of memory and mourning, triggered by a period of intense stress or change such as the birth of a child or the death of a parent. Therefore, the work of traumatic healing, as it is parsed above, is not as neat as it may seem. The importance of relational and social support, however, threads all stages of healing together.

Social relationships of support propel the entire process of recovery. As Herman puts it, "It cannot be reiterated too often: *no one can face trauma alone.*"[86] No one can secure safety for herself without another's listening ear as well as their concrete, material assistance. No one can bear the weight of memory and mourning without the compassion and solidarity of another. No one can reconnect with everyday life without the welcome and companionship of others. Traumatic recovery is the restoration of right relationship.[87]

A survivor must be connected to a community of support in order to recover. If a survivor is already enmeshed in a supportive community before the traumatic event, it can be extremely helpful to her recovery efforts if this community validates her traumatic experience. There are many reasons, however, that social communities can fail to do this; most frequently because validation of the traumatic experience seems to threaten the (apparent) integrity of the community itself.[88] For this reason, not only individual survivors, but also the communities to which the survivor belongs, must practice courage so that a different world can emerge.

Pain Transformed, Not Erased

Traumatic healing does not consist of returning to a pre-traumatized way of living. Traumatic healing involves the ability to elect to focus on traumatic memories when desired, rather than unintentionally becoming overwhelmed by traumatic memories without any sense of control over where and when this might happen. Traumatic memories can be managed but not erased.

Traumatic healing is the restoration of the capacity for relationship. The survivor regains relational functionality. She is able to form and sustain relationships *despite* the ongoing challenges that her traumatic history presents—rather than arrive at a state in which her relationships are not affected at all by her traumatic past.

Despite survivors' strong desire that the pain of trauma disappear over time, trauma researchers document that survivors' traumatic pain has been *transformed*. One study that attempted to quantify this sentiment found, as sociologist Catherine Cameron reports, "[o]verwhelmingly (92%), the respondents were convinced that the past abuse lost its power in their lives rather than disappearing. This conclusion, however, did not seem to dismay them."[89] Those who had the strongest desires for the erasure of their traumatic past through therapeutic interventions found those therapeutic recovery efforts lacking. Psychological treatment does not erase traumatic memories or reinstate confidence that the world is a safe place. In fact, therapeutic recovery efforts can often *increase* patients' pain before it helps them to manage pain effectively. Cameron explains:

> The flaw in their expectations lay in their belief that life was going to change—to become much kinder to them—that there would be changes in their outward existence, and the world would be a better place. However, in some ways, the world, or certainly their view of it, became worse. They discovered evil in men and women that they had never conceived possible in the process of understanding their own background and the experiences of others like them. They recognized events in the lives of little children that were nearly incomprehensible. And yet they had to acknowledge that these things not only happened to other children but had happened to themselves. They learned about human depravity.[90]

Erasure of traumatic pain is not the goal of traumatic healing. An expectation that traumatic pain can be erased, fails to do justice to the gravity of the original act(s) of violence. Cameron quotes a study participant, Norma, "Will we get over it? The question itself is an insult. It diminishes the wrong that was done to us, and the achievements we have made in working it through. We are forever changed, but we have turned that change into a positive." Traumatic recovery efforts should respect the harm that has been done and aim to transform pain into reserves of resistance to evil and conversion of the world.

This sentiment propels trauma researchers Kim Anderson and Catherine Hiersteiner to make a terminological distinction between "recovery" and "healing," arguing that "[r]ecovery is possible; healing is not."[91] By eschewing the term "healing," they are trying to avoid the idea that, with therapeutic treatment, survivors can be "cured" of the wounds of violence. "Recovery" more clearly indicates the ongoing nature of posttraumatic efforts toward wholeness. But I argue that, in a Christian context, the idea of healing can be reclaimed if it is heard in an eschatological register: that is, with an attention to the awareness that comprehensive healing is not yet complete. To simply insist that "healing is not possible" risks foreclosing fertile, imaginative space to envision fully redeemed human life. The fullness of posttraumatic recovery requires this kind of theological imagination.

A Theological Account of Healing

The pervasive nature of sexualized forms of violence, and the failure of the majority of institutions to provide accountability[92] should, by most rational accounting, make imagining and yearning for a just future that has never existed impossible. If not impossible, perhaps we can say that the effort required in continuing to protest injustice, to imagine a better future, and to work to bring about that future, would leave most of us exhausted and drained of all resources. As Herman notes, sexual trauma is largely "without formal recognition or restitution from the community. There is no public monument for rape survivors."[93]

Survivors of sexual trauma live with the reality of a damaged world, yet courageously pursue comprehensive healing—personally, interpersonally, and socio-politically. When the goal of comprehensive healing continually remains illusive, what empowers this work? Survivors do not have the privilege of knowing that if they simply gather enough courage to tell their stories, they will be heard. They cannot be sure that if they bring the crimes of perpetrators to light, justice will be served. And, from a broader perspective, there is no clear sense, over the course of history, that humans in their communities have secured a greater degree of safety for children, women, and sexual and gender minorities. The idea of social progress is a beloved illusion. Given these cold realities, how are survivors and their allies able to proceed in the difficult and long work of recovery, especially when progress cannot always be perceived?

The fullness of posttraumatic healing requires reserves deeper than that which can be articulated by the secular field of psychology alone: healing requires hope solidly grounded in the genuine expectation that transformation is possible through God's creative work and our free, creative, and courageous cooperation. Hope sustains survivors and their allies in imagining the impossible. Hope gives us the energy we need to endure the long and slow work of personal, interpersonal, and socio-political recovery.

Because the word "hope" has been evacuated of much meaning in contemporary culture—often standing in for a mere wish or an optimistic feeling—it is important to be specific. By "hope," I mean Christian eschatological hope. It is only in the tension between the already and the not yet carved out by eschatological hope that we can adequately speak of posttraumatic healing: there is much that is within our reach, but the fullness of healing still runs out ahead of us.

Eschatological hope is fueled by the faith that "good must have the last word."[94] Human action empowered by eschatological hope is neither timid (since the Christian is confident that her activity is a necessary part of salvation) nor hubristic (since she does not mistakenly believe she can bring about the fullness of healing on her own). Efforts toward posttraumatic healing, empowered by eschatological hope are, instead, both courageous and self-consciously provisional. To diminish the provisional nature of these efforts is, paradoxically, to limit the possibilities of human good. Without the permanent criticism that eschatological hope affords, we fall into the trap of ideologically limiting the possibilities of healing.[95]

Eschatological hope functions in a critically negative way to ensure both a perpetual discontent with the world *and* a perpetual commitment to its good. Eschatological hope commissions the Christian to transform in, imaginative ways, what *is* into what *should be*, converting the basic human impulse to imagine and expect into a responsibility to resist and create. Eschatological hope empowers resistance to sexual violence and helps promote the creative dismantling of rape culture since it supports a deep critique of structures of evil alongside a tireless love of the world, and a genuine expectation that the world can be different.

An Incarnational Account of Healing

In philosophical circles, theorists have intuited that posttraumatic healing begs for theological language, but they often do not have the conceptual tools to fully flesh out the nuances of such language. For example, philosopher Susan Brison argues, to survive rape is to "outlive oneself" as if one has "stayed on a train one stop past [one's] destination."[96] One has been "virtually annihilated"[97] and healing is nothing less than "remaking oneself"[98] in a new way, a kind of "resurrect[ion]."[99] Riffing on Brison's argument, philosopher Ann Cahill elaborates, "This resurrection is not a rebirth of the same self who existed prior to the attack, but rather a replacement of that self with a new being."[100]

That both philosophers use the language of resurrection in connection with posttraumatic healing, without much additional explanation, suggests that there is an implicit theological point in need of refining: healing from the death of sexual violence is not a resuscitation, but a resurrection. In the Christian tradition, where resuscitation is typically conceived as the restoration of continuity of life after an experience of death, resurrection dialectally involves both a restoration of continuity as well as a radical sense of discontinuity.[101]

Life pre-trauma and life post-trauma (especially as healing has already begun) is continuous (i.e., one can be "recognized as identically the same person"),[102] yet is radically transformed in such a way that one lives according to a "new mode of being and presence."[103] As Jürgen Moltmann describes the transformation of resurrected bodies, "what comes into being is not a different life, it is this lived, loved, and mortal life which becomes different; it will be healed, reconciled, and perfected, and in this way arrives at its divine destiny."[104] An incarnational approach to posttraumatic healing (especially one that takes the integrity of bodily experience seriously) demands—perhaps against the intentions of Brison and Cahill—that the resurrection of healing from rape not be understood according to an apocalyptic model of "destruction and new creation,"[105] in which the healed self is exclusively new, but instead a transformation model without destruction. As biblical scholar Raymond Brown argues, "What will be destroyed can have only a passing value; what is to be transformed retains its importance. Is the body a shell that one sheds or is it an intrinsic part of the personality that will forever identify a man?"[106] One's traumatic experience remains an intrinsic part of one's life story, even with the fullness of healing. As Anthony Godzieba explains, "At Easter, we are promised that our constituted embodied selves, with all their history, will be redeemed and transformed,"[107] including our experiences of suffering, betrayal, and violence. This history is not erased. At Easter, Jesus's own experience of violence is transformed and "fill[ed] . . . with meaning" "despite"[108] God's desire that this violence never be committed in the first place.

From its inception, the Christian tradition has been formed in the shadow of violence, but theologians have only self-consciously been working to formulate trauma theologies for the past three decades. Theologians prepare the soil for a rich theology of posttraumatic healing by correlating posttraumatic healing with Christian salvation. As one reviews the breadth of conversations within the Christian tradition on salvation, this correlation should not be taken for granted. Christians have frequently emphasized the spiritual, personal, and other-worldly nature of salvation at the expense of the material, interpersonal, and this-worldly components of salvation.[109] Christians have traditionally failed to condemn, unequivocally, violence against women and children,[110] and have tended to lift up the dynamics of victimization as preferred pathways for expressing obedience to God.[111] An insistence that salvation involves posttraumatic healing from sexual violence assumes that salvation itself is more than a heavenly reward and, instead, that salvation involves struggling with God for one's own and others' holistic well-being in this life.

Trauma theologians have begun to set the stage for arguing that the conceptual relationship between posttraumatic healing and Christian salvation can be mutually clarifying. The shape of posttraumatic healing reveals to us something about the shape of Christian salvation, and the Christian tradition of imagining the fullness of salvation reveals to us something about the shape of posttraumatic healing.

For example, theological ethicist Jennifer Beste argues that the interpersonal nature of traumatic wounds correlates with the interpersonal nature of both recovery and Christian salvation. Traumatic experiences of severe interpersonal harm can threaten salvation insofar as it can impair one's ability to accept God's self-offer. Yet, it is also true that instances of posttraumatic social support and love mediate God's grace and strengthen the survivor's capacity to respond to this grace. In other words, we are both harmed and healed in relationship, in community. By extension, when we work towards healing, we participate in both our own and each other's salvation.

It is clear from Beste's account, as well as from non-theological trauma theorists, that a repaired sense of the traumatized person's agency is salient to recovery,[112] yet the more precise ways in which human action and divine action relate in the work of recovery remain undertheorized. The eschatological shape of the Christian tradition calls for a theology of healing that understands humans as co-agents with God in bringing about salvation, yet also clearly articulates that salvation exceeds that which we are able to bring about through human effort. A *proviso* always remains. An explicit reflection upon the eschatological structure of Christian salvation can prioritize human agency without risking totalization of human achievement.

As much as trauma theologians have been able to find positive resources in the Christian framework for thinking carefully about the dynamics of trauma and healing, they have also identified the ways in which the Christian framework can function as a hindrance to thinking clearly about posttraumatic healing. Taking their cue from psychological researchers and clinicians who have observed the hard, comprehensive, and long nature of trauma recovery, and the ways in which those who suffer from traumatic violence never "get over" their pain, many theologians have reflected on the ways in which a Christian framework can sometimes rush the healing process or create false expectations. In particular, theologian Shelly Rambo argues that the shape of traumatic wounding warns Christians of the dangers of passing too quickly from narratives of death to narratives of resurrection.[113] For the traumatized person, God's salvific presence is experienced, not as an erasure of the traumatic experience, but rather as the tenacity of love in the middle space between death and life. The Spirit works in this middle space to inspire the traumatized person to imagine the arrival of life before it has been inaugurated. Held by the Spirit, the traumatized person has a "pneumatological confidence" in the persistence of love. Rambo describes this confidence as not "absolute" but instead as "resolute": the trauma survivor resolves to persist as a witness to the presence of God within herself and within the world.[114] The trauma survivor experiences grace as the strength to continue to watch, to wait, to notice love's survival, and to proclaim this (modest) good news—love remains alongside of death.

Trauma psychologists similarly describe recovery in modest terms, avoiding the language of triumph or militaristic obliteration of the enemy and instead favoring the language of precarious, but persistent, survival. As Judith Herman argues, "[The survivor's] recovery is not based on the illusion that evil has been overcome, but rather on the knowledge that it has not entirely prevailed and on the hope that restorative love may still be found in the world."[115] On this point, Rambo follows, perhaps too closely, the direction of non-theological trauma theorists, since she does not signal any eschatological future in which the triumph of life over death can be expected (however deferred or "not yet"). What can ground persistence, if not a robust hope for the future? How can the traumatized person remain in the middle space without an awareness that this is in fact a *middle* space, i.e., that we can expect a transformation which is not yet?[116]

For Rambo, the ungrounded nature of posttraumatic hope is further evidence that posttraumatic hope is the work of the Spirit upon the imagination, pushing us beyond the bounds of logic.[117] Rambo's account of the impossibility of healing as both non-rational and non-natural, and yet also the work of the Spirit, relies upon an implicitly dialectical understanding of faith and reason, revelation and experience. I worry that this portrait of divine action as illogical (or perhaps meta-logical) and Christian hope as radically miraculous—while reflective of the gravity of traumatic harm—might truncate a richly incarnational, fleshy theology of creation that is critical to affirm in the particular context of sexual violence. Sexual healing demands an attention to the fundamental goodness of the material and of natural processes, it demands an affirmation of the trustworthy nature of experience as a ground for judging reality, and it demands an attention to the body as the hinge of salvation.[118] In other words, it demands an incarnational mystical approach.

Salvation as Mystical-Political Healing

Posttraumatic healing is the restoration of relationship. Because the Christian story is the story of the persistence of relationship in the face of violence, the Christian tradition contains rich resources to animate (etymologically, to instill with Spirit) posttraumatic healing.

The fullness of posttraumatic healing—personal, interpersonal, and social-political—takes the full breadth of Christian salvation. Christians have traditionally gestured toward this breadth of salvation with two interlocking images: the resurrection of the body (representing personal-material well-being) and the kingdom of God (representing interpersonal and social-political well-being). These images work together to indicate the holistically mystical-political shape of Christian salvation.[119] The tradition holds both of these images together, remembering Jesus as one who announced and initiated both. The resurrection of Jesus's own body, and the promise that it contains for our bodies, is recognized in the community; in the collected friends who gather to re-member Jesus after the violent dismemberment of his body, and the intended dismemberment of his group through political tactics of terror by public execution. The communal activity of re-membering Jesus embodies—politically and religiously—the conviction that death is not the end and hope lies in the resurrection. Posttraumatic restoration of relationship consists of the gathering of friends to recognize a "body broken" and to strive to re-member this body.

The body broken encompasses both the individual survivor's damaged body—including a damaged psyche, damaged capacity for interrelationship, and damaged spirituality—as well as the social body, broken by betrayal. One broken body cannot be healed apart from the other. Without the social-political transformation of rape culture, sexually traumatized individuals know that they can never secure full safety (the first step of trauma recovery). And, without a healed and whole individual (i.e., one who has received recognition and restitution) any degree of social "wholeness" is an illusion, frequently weaponized against those who threaten to expose violence within the community.[120] The work of recognizing and re-membering the body, broken by sexual violence, is a long and arduous mystical-political practice, necessitating both courage and hope. Because God is "for us" and desires our wholeness, this is God's eschatological saving work. Yet we don't do nothing for our salvation.[121] God animates us for the creative and courageous transformation of ourselves and our communities.

Let us turn to the life and thought of Teresa of Avila who can offer survivors of sexual violence a vision of union with God as a patient, lifelong process of coming home to one's body and receiving God there. For Teresa, God is the Friend who, despite God's inherent inequality with humanity, invites us into egalitarian relationship. Because God is unconcerned with distinctions of honor, God desires our freedom from concern over social distinctions for true friendship with ourselves and others. Since the primary site of woundedness from sexual violence is one's capacity for relationality, this kind of freedom is truly healing. For Teresa, to be saved (or made whole) is to be set free for authentic friendship. For those who have survived grave harm at the hands of another, friendship with God, oneself, and others, requires both courage to persist in the *arduum bonum* and, at root, a fundamental hope that evil does not have the final word.

2
Teresa of Avila: A Saint for Survivors

Although not necessarily a trauma survivor herself, Teresa of Avila has much to offer survivors of sexual violence—especially her understanding of God as the Friend who sets us free to embrace friendship with ourselves and others. This chapter, and the two that follow, will focus on Teresa as a saint for survivors. I will begin with what we know about her life, highlighting her political and social context, to help us understand the ways in which she aimed to transform her culture's patriarchal system of the exchange of women's bodies, into networks of female friendship and mutual support. Teresa is, of course, mostly remembered in the Christian tradition, not as a social or political critic, but rather as a mystic. But, as we will see, Teresa's mystical theology cannot be separated from its political and social implications.

Teresa's Incarnational Mysticism

When people think of "mysticism" or "mystical prayer," they imagine a dreamy, out-of-body experience in which one encounters *the Ultimate*. For those who have suffered from sexual trauma, this version of prayer is, at best, not helpful and, at worst, dangerous. The threat of dissociation between the mind and the body is both debilitating and ever-present for trauma survivors. For survivors, imagining prayer as a "mystical flight" away from the realm of bodies (both personal and social-political) is a profoundly bad idea—theologically and psychologically. The idea that mystical prayer might push one beyond or away from the body is psychologically dangerous, because dissociation from one's body is a costly mode of coping with trauma, and bodily reintegration is extremely difficult once this breach has occurred.[1] And for Christian survivors of sexual violence, the idea of prayer as mystical flight is inadequate because the Christian tradition is an incarnational tradition—one that centers revelation on the disclosure of God in flesh. According to the Christian tradition, prayer orients us more profoundly to God incarnate—God disclosed sacramentally in our lives, in history, in the world. Therefore, Christian prayer is always and everywhere an embodied practice.

Teresa of Avila, the sixteenth-century Spanish saint and mystic, is one of Christian tradition's most celebrated authors, describing the deep and enduring connection between the life of prayer and the body. In her autobiography, she narrates a vision that she occasionally has of a small angel in human form who repeatedly pierces her heart. This action arouses in her such an intensely painful desire for God that it rages through her soul and, as she describes, spills over into her body. She writes:

> I saw in his hands a large golden dart and at the end of the iron tip there appeared to be a little fire. It seems to me this angel plunged the dart several times into my heart and that it reached deep within me. When he drew it out, I thought he was carrying off with him the deepest part of me; and he left me all on fire with great love of God. The pain is not bodily but spiritual, although the body doesn't fail to share in some of it, and even a great deal.[2]

Although this scene from Teresa's autobiography is not Teresa's most compelling illustration of the integration of the body in the life of prayer, it is certainly one of her most famous ones. In the seventeenth century, Gian Lorenzo Bernini memorably captured the erotic undertones of Teresa's account in his sculpture "Ecstasy of Saint Teresa." In the piece, Teresa reclines beneath an armed angel—magnified from Teresa's original account to the size of an ordinary human male—poised to receive his spear into her heart. Reflecting Teresa's own description of this as a "loving exchange"[3] rather than a violent one (though many survivors have good reason to be suspicious of the coincidence of pain language, stabbing with a weapon, and sexual imagery), the depiction of Teresa's face suggests (at least to some) that she is mid-orgasm.[4] Upon seeing Bernini's masterpiece, Charles de Brosses famously remarked, "If this is divine love, I have known it well."[5] The scene speaks plainly to its reader or viewer: divine encounter is never exclusively spiritual in nature, but also, always profoundly material.

Physicians in the late nineteenth and early twentieth centuries saw a deep resonance between Teresa and the female patients they labeled "hysterics." This psychological disorder, a so-called "women's" disease and so named from the Greek for uterus (*hystera*), was thought to cause strange symptoms including "motor paralyses, sensory losses, convulsions, and amnesias."[6] Josef Breuer, a mentor to Sigmund Freud, famously referred to Teresa of Avila as the "patron saint of hysteria," and Jean-Martin de Charcot photographed a woman that he treated for hysteria in stylized portraits, evoking Bernini's Teresian sculpture. He titled them, "Ecstatic State," "Beatitude," and "Crucifixion," and published a three-volume analysis of medieval artwork, arguing that religious experiences of both ecstasis and demonic possession could be medically explained as manifestations of hysteria.[7] For these physicians, the tradition of Christian mysticism was simply undiagnosed hysteria, and Teresa of Avila was "the definitive and most legible metonymy of Christian mysticism."[8] Helpfully, Breuer, Charcot, Janet, and Freud's work on hysteria brought a level of seriousness to women's mental health that could not be taken for granted.[9]

Yet, as soon as progress was made linking hysterical outbursts to traumatic experiences of childhood sexual abuse, Freud and his colleagues repudiated their own findings, refusing to believe that sexually violent treatment of children could possibly be as widespread as hysteria among adult women seemed to be.[10] In order to recant their previously published findings regarding the connection between hysteria and childhood sexual abuse, physicians rejected the authentic subjectivity of their female patients, denied the reality of their experiences, and demonized their reported violations as unfulfilled erotic fantasies.[11]

Thus, hysteria came to have the negative connotation that we recognize today—a frenzied, emotional (and fundamentally delusional) response to reality. In consistently looking toward Teresa of Avila as the model of this kind of response to reality, turn-of-the-century physicians discredited and pathologized women's experiences of mystical encounters with God, intending to refute religious explanations of women's experiences and to free them from outdated dominion by the Church for dominion by (male) scientists.[12]

These early psychologists saw themselves as "benevolent patrons" or "rescuers" of hysterics, in contrast to what they imagined religious men would do to these women without the benefit of scientific rationality—namely, burning them at the stake.[13] Ironically, these men failed to listen to what women said about their own lives, and they failed to follow their own research to its natural conclusions. By positioning the world of faith in dualistic opposition to the world of scientific rationality, rather than rescuing women from the shackles of backwards belief, they reinforced women's coerced dependence upon the authority of others to validate their own interpretations of their experience.[14] In the same way that nineteenth-century physicians pathologized Teresa's experiences of her mystical encounters with God, repressing their supernatural content and dismissing her stated descriptions as fantasy, they saw themselves as the arbiters of reality and fantasy in the lives of their hysterical patients.[15]

Some turn-of-the-century women resisted the erasure of their own recovered traumatic memories by disbelieving physicians. Most notably, Josef Breuer's famous patient "Anna O" actively developed Breuer's method alongside him, referring to their mutual process as the "talking cure."[16] After her treatment with Breuer ended, "Anna O" rose to prominence under her own name—Bertha Pappenheim—as the founder of a feminist organization for Jewish women and an advocate for women's and children's human rights, especially sexual safety. She established schools, orphanages, and community homes for trafficked women and their children. She gained notoriety for her intellectual work as a playwright, poet, author of short stories, and translator of feminist and religious texts; first under the pen name Paul Berthold and then later under her own name.[17] Ironically, the saint, whom late nineteenth- and early twentieth-century psychologists singled out as the "model and protectress"[18] of hysterics, practiced the same kind of resistive writing and social action that characterized the most resilient of hysterical patients.

While not in the same way that psychoanalysts intended it in the nineteenth century, Teresa might very well be a patron saint for those who have suffered from sexual violence. Teresa's own descriptions of her life, and her understanding of God, are shaped in resistance to those who would describe her as deluded and possessed. Instead, she constructs her own life as a model for those who desire to know themselves deeply and to experience God intimately.[19] Teresa of Avila articulates a mystical theology that disturbs the presupposition that mysticism is inherently neurotic through a skillful defense of her experience as authentically gifted by God, the Friend and Source of loving action in the world. This self-defense produces a rich theology of friendship, a vision of the human person as created in the "image of God," and insistence on the revelatory nature of the body. These sixteenth-century ideas are fertile ground for a contemporary theology of posttraumatic healing.

If we analyze what Teresa has to say about her experiences of God in prayer, we discover that her mystical theology is neither dreamy nor neurotic, and it is certainly not one that trades ordinary, embodied life, for a so-called "higher" or more "worthy" spiritual life of ecstatic experiences. Because, before the twentieth century, women have infrequently been given the opportunity to textually narrate their own experiences,[20] we have a rare opportunity with Teresa's writing to examine what she has to say about her own life, rather than rely exclusively on others' representations. Despite Teresa of Avila's reputation—immortalized by Bernini in the seventeenth century and then later pathologized by the nineteenth-century founders of psychoanalysis—as one who has had extraordinary experiences of encounter with the divine in prayer, the majority of her writings speak to the continuity of her mystical experiences within a normal life of faith.[21] Her writings detail the interplay of the supernatural with the very ordinary, daily joys and sufferings of the body—namely, the pain of chronic illness, the patience and endurance required in making prayer a daily practice, and the challenges of loving others.

Teresa's mystical theology is fundamentally incarnational. It is a mysticism that particularly emphasizes the role of the mundane body in consciousness of the presence of God. Teresa holds in tension two ideas about the role of the body in the life of prayer: first, the well-being of the body positively affects spiritual well-being and vice versa; second, bodily suffering is not annihilating, but can present an opportunity to serve God. In fruitful tension, these two ideas together produce a vision of the body as an integral component of service to God, especially as one pursues posttraumatic healing. The writings of Teresa of Avila can help us, therefore, affirm the destructive realities of bodily harm, while at the same time preserving a deep foundation of human beauty and integrity. Discussions of the body, and bodily well-being, do not remain abstract notions for Teresa, but are instead enfleshed through a compelling narrative of her own experiences of suffering in illness, distress, depression, and bodily pleasure.

Teresa as Trauma Survivor?

While Teresa's work is helpful for constructing a theology of trauma, it is important to avoid characterizing Teresa herself as a traumatized individual. She certainly underwent much suffering in her life—the multigenerational suffering inherited through her Jewish heritage in an antisemitic, social-political context; the loss of her mother when Teresa was a teenager; experiences of chronic illness (including coma and near death); ongoing suspicion of her as demonically possessed; and a well-founded, persistent anxiety over the unpredictable and volatile power of the Inquisition. Some have even described her participation in the luxuries of convent life at the Monasterio de la Encarnación, where social classes were sharply stratified, as traumatizing.[22] The cumulative effect of these experiences of suffering could provoke a traumatic response in any of us, but retrospectively, there is no way to tell whether this was the case for Teresa.

Certainly, some trauma survivors will find her descriptions of the intense spiritual and physical pain that she experienced over the course of her life to be eerily resonant with their own experiences. Survivors may identify with her description of an experience of hell where she could feel her own soul tearing itself into pieces.²³ Survivors might resonate with her description of a spiritual pain so intense that it feels as though one's bones have been pulled apart after a profound encounter with God in prayer.²⁴ Survivors might recognize themselves in her descriptions of feeling frustration with—or at times, hatred for—her chronically ill body.²⁵

We do not need to know whether Teresa suffered from trauma herself to argue that her writings provide some resources for a constructive account of posttraumatic healing. Her dynamic and incarnational mysticism offers a vision of the human person as created in the *Imago Dei* to be a friend of God and others. This vision can provide a theological foundation for a description of healing from sexual violence without the need to diagnose Teresa retrospectively.

Teresa in Context: Honor, Shame, and Lineage

Let us begin with what we know about Teresa's life, in order to place her theological ideas in context. Understanding Spanish cultural constructions of honor and shame, assigned through family lineage, will help to underscore the revolutionary impact of Teresa's formation of egalitarian women's communities that claimed friendship with God, irrespective of "purity of blood."

Teresa de Ahumada y Cepeda was suspect from birth. She had inherited the "stain" of dishonor from her Jewish ancestors, but she also inherited from them skillful strategies for navigating constant threats of violence in antisemitic Spain. Her paternal grandfather, Juan Sánchez, a Jewish convert to Christianity, moved to Avila from Toledo after he was prosecuted in 1485 as a *judaizante* for secretly practicing Jewish customs.²⁶ As punishment for his "crimes," he had been forced to commit public penance by processing down the streets of Toledo wearing the *sambenito*, a yellow garment made to parody a monk's robe, and *la coroza*, a pointed cap, fashioned to make the wearer look like a fool.²⁷ Juan most likely accused himself of Jewish crimes as a tactic to take advantage of the so-called "pardon" that the Tribunal of the Inquisition offered that year to all those who turned themselves in.²⁸ Yet, as historian Marcelin Defourneaux argues, the seriousness of even mild punishments by the Inquisition should not be underestimated—a man who wore the sambenito was "forever dishonoured and so were all his descendants."²⁹ Teresa, his granddaughter, would have to navigate this suspicion of dishonor her whole life.

Throughout fifteenth-century Spain, all Jews faced increasing restrictions on their freedom and economic well-being and were forced to live in crowded ghettos. As early as 1449, even converted Jews were barred from positions of civil authority and entrance into religious orders.³⁰ The legal suffocation of Spanish

Jews climaxed in 1491 with the infamous Santo Niño de la Guardia trial in Avila, where several Jews from Toledo were tried and convicted of kidnapping and crucifying a boy. Using torture tactics, officials had coerced the accused Jews into a false confession that they had used a consecrated host and the boy's heart in demonic ceremonies.[31] This elaborate, public theater sparked violent attacks against Avila's Jews by their Christian neighbors.[32] In 1492, it also provided the rationale for Catholic monarchs to force Jews to choose either losing their religious and cultural identity through conversion to Christianity, or face expulsion from Castile and Aragon.[33] Although many Jews elected to convert, these New Christians—or *conversos*—were regarded with continual suspicion for secretly practicing Judaism in the privacy of their homes and their relatively closed ghettos.[34]

Despite the systemic persecution of Jews in Spain through the late fifteenth century, Juan Sánchez skillfully built wealth as a silk and fine wool merchant in Avila,[35] and was able to secure a *plieto de hidalguía* around the year 1500, establishing himself as a person of lower nobility (signified by the title *Don*) and exempting himself from taxation.[36]

Juan's son Alonso—Teresa's father—had participated in his father's penitential processions in Toledo and had witnessed his father's strategic practices to secure safety for himself and his family. Alonso and his brothers took on their father's legacy of careful political and economic calculation and secured a *pleito* for themselves in 1522.[37] Alonso married into an old Christian family from Avila, and when his first wife died, he married her cousin in order to continue benefitting from his marital family's "pure" heritage. Alonso's second wife, Beatriz, was Teresa's mother.

Sixteenth-century Spanish nobility traded on the dual social concepts of honor and lineage, and Teresa's father and grandfather needed to manufacture an alternative lineage that obfuscated their Jewishness and imputed military valor.[38] Scholars disagree as to whether Teresa knew about her Jewish ancestry.[39] Regardless, this antisemitic history impacted her life, generally and personally. Generally, Spanish antisemitism created conditions of religious suspicion against Christians who advocated for so-thought "Judaizing" spiritual practices like mental prayer (i.e., mental prayer appeared suspiciously private), as well as the economic and social conditions that made reform of the Carmelite order possible.[40] Individually, Spanish antisemitism instilled in Teresa cross-generational skills of self-advocacy and the ability to carefully read social and legal subtleties.[41] As we will see, self-advocacy becomes a critical skill for Teresa's work later in life. (Many Spanish authorities did not trust that her vision was animated by God's spirit and she needed to demonstrate considerable persistence as her critics continually demonized her.) Notably, Teresa's

Jewish ancestry was actively suppressed by historians and religious scholars until the 1940s.[42]

Survivors of sexual violence may recognize in Teresa's background some of the same skills that have enabled them to persist when others attempt to silence or discredit them. Audrey Savage, survivor of rape by a stranger while camping in Wales, describes the trial against her attacker as a "second rape" by the defense barrister, Trevor Halbert.

> I was listening to this man take my words and twist them to suit his own purposes. I was listening to him distort and misrepresent what I had said. I was listening to him malign my person and my character. I was hearing him belittle me with his tone and with his words. He had taken my truth and used insinuations and innuendos to distort it until it was almost unrecognizable. It seemed as though he had taken my persona and turned it inside out, saying, "This woman is a liar."[43]

In response to the jury's verdict of "not guilty" on the charges of rape, Savage resolves, "Halbert, and the like, may have won the battle, but they haven't won the war."[44] Savage, like many survivors, made the decision to persist in seeking justice for herself and others. In her case, this took the shape of committing to writing about her experiences and working with victims as a psychotherapist.[45] Analogously, Teresa struggled for validation as one inspired by God in her own social and political climate, and refused to be silenced by those who wished to intimidate her.

During Teresa's lifetime, Avila was a growing center for wool production. Teresa witnessed Avila's population double, as migrants from the countryside flooded the urban center, seeking the opportunity to invest in the production of luxury wool or to work as textile laborers, construction laborers, or domestic servants supporting the increasing urbanization of Avila.[46] Despite large investments in infrastructure development—i.e., construction of roads and new buildings (including new religious institutions), Avila's growth generated overcrowding, homelessness, conflicts over public and private space, and food shortages.[47] Most especially, Avila struggled with water management. Avila's arid and rocky climate made rainfall a scarce resource and residents did not often have reliable ways to store or transport water.[48] Those who lived on high ground never had enough access to water and those who lived in low land often experienced flooding.[49] These social conflicts provided friction in Teresa's life as a religious reformer, and she constantly needed to defend her communities from accusations that they were unfairly depleting the city's resources. But these frictions also provided inspiration for some of her most memorable metaphors for God's love. To Avila residents, it would have felt like nothing short of divine favor to have access to just the right amount of water to make life livable. It makes sense, as we will see later, that in Teresa's first major writing project, she used metaphors of irrigation to describe her method of prayer.[50]

The Comfort of the Convent

The combination of economic growth in Avila and the emergence of "new men"—previously non-noble individuals gaining provisional access to nobility through the *pleito* system—caused great interest among newly wealthy individuals to reconstruct or found new monastic houses and churches.[51] This practice helped to cement wealthy individuals' legacies of honor—e.g., often a family's coat of arms might adorn the reformed monastic church's walls[52]—especially for those individuals who had limited access to power and influence through other means. To this point, most of Avila's new religious houses were established by elite women.[53] It is in a house such as this that Teresa spent nearly the first half of her adult life.

Teresa would eventually come to abhor the honor systems that birthed these religious houses and seek to found her own houses in which vowed community members might find "holy freedom" from exploitative wealth and honor-accumulating practices. Survivors of sexual violence may resonate with Teresa's desire for freedom from exploitation and transactional relationality. Calling to mind Jesus's teaching in the Gospel of Matthew that the rich need to give up their wealth in order to participate in the kingdom of God—"it is easier for a camel to go through the eye of a needle than for someone who is rich to enter the kingdom of God" (Mt 19:24)—author and poet Maya Angelou describes her experience of childhood rape as the inversion of Jesus's ethics. The rape of an eight-year-old girl is "a matter of the needle giving because the camel can't. The child gives, because the body can, and the mind of the violator cannot."[54] The rapist forces himself upon the child, unwilling to give up any of his own desires for the sake of the well-being of another. The child is a mere means of pleasure. Teresa found that poverty provided her and her sisters with freedom *from* transactional relationality—where people serve as means to ends—and *for* true friendship—where others can be honored as images of God.

After Teresa's mother died in November of 1528, and her oldest sister married and moved out of the family home in 1531, Teresa's father observed that his maturing teenager was dangerously without female mentorship and (prompted, in part, by Teresa's apparent romantic interest in a cousin) sent her to live as a boarder in the Augustinian convent, Our Lady of Grace, in Avila. Here she was schooled in home economics and basic religious doctrine.[55] As she developed a deep friendship with one of the sisters, Doña María Briceño, she began to consider becoming a nun herself.[56]

Teresa was deeply conflicted about whether to take vows, grew seriously ill[57] (perhaps due to anxiety about her vocational decision, as some scholars suggest[58]), and needed to leave the convent. This would be the first of many instances of extreme illness in Teresa's life. She struggled, not just physically but also spiritually, from chronic illness, and yet she continued to encounter God in her profound suffering. This may be another aspect of Teresa's life that resonates with survivors of sexual violence: many traumatized individuals suffer from a diversity of chronic illnesses, triggered by the stress of traumatic violence, and struggle over a lifetime with how to connect to God in the midst of ongoing physical and spiritual suffering. Philosopher Shannon Sullivan presents the case of Ginette as an example of the ways in which long-term medical issues—particularly related to urinary, genital, and the lower intestinal tract—plague individuals with histories of sexual abuse. At twenty-nine years old, Ginette began seeking outpatient and emergency medical treatment for severe urinary issues. After six years of unsuccessful treatments, a nurse who performed an extended medical interview and exam discovered some helpful information: Ginette also had issues with defecating, painful vaginal sexual intercourse, and (most revealingly) had experienced eleven years of incestual abuse, beginning as a child. Sullivan explains:

> When Ginette's father began sexually abusing her as an adolescent, he would give her quarters so that she would "shut up" and not tell anyone about what he did. . . . [Ginette's doctor observed] "he told you to shut up, and you closed up everything. You closed the exit to the urinary tract and you have urinary problems. You closed the vagina and you have pain at penetration during sexual intercourse. You closed yourself to pleasure and you never achieve orgasm. You closed your anus and you are constipated."[59]

With this information, a year of biofeedback training, and several forms of psychotherapy, Ginette was able to improve her health significantly, yet the challenge of navigating physical suffering will likely last a lifetime.[60]

In response to her first bout of serious illness, Teresa returned to her father's house in order to recuperate and spent some time living with other relatives.[61] During a stay at the home of her uncle, Don Pedro Sánchez de Cepeda, who lived as a hermit in Hortigosa, she made her final decision to become a nun. Her father did not approve, but she ran away from home to enter the Carmelite convent, la Encarnación, as a novice on November 2, 1535.

Life at la Encarnación included vocal prayer of the Divine Office, fasting, and keeping silence. No time was designated for mental prayer and no instruction about mental prayer was provided during the novitiate.[62] In a system of patronage, such as la Encarnación relied upon, vocal prayer was critical, since it helped measure whether or not the sisters of the convent were fulfilling their commitments to pray for their patrons. One such patron—Bernardo Robles—exacted a particularly high toll on la Encarnación throughout Teresa's residency. According to the terms of his 1513 endowment, the sisters were required to commit to perpetual vocal prayer for the salvation of his soul. The sisters kept up this commitment for twenty years, rotating in one hour shifts all day and night. But when they abandoned their perpetual vigils in 1533, Robles' heirs threatened to terminate payments to the convent. Legal negotiations between the sisters and Robles' heirs extended laboriously until 1574, with a final judgment in favor of the sisters. Teresa was witness to the strain that patronage agreements placed on endowment recipients.[63] She eventually envisioned a different kind of community—one that could embrace voluntary poverty and eschew the constraints of donors' demands[64]—but not before she spent some time benefitting from la Encarnación's social and class distinctions.

Even though Teresa's father disapproved of her decision to join la Encarnación as a young woman, he provided her with a large enough dowry to secure a private room, signaling his reluctant acceptance (or perhaps resignation).[65] At the convent she lived in a private, two-level apartment with enough room to house several other relatives with her.[66] Teresa's life at la Encarnación was not austere (certainly, not as austere as her life would later become). Because la Encarnación was "one of the largest religious houses in Avila and a center for the city's upper classes," it allowed the women who entered to remain elite.[67] As historian Jodi Bilinkoff explains, wealth disparity was great at the convent: "nuns without private incomes lived in a state of near destitution [and malnutrition][68] while other nuns maintained a style of life not very different from that enjoyed in the houses of their fathers and husbands."[69]

Despite Teresa's desire as a novice to reject her society's conceptions of class and honor,[70] her life at la Encarnación resembled, very closely, the luxuries that she would have had access to if she had never taken vows at all.[71] While poor nuns slept in a common dormitory together, Teresa benefitted from living in a comfortable and private room with cooking, dining, and parlor areas.[72] Because Teresa was a good conversationalist and known for her sense of humor, her parlor became a popular place for friends and relatives to gather.[73] Ironically, during these parlor conversations, Teresa and her collaborators planned reform of the order—reflective of a more authentic rejection of her culture's ideas of class and honor.[74]

Mental Prayer: A Revolutionary Practice

In the fall of 1538, Teresa became seriously ill again—frequently fainting, experiencing chest pains and, in her words, "many other illnesses all together."[75] Her father, desperate to help her, sent her to Becedas to a famous *curandera* who administered herbal treatments and purges.[76] Along the way, she stopped again at the home of her uncle, Don Pedro Sánchez de Cepeda, the same uncle at whose house she first decided to become a nun—and he gave her Francisco de Osuna's *The Third Spiritual Alphabet* to read.

The Third Spiritual Alphabet had been revolutionizing religious practice in Europe. It was critical to the popular *devotio moderna* movement of spiritual renewal, which introduced a practice of mental prayer called "recollection."[77] Teresa describes this prayer technique as a significant catalyst in her life, teaching her to gather together her senses, imagination, and memories—to enter within herself to be with God.[78] This practice was not only spiritually revolutionary for Teresa, but also socially and politically so. She found that mental prayer opened the practitioner to "friendship with God" and authentic friendship with others. As she memorably puts it, "mental prayer in my opinion is nothing else than an intimate sharing between friends; it means taking time frequently to be alone with Him who we know loves us."[79] True friendship with others, she came to believe, must be supported by alternative modes of organizing religious life apart from the freighted system of patronage and vocal prayer, dominant in sixteenth-century Spain.

Extreme Suffering

Teresa spent the spring and early summer of 1539 in Becedes undergoing the *curandera's* treatment, which proved to be harsher than the original illness it intended to cure. She suffered greatly. As Teresa explains:

> I spent three months in that place, for the cure was too harsh for my constitution. After two months, because of the potent medicines, my life was almost at an end. The severity of the heart pains, which I went to have cured, was more acute. For sometimes it seemed that sharp teeth were biting into me, so much so that it was feared I had rabies. With the continuous fever and the great lack of strength (for because of nausea I wasn't able to eat anything, only drink), I was so shriveled

and wasted away (because for almost a month they gave me a daily
purge) that my nerves began to shrink causing such unbearable pains
that I found no rest either by day or by night—a very deep sadness.[80]

Her intense physical pain produced emotional and psychological difficulties, as indicated in her pointed, brief, and almost disjointed comment, "a deep sadness."[81] This rich interconnection between the physical, spiritual, and psychological is a persistent theme in her writings: bodily well-being does not remain in the personal-material realm alone, but dynamically affects other forms of well-being.

Her poor condition came to a climax on the evening of the feast of the Assumption in 1539—notably, a feast celebrating the integration of the body and the soul[82]—when she fell into what seems to be a coma. She remained completely incapacitated for four days, bedridden for eight months, and with some kind of enduring symptoms of paralysis for three years.[83] For the first days of her incapacitation, those around her assumed that she had died or, at the very least, that she was on the brink of death. As she narrates:

> At this time they gave me the sacrament of the anointing of the sick, and from hour to hour or moment to moment they thought I was going to die; they did nothing but recite the Creed to me, as if I were able to understand them. At times they were so certain I was dead that afterward I even found the wax [from the candle ceremoniously used to prepare for burial] on my eyes.[84]

Looking back on her life, realizing that not only did she recover, but that she had come to live a life of long spiritual and material fruitfulness, she later wrote, "I am so startled in arriving at this part of my life and in seeing how apparently the Lord raised me from the dead that I am almost trembling within myself."[85]

Trauma survivors often use the language of death in life as a description of the depths of interruptive pain that sexual violence introduces into their lives. For survivor and anthropologist Cathy Winkler, rape is "social murder."[86] To survive rape is, in the words of survivor and philosopher Susan Brison, "to outlive oneself."[87] Theologian Shelly Rambo explains, "Surviving is not a state in which one gets beyond death; instead, death remains in the experience of survival and life is reshaped in light of death—not in light of its finality but its persistence."[88] Healing from trauma, then, does not consist of the erasure of traumatic memories as if the experience of annihilation never happened, but rather in the management of the memory and effects of trauma within an integrated, relational life, after an experience of death.

For Teresa, God's healing from extreme paralytic sickness did not grant her perfect health—she continued to struggle for the rest of her life with persistent digestive issues and heart pains[89]—but rather, God's healing granted her a new life of managed illness. Teresa never received clarity about the root of her varied health problems.[90] Survivors of adverse childhood experiences, particularly survivors of childhood sexual violence, may resonate with this aspect of Teresa's biography. The bodies of childhood trauma survivors collect an amazing arsenal of (apparently non-psychological) health problems, including a range of digestive and autoimmune illnesses, diabetes, obesity, and cancers.[91]

The Courage to Persist in Prayer

When Teresa returned to la Encarnación, in the midst of her recovery, the benefits of her new practice of mental prayer were clear for some time—she was patient with others and would not tolerate gossip, she enjoyed solitude, and she desired to speak about God and read spiritual books.[92] But she began to lose her taste for mental prayer after a while since, as she explained, "it was better to go the way of the many, to recite what I was obliged to vocally and not to practice mental prayer and so much intimacy with God."[93] After her father died in 1543, Teresa recommitted to a mental prayer practice, persisting through spiritual dryness and distraction.[94]

Teresa discovered that the practice of prayer required profound endurance. The courage required to persist in the daily discipline of prayer was significant, even for Teresa, who had a naturally courageous temperament. As she describes:

> It is certain that so unbearable was the force used by the devil, or coming from my wretched habits, to prevent me from going to prayer, and so unbearable the sadness I felt on entering the oratory, that I had to muster up all my courage (and they say I have no small amount of that, and it is observed that God has given me more than women usually have, but I have made poor use of it) in order to force myself; and in the end the Lord helped me. After I had made this effort, I found myself left with greater quiet and delight than sometimes when I had the desire to pray.[95]

After many years, she began to be awakened to prayer.

On one occasion, prompted by the sight of a statue of the tortured Christ before his crucifixion, she threw herself on the floor in front of the statue, crying and commending herself to the care of St. Mary Magdalene (with whom she greatly identified).[96] Another time, in 1554, during Lent, as she read

Augustine's *Confessions*, she became overwhelmed with tears and felt, acutely, the call of God upon her soul.[97] These experiences prompted a desire to spend more time in prayer, grow in virtue, and opened up a new level of union with God.[98] Recognizing a connection between her experiences in prayer and other behaviors in life, she gradually adopted a greater commitment to simplicity.[99]

Teresa turned to Gaspar Daza—a popular and charismatic preacher with converso roots who organized Avila's ecclesial "reform party"—as a spiritual director to help her interpret these spiritual experiences.[100] She made Daza nervous, in part, because he was ill-equipped to advise someone about mystical experiences, since he had never had them himself, and he concluded that she was deluded by the devil. Daza was the first of many who suspected that Teresa was under demonic influence. Teresa was likely unsure herself as to whether she could trust her own experiences of God,[101] but she eventually came to trust her interpretation of her experiences and actively sought to partner with those who would understand and support her. Thankfully, Daza recognized that he was not competent enough to handle Teresa's case, so he referred her to the Jesuits of the College of San Gil.[102]

Seeking Support for Her Mission

Teresa found sympathy with the young Jesuits. They understood the kinds of experiences that she talked about, presumably because Ignatius himself had been influenced by some of the same *devotio moderna* texts that had been so formative for her. Teresa's first Jesuit confessor reversed Daza's previous decision that she was under demonic direction and professed that she was under the direction of God.[103] The Jesuits and Daza were key players in Avila's ecclesial reform party, and they eventually became eager supporters of Teresa's reforming efforts.[104]

Teresa's Jesuit spiritual directors helped her (sometimes even against their own intentions) to work through ways to sever social ties that were unhelpful to Teresa's spiritual growth, assisting her in setting up healthy boundaries, and acting against the conventions of polite social expectations when needed.[105] All the while her visions and experiences of union increased. As Bilinkoff puts it, "As she severed her attachments to things of the world, so her experience of Union with God deepened. She was replacing one form of 'friendship' with another."[106] As we will see, Teresa's own theology of friendship, which grounds friendship with (trusted) others in an experience of God as Friend, is important for posttraumatic healing relationships.

Many were unhappy with Teresa's behavioral changes and formally complained to her confessors, but her colleagues at the Jesuit college came to her public defense. Teresa's confessors' support for the mystic, however, did not come easily. Teresa needed to work continually to convince her spiritual directors that her experiences were generated from God, rather than from her own imagination or, even worse, from the devil.[107]

Despite (or, even *by* skillful means of, as some scholars have suggested)[108] Teresa's constant denigrations of herself as a mere woman—uneducated and naturally weak—as well as a *sinful* woman, she persistently defended her own interpretations of her experiences, and refused to allow her skeptics to scare her into paralysis. Survivors of sexual trauma similarly struggle to direct the thread of their own narratives, safeguarding their stories from those who insist that they misinterpreted or misremembered what happened to them. In an essay titled "It Began for Me," Jill Morgan (a pseudonym) describes her experiences of brutal sexual abuse by her father. Throughout her childhood, she explains:

> I told adults of the horror I was enduring, but no one listened. . . . Or they believed that my parents were such pillars of the community that they could not be guilty of the crime. Later, therapists referred to Oedipal fantasies instead of listening to what I was saying.[109]

Yet, as an adult, Morgan continued to assert the validity of her experience by writing publicly about incest. Teresa can be a model of refusing to relinquish one's role as interpreter of one's own life, despite persistent efforts by those who try to convince us that we have no grasp of the truth.

In 1561, Teresa experienced a vision that elicited a different kind of response; this time, "organizational" in nature about how to serve God and to express God's love for human beings in the world.[110] She saw her own place in hell—"dark and confined" with a floor of "dirty, muddy water emitting a foul stench and swarming with putrid vermin"[111]—and she experienced the spiritual pain of hell's alienation from God. As she later described:

> [I experienced] a constriction, a suffocation, an affliction so keenly felt and with such a despairing and tormenting unhappiness that I don't know how to word it strongly enough. To say the experience is as though the soul were continually being wrested from the body would be insufficient, for it would make you think somebody else is taking away the life, whereas here it is the soul itself that tears itself in pieces.[112]

Writer Cathleen Medwick observes that this vision functions as "a diabolic inversion of sacred imagery. Instead of the marble saint ensconced in its niche, there is the flesh-and-blood sinner stuffed into a hole in the wall."[113] Teresa interprets this vision as an invitation from God to do all that she can to avoid hell (enduring alienation from God), and she decides to reject the comforts of social stratification and to embrace a more austere, but also more egalitarian, religious life.[114]

Seeking *Santa Libertad*

On August 24, 1562, four nuns officially entered Teresa's new convent of San José, under a primitive Carmelite rule.[115] This was the birth of a monastic order that embodied the goals and values of Avila's reform party and Gaspar Daza presided over the ceremony. Other members of Avila's ecclesial reform party were also present.[116] Teresa founded the convent of San José in strict poverty, rejecting regular fixed income from land investment or wealthy benefactors, and instead relying on donations and the sisters' own income-generating labor to support the house.[117]

Teresa wanted the sisters at San José to achieve *santa libertad*.[118] She believed that holy freedom would open up the sisters to true friendship with those outside the monastery by releasing them from the pressures of pleasing benefactors. For Teresa, freedom is always for "friendship"—deeper and truer relationships with others. As she expressed in her rule, *The Way of Perfection*, "It is certain that in having need of no one a person has many friends."[119] She was convinced that adherence to strict poverty opened up the possibility of true friendship between sisters, ensuring an egalitarian convent community in which class distinction had no place. All property was to be held in common, social titles or family names were not to be used, manual labor was to be done by all, and no interested women would be turned away for lack of a dowry.[120] In order to keep the convent small, she set an upper limit of thirteen nuns, allowing herself the ability to select the most emotionally and spiritually mature candidates and discourage social factions.[121] Teresa, serving as an example to the rest of her sisters, dropped her own family name—Doña Teresa de Ahumada—for the simple title, Teresa of Jesus.[122]

Clearly, a critical component of Teresa's conversion and reform was a rejection of her own society's emphasis on honor and lineage. As some scholars have suggested, her own Jewish heritage and her experiences as a woman may have played a role in her critique of society's obsession with lineage.[123] San José monastery, and the others like it that Teresa would later found, provided both material and spiritual refuge for women, especially marginalized women of *converso* descent and domestically abused women. As Teresa detailed in her *Foundations*, members of her monasteries included women who had experienced nearly lethal forms of abuse and neglect as infants,[124] forced child marriage,[125] and domestic whippings and choking.[126] By providing a home and a future for these women, the monastery not only established safety for them—notably, the first stage of traumatic recovery—but also provided an alternative model of social organization, thus beginning the work of cultural and structural transformation. As Carol Slade argues, "replac[ing] the patriarchal system of exchange" of women's sexual availability for the family's economic well-being "with a network of female kinship."[127]

Openness to Relationship with God

Teresa never had any dramatic, lightning rod moment of conversion. Instead, her transformation was gradual. She experienced a small conversion when she encountered Osuna's mental prayer method in the midst of intense illness in 1538. She experienced another small conversion in moments of prayer before the statue of the tortured Christ in 1554, and upon reading Saint Augustine's *Confessions* in the same year. But there was no singular, spectacular moment of clarity and commitment to action in her life.[128] Rather, God called Teresa throughout her life, quietly but persistently, to a fuller life of love and freedom.

This is also the shape of grace in the life of the trauma survivor. There is no dramatic, pivotal moment in which suffering is left behind and everything is light and butterflies. The healing from trauma that God desires for all who suffer is typically slow and infrequently linearly progressive. This is not because God desires hardship for survivors. The difficult and uneven nature of posttraumatic healing comes from the depth of violation that perpetrators have inflicted, and the breath of integrity for which we were created by God. We are created for relationships. This relationality leaves us vulnerable to harm by others, but as Teresa's theology also witnesses, it is this same openness to relationality that makes genuine love, friendship and, ultimately, salvation possible.

Resistance to Exploitative Others

A few months before the foundation of San José, Teresa submitted the first draft of her *Vida* to a confessor, García de Toledo, so that he might judge whether her experiences were authentically from God. After García read the first draft of her *Vida*, he suggested that she add details about the founding of San José.

Now living in the reformed Carmelite convent, she wrote a second draft of her *Vida* in 1563–65 with twenty additional chapters—detailing the foundation of her new home and adding a treatise on prayer, including her allegory of the four ways of watering a garden.[129] This is the draft that we have access to today. Her choice of metaphors was likely influenced by the tumultuous experience of living at San José, where the house's garden was both the most beautiful part of the property as well as a source of significant conflict with local authorities. Lázaro Dávila, a municipal water inspector, who had previously campaigned against the establishment of San José in Avila, based on the argument that the monastery would overburden the city's water supply, brought an outlandish suit against Teresa.[130] He claimed that the small hermitages (tiny structures for solitary prayer) located in the garden produced such excessive shadows that they would cause the city's water to freeze in the winter. Despite the absurdity of his claim, Teresa lost the suit, and was ordered to demolish the garden wall and all hermitage structures. But Teresa—resourceful and resilient as ever—quickly rebuilt the garden on another side of the convent. The life of prayer, then, is like the landscape in which the sisters pray: beautiful and birthed in trial and determination.[131]

As this anecdote hints, the convent of San José was met with ample resistance from city officials on several accounts. First, city officials feared that the convent's commitment to complete poverty would put too much strain on municipal resources.[132] Medwick describes:

> when the bells rang for the first Mass at San José, the townspeople acted as if plague, fire, and an invading army were rushing over them. There were demonstrations in the streets; shops were closed . . . The town council called an emergency meeting and announced that on the next day, August 25, they would hold an assembly (*junta*) and hear complaints. Meanwhile, a horde of citizens stormed the convent, hoping to flush the four nuns out. The *corregidor* of Avila, surrounded by his officers, threatened to break down the doors. The nuns said they could not obey him, as they were under orders from the bishop; the officers could invade the premises at the peril of their souls. The men began to hammer away, but the nuns buttressed the doors with thick wooden planks, then settled in to pray.[133]

Bilinkoff argues that at the root of the city's panic was likely a deeper fear: Teresa's reform would threaten the very foundation of Spanish society—namely, its values of honor and lineage.[134]

Second, because San José was a community of poor women, practicing mental prayer, it aroused the suspicions of the Inquisition, poised to root out heresy in Spanish society and already primed to target women and conversos.[135] Inquisitional authorities were particularly anxious that unregulated, silent prayer, would lead individuals—especially members of the weaker sex—into the control of the devil, or Protestants, or both.[136] Vocal prayer could be more easily monitored for orthodoxy, and mental prayer threatened the benefactor system in which prayers were chanted aloud for the salvation of benefactors' souls.[137]

Priest members of the reform party in Avila (i.e., Gaspar Daza, Peter of Alcántara and his colleagues, and the young Dominican, Domingo Báñez, who later became Teresa's confessor) defended Teresa to the local bishop—Alvaro de Mendoza. Because these priests were respected throughout Avila, Teresa's cause was narrowly preserved.[138]

As Teresa set up other houses throughout Castile,[139] she compromised some of her convictions. She allowed some rural convents, which were less likely to receive alms, to collect rent from land investments and to form benefactor relationships.[140] But Teresa never compromised her refusal to allow class and lineage distinctions to bar socially disenfranchised women from entering the convent. She always refused to demand documentation of *limpieza de sangre* from entering nuns.[141] As a result, conversos were particularly interested in Teresa's reformed Carmelite houses.[142]

Teresa intentionally kept monastic options open to conversos even after 1566, when the unreformed Carmelites began formally demanding proof of "purity of blood" for applicants, prohibiting entrance to Muslim and Jewish descendants. Indeed, conversos made up such a large percentage of those involved with Teresa's foundations (both as applicants and as financial backers), that some foundations suffered from local opposition precisely on these grounds.[143]

Soon after Teresa's death, however, the Discalced Carmelites amended their constitution to exclude those who could not produce evidence of "purity of blood," thus compromising Teresa's vision.[144] As Bilinkoff notes, "In an ironic twist, the *Constitutions* adopted by the Spanish Chapter in that year blocked entrance to the descendants of conversos extending back four generations, a proviso that would have prevented Teresa de Ahumada from joining the order she founded."[145]

In 1575, Teresa came under formal investigation by the Inquisition, prompted by a complaint from the Princess of Eboli, Ana de Mendoza, a significant financial backer of Teresa's reforms, who felt scorned after an unsuccessful attempt to join the Carmel of Pastrana community.[146] Teresa's confessor Domingo Báñez was appointed sensor, and gave her *Vida* formal doctrinal approval. Yet, because Báñez did not think that it was prudent for women to have access to a book that advocated their engagement with mental prayer, he recommended formal censure. Teresa's case was not formally cleared until 1588, six years after her death.[147]

Shortly after the investigation of her *Vida* was opened, in early 1576, a disgruntled novice, María del Corro, added her complaints, accusing the Discalced Carmelites of moral misconduct and unregulated mystical fervor. Inquisitional authorities investigated the order on these charges, and they were acquitted. Teresa was spared the public, corporeal punishment that was standard for women accused of similar crimes.[148]

Amidst these controversies, Teresa continued to add to her theological canon—including *The Way of Perfection*, about her monastic rule (1565–66), and *Meditations on the Song of Songs*, reflections on divine love (1566–67 first draft, and an additional draft between 1572–75).[149] Because her autobiography was delayed in the hands of the Inquisition, her confessor Jerónimo Gratian asked her to write another extended work on prayer, in order to make the most critical contents of her *Vida* available for reading to sisters. This new work was completed in 1577 and titled *Las Moradas*, literally "Dwelling Places," but usually referred to as the *Interior Castle* in English. This treatise on prayer was not a mere recitation of whatever she could recall from her *Vida*. Instead, it was a substantially expanded work, reflecting the deeper understanding of her relationship with God that had developed in her life since the composition of the *Vida*.[150]

During the short period in which Teresa wrote the *Interior Castle*, she and the Discalced Carmelites faced significant tribulation as clerical officials tried to halt her reforming work, circulating a pamphlet throughout Avila denouncing her as a heretic and a criminal.[151] But these interruptions deterred her progress very little. She wrote the entire work in five months (and only two of those were active writing time).[152]

Teresa was again investigated by the Inquisition after the completion of the *Interior Castle*, in response to an accusation that Teresa was acting as a confessor to her nurse, Ana de San Bartolomé.[153] Again, she was acquitted, but only after two prolonged years of investigation.

Between 1567 and the end of her life in 1582, Teresa founded fourteen new houses and traveled more than two thousand miles.[154] The Spanish papal nuncio, Felipe Sega, derisively called Teresa the "restless gadabout."[155] The extent of her travel is more remarkable given the cultural presupposition that women should stay at home. Francisco de Osuna, whose own writing inspired Teresa, recommended domestic violence as a remedy for women who insisted on travel.

> Since you see your wife going about visiting many churches, practicing many devotions, and pretending to be a saint, lock the door; and if that isn't sufficient, break her leg if she is young, for she can go to heaven lame from her own house without going around in search of these suspect forms of holiness. It is enough for a woman to hear a sermon and

then put it into practice. If she desires more, let a book be read to her while she spins, seated at her husband's side.[156]

Unsurprisingly, Teresa's travel added even more suspicion to an already suspect body of written work and reforming activities. Yet she persisted in her vision of reform until the very end of her life, animated by her own experiences of God as Friend and a desire to invite other women—especially those marginalized and endangered by violence—to share in those experiences. She died on the road on October 4, 1582, surely affected by the stress of travel and the labor of establishing new communities.

Teresa's Buried Legacy

Teresa enjoyed near-instant legacy status after her death, though for reasons that often had little to do with the socially transgressive details of her life. As early as nine years after her death, ecclesial officials had already begun the process of beatification.[157] Just thirty-five years after her death, the Spanish courts declared Teresa the patroness of Spain.[158] And, only forty years after her death, Teresa was officially canonized as a saint by Spanish Pope Gregory XV.[159]

During the seventeenth century, some elements of her story were amplified and exaggerated—such as her orthodoxy and obedience to ecclesial authorities—while other parts of her identity were intentionally obscured or forgotten—particularly her insistence on material austerity and freedom, as well as her Jewish heritage.[160] However, it is precisely these buried elements of Teresa's story that are most relevant to survivors of sexual violence: a marginalized identity, persistent struggle with those who do not believe the accounts of one's own experiences, courage in the face of adversity, and an insistence on freedom from exploitative dependencies. In the next two chapters, we will examine in a deeper fashion the theological ideas that animated Teresa's commitment to friendship with God, friendship with others, and holy freedom.

3
Teresa's Embodied Anthropology

For Teresa of Avila, the human person is in all ways an embodied person. Salvation, or healing, comes to the human person not by circumventing or bypassing the body, but in and through the body. This is important for survivors of sexual violence who have experienced a profound kind of bodily harm that spills over into so many other forms of wounding—psychological, spiritual, and relational. American philosopher Susan Brison describes the comprehensive wounding that she suffered in the aftermath of a brutal rape while on a walk in the French countryside, just six months after beginning to try to conceive a child with her husband.

> My body was now perceived as an enemy, having betrayed my newfound trust and interest in it, and as a site of increased vulnerability. But rejecting the body and returning to the life of the mind was not an option, since body and mind had become nearly indistinguishable. My mental state (typically, depression) felt physiological, like lead in my veins, whereas my physical state (frequently, one of incapacitation by fear and anxiety) was the incarnation of a cognitive and emotional paralysis resulting from shattered assumptions about my safety in the world.[1]

In light of survivors' experiences, serious attention to the body is theologically necessary. For Brison, and many other survivors, posttraumatic healing cannot be psychological, or even spiritual, without also being bodily.

In this chapter, I will detail Teresa's attention to the body in the life of prayer and, ultimately, in the process of salvation. This will allow us to turn to other (though related) aspects of Teresa's thought; the human person as created in the image of God and oriented toward friendship with God and others.

As we will see, Teresa's embodied anthropology highlights the fluidity of spiritual and physical experiences and, relatedly, human embodiment as an occasion for vulnerability (both positively and negatively). For this reason, human embodiment is an opportunity to practice patience, trust, and hope for the dynamic salvation of the created order. Care for the human body (especially one's own) also presents an opportunity to practice fidelity to God and to each other.

Teresa's ideas about the embodied nature of the human person are incomplete for our contemporary context, but they do provide a generative starting point for constructing a contemporary theology of healing. Teresa can provide us with a dynamic account of union with God from the perspective of one who has experienced significant suffering over the course of her life. Because the human person is created in the image of God, she is capable (through grace) of fully embodied union—within and without. This completeness of union of body and soul is patterned after the unity of the two natures in the one person of Christ and the unity of the three persons in one Godhead.

The textured and uneven nature of Teresa's descriptions of the divine-human relationship can frame the pulsing character of engagement with traumatic memories, as well as struggles with self-frustration within the broader arc of God's saving activity of the traumatized person. The way that Teresa understands patient care for the body as part of fidelity to God, and fidelity to others, can frame survivors' recovery efforts as participation in God's saving work. Teresa is able to help us insist on the importance of the body as that which mediates God to the self and to others—highlighting the ways in which bodily well-being can positively condition spiritual well-being. Bodily harm is not simply a secular problem but also creates spiritual wounds. Yet, illness and injury do not pose insurmountable barriers to union with God, thus providing space to defy perpetrators' attempts to make totalizing claims over their victims' lives. Teresa's honesty about her frustrations with chronic illness can, at times, veer into a denigration of embodied life as an unfortunate, but temporary, purgation intended to prepare us for a more perfect life in heaven, free from this "wretched guest"—the body. For this reason, she fails to be incarnational enough for a posttraumatic theology of healing.

The Bodily Texture of the Life of Prayer

Teresa's account of the life of prayer profoundly involves the body. The life of prayer is thoroughly embodied and therefore *dynamic*—changing with the temporal movements of the body and blotting out any demarcation one might assume between the spiritual and physical realms of Christian life. Teresa offers her readers an incarnational mysticism. Hers is a fleshy account of the life of prayer, detailing its multiple manifestations, shifts, and developments. She maps these details, collecting data, and organizing it into stages of development, as a scientist might document the results of an observational experiment, or a cartographer might lay out examined terrain.[2] Her writings are not abstract treatises on the nature of the human person or on the nature of prayer. Instead, they are narratives that flesh out the life of prayer—the dynamic movement of prayer in the life of the human person who is created for friendship with God, and who experiences the joys and stresses of embodied life. She details these dynamic movements through her own narratives of illness, depression, and distress, as well as pleasure and delight. These narratives construct general patterns of progression in their own way (i.e., she organizes her autobiography into a four-part structure and the *Interior Castle* into seven), but they also preserve the uneven terrain of divine-human relationality.

At times, Teresa narrates that the contemplative at prayer consciously exerts full effort in drawing near to God. At other times, she describes the contemplative as abandoning effort and feeling as if she is passively taken up by God. At some moments in prayer, Teresa describes that the contemplative is drawn both inward and upward to God, while at other times the contemplative is drawn outward to meet others and work for the common good.

Psychologists and other trauma theorists describe the healing process as similarly uneven, pulsing between periods of intense engagement with traumatic memories and periods of rest and healthy distraction: sometimes engaging in relationships with others, sometimes needing to retreat as much as possible into solitary reflection, sometimes sitting comfortably with pain as part of one's story, sometimes assaulted and overwhelmed by memories of abuse that seem to take over every part of one's consciousness. These apparently conflicting dispositions and behaviors are not setbacks from healing. Instead, these are movements within the arc of the healing process.

Because, for Christians, posttraumatic healing involves, among other movements, restoring one's relationship with God, an examination of the movements of divine-human relationality is not only helpful, but essential. If it is true, as trauma theologian Jane Grovijahn argues, that "the incredible witness contained in sexual abuse narratives is precisely all about bodily loss of God,"[3] then posttraumatic healing must involve the kind of (re)union with God that Christian mystics have been talking about for centuries—an *incarnational* mysticism. Teresa's narrative account of divine-human relationality leaves space for these varied movements, while still placing them all within the arc of an incarnational union with God.

An Incarnational Mysticism

Teresa recognizes the body as having a profound significance in the life of prayer because it is only in and through the body that a person experiences God.[4] Teresa reminds her readers, "we are not angels but we have a body."[5] *Positively*, because we are fully embodied creatures, bodily pleasure is a gift from God and sensual delight is one of the purposes of intimacy with God in prayer.[6] *Negatively*, because we are embodied creatures, we are vulnerable to intense forms of suffering. In Teresa's own case, she reflects on the suffering of illness and depression, but we might also add interpersonal forms of harm inflicted by others.

For Teresa, it is also the body (even the wounded and ill body) that can mediate God's love, both to oneself and to others in need of healing. In the context of sexual violence, it is of vital importance to affirm the profoundly embodied nature of the human person. Riffing on Tertullian's classic theological maxim, Grovijahn argues that sexual abuse highlights the reality of "flesh as the very condition on which the soul hinges."[7] She explains that in sexual abuse, "God is ripped out of a woman's body in the *very same acts* that violate her, pummeling her into a visceral location of deicide [. . . and thus,] survivors come to know a profound interdependence between the well-being of their visceral, physical self and their access to God."[8] Therefore, Grovijahn concludes, "the body, in all its physicality and corporeal characteristics is the only way to God."[9]

The persistence of illness throughout Teresa's life significantly shaped her thoughts about what it means to be embodied. Yet chronic illness did not prevent Teresa from accomplishing great deeds, including a radical reform of the Carmelite order that allowed for an expansion of spiritual and social opportunities for women and *conversos*. One can assume that those who opposed her wide-ranging reform activities would have been glad to see her submit to her maladies and refrain from the travel that allowed her to establish her foundations. On the one hand, the body mediates God and bodily well-being and positively conditions spiritual well-being. On the other hand, illness and injury do not pose insurmountable barriers to union with God. It is only in this dialectical space, carved out with assistance from Teresa, that a posttraumatic incarnational mysticism can thrive.

Chronic Bodily Suffering

One of the few childhood stories that Teresa shares in her autobiography is the plan that she hatched with her brother Rodrigo to die as martyrs. They decided to run away to a neighboring Muslim region and ask the local inhabitants to chop off their heads. But, as she tells it, "Having parents seemed to us the greatest obstacle."[10] Her aim was "to get to enjoy very quickly the wonderful things I read were in heaven."[11] To their chagrin, they were stopped not far from the city walls by their Uncle Francisco, who carried them home on horseback. Their plans for glory were thwarted, and heaven would have to wait.

She tells this story with palpable affection for her younger self, relating that the desire for martyrdom, however ill-conceived, was evidence of an early desire to serve God courageously. Yet, she acknowledges that the allure of this kind of act was that it was "cheap."[12] A quick, painful, heroic, and very visible form of death is not true courage, or at least the kind of courage to which God called Teresa. Instead, her path would be one of slow and patient service to God, coping with chronic suffering over the course of a long life.

Even before she gained personal experience of chronic illness, the realities of intense physical suffering made an impression upon a teenaged Teresa when her mother died in 1528. She praises her mother for the "many virtues" she exhibited during her life, despite the "great trials" she suffered due to lifelong illness.[13] Certainly, her mother served as a model for Teresa's own struggles with chronic illness.

In her novitiate year, Teresa lived with a seriously ill Carmelite nun who shaped Teresa's theology of suffering significantly. The nun suffered from holes in her abdomen that ejected all of her food. While many other sisters in the community reacted to this nun's illness with fear (presumably that they might suffer a similar fate), Teresa looked upon this nun with envy. She was jealous of her fellow sister's patience with her illness, and prayed that God would give her an illness of her own by which she might similarly serve God.[14] She reports, "So well did His Majesty hear my prayer that within two years I was so sick that, although this sickness was not the same as the nun's, I don't think it was any less painful or laborious during the three year period that it lasted."[15]

This can sound like Teresa understood suffering as salvific and God as desirous of human suffering and is a particularly unhelpful way of thinking about suffering in the context of sexual violence. This would not be an incorrect interpretation of Teresa, but it does require nuance.

Teresa believed that suffering presented an opportunity to grow in intimacy with God. In a popular story, found in both scholarly and devotional literature on Teresa, she complains about all of the suffering that she had faced and God responds, "This is how I treat my friends."[16] The story is often repeated to demonstrate Teresa's wit—as evidenced by her comeback, "This is why you have so few." But the anecdote can also suggest that suffering is a gift from God, for the purpose of *generating* intimacy with God.

There are some elements of Teresa's theology, however, that mitigate the wholesale valorization of human suffering itself as desired by God. Teresa understood suffering as an opportunity to serve God if it was borne well. It is not suffering itself which Teresa sees as service, but instead it is the opportunity to practice the patience that suffering presents.

For Teresa, the blessed opportunity of suffering is one's response to the suffering, particularly the extent to which one persists in activities that are worthwhile (namely, good works and the disciplines of prayer). Furthermore, care for the body in the process of healing is an opportunity to express one's love of God. "Patience," thus, is understood as patience with oneself; particularly patience with the limitations of the suffering body and a commitment to serve God within these limits.

Despite these nuances, I do not think that Teresa guards sufficiently against a dangerous theology of suffering. In a posttraumatic context, any sense that God desires human suffering is extremely harmful. God does not desire some human beings to suffer from rape in order to grow closer to God, learn a "lesson," or avoid some greater suffering. The suffering of rape is not redemptive. Those who claim that God desires the suffering of sexual violation proclaim a God who metes out evil.

For these reasons, Teresa's embodied anthropology—though having much to offer by way of asserting the value of the human body and the possibilities for union with God, despite the fullness of health—fails to sufficiently proclaim that God does not desire human suffering. Teresa's theological framework needs the correction of contemporary theologians who have thought carefully about the absurdity of suffering. Later, we will turn to one such theologian—Edward Schillebeeckx—to construct a clearer account of sexual violence as senseless suffering. For now, however, let us continue to detail the ways in which Teresa can positively contribute to a contemporary theology of healing.

Total Well-Being Is Not Necessary for Union with God

Teresa makes it clear that total physical well-being is not a prerequisite for union with God. This is a necessary clarification in a posttraumatic context, where victim-survivors perpetually bear the wounds of their violations. Those who have been wounded by sexual violence never experience a kind of healing that somehow erases that which has been done to them. Survivors are forever, as Serene Jones posits, "death-carrying selves."[17] As Teresa argues, "bodily strength is not necessary but only love and a habit; and the Lord always provides the opportunity if we desire."[18] Although the care needed from others can sometimes limit an ill person's ability to devote time to solitude, "it would be incorrect to think that if there is no time for solitude there is no prayer at all. With a little care great blessings can come when because of our labors the Lord takes from us the time we had set for prayer."[19] The one who seeks union with God prepares herself for the gift of God's grace, making time for solitude, if she is able. But she does not manufacture it. Teresa explains, "prayer is the door to favors as great as those He granted me. If this door is closed, I don't know how He will delight in a soul and favor it, there is no way of doing this, for He wants it alone and clean and desirous of receiving His graces. If we place many stumbling blocks in His part and don't do a thing to remove them, how will He be able to come to us?"[20]

We play a role in preparing ourselves to receive God's healing grace, but at the same time, our preparatory efforts themselves are already animated through the gifts of strength and courage by God, who is always seeking union with us. Teresa writes:

> Indeed a great mercy does He bestow on anyone to whom He gives the grace and courage to resolve to strive for this good with every ounce of energy. For God does not deny Himself to anyone who perseveres. Little by little He will measure out the courage sufficient to attain this victory. I say "courage" because there are so many things the devil puts in the minds of beginners to prevent them in fact from starting out on this path.[21]

This is good news for those whose bodies and souls are wounded by sexual violence. Our wounds do not place us beyond the reach of God. By emphasizing our responsibility to prepare ourselves for the reception of God's healing grace, and affirming that our limitations of sickness and injury do not pose barriers to God, Teresa is able to encourage the cultivation of personal agency—which is so integral to the trauma victim's healing process[22]—without foreclosing the possibility that God's healing grace may transcend our capacity to effect healing wholly on our own.

The Body Mediates God

While physical illness and suffering are not barriers to union with God in prayer, one's physical state does affect one's prayer life, echoing contemporary trauma theologians' convictions that access to God is mediated by the body. Teresa advises practitioners of prayer to be sensitive to the movements of the body and its limitations, never forcing it beyond that of which it is capable. Though she never advises the practitioner to give up the practice of prayer, she suggests modification of spiritual disciplines in sensitivity to changing bodily conditions and limitations[23]—such as limiting fasting, prioritizing sleep, etc.[24] She writes:

> We are so miserable that our poor little imprisoned soul shares in the miseries of the body; the changes in the weather and the rotating of the bodily humors often have the result that without their fault souls cannot do what they desire, but suffer in every way. If they seek to force themselves more during these times, the bad condition becomes worse and lasts longer. They should use discernment to observe when these bodily disorders may be the cause, and not smother the poor soul. *They should understand that they are sick. The hour of prayer ought to be changed, and often this change will have to continue for some days.* Let them suffer this exile as best they can. It is a great misfortune to a soul that loves God to see that it lives in this misery and cannot do what it desires because it has as wretched a guest as is this body.[25]

She warns against pushing through with any generic program of spiritual discipline, but instead she urges her reader to know herself well and to have compassion toward her own limitations even (and especially) when these limitations cut against one's desires and plans.

Honesty about the Body

Some scholars are uncomfortable with Teresa's negative language toward the body—especially as she refers to the body as a "wretched guest" or plagued with "miseries." But I argue that her negativity has the potential to give voice to the frustrations that many suffering people have with their bodies (especially survivors of sexual violence), when their bodies made them vulnerable to abuse in the first place and often do not work the way that they want them to (perhaps, freezing or producing overwhelming memories at unwanted times). While it is true that bodies also provide the opportunity for positive forms of intimacy and pathways for healing, awareness of the positive gifts of the body does not undo its burdens and vulnerabilities. Survivors are not served by anything less than honesty about the ambiguities of the body.

Bodily Self-Care: The Body as a Sacred Vehicle for God

Although Teresa did recommend disciplines of bodily mortification to practitioners of prayer in certain circumstances, she was careful to recommend them in strict moderation; giving specific instructions about getting enough sleep and enough food to eat. She was more worried for those who are ardent in the path of prayer and might *deprive* themselves to excess, than those who might treat the body too indulgently. Teresa made it clear that any desire for penance and purgation must be balanced by a desire to preserve and safeguard one's health.[26] She believed that women were particularly prone to the dangers of penitential exuberance.[27] She advised sisters who began to notice a feeling of stupor following penitential practices to inform their superiors and receive assistance in avoiding these practices in the future.[28]

Teresa, an avid letter writer, made matters of bodily care a frequent topic of correspondence in communication with those to whom she was closest.[29] In letters to her spiritual director and spiritual "son," Jerónimo Gracian, she repeatedly expressed her concern that he make sufficient time to sleep no matter how many things pressed upon him to get done.[30] To her spiritual "daughter" and prioress of Seville Carmel, María de San José, she similarly prescribed prioritization of bodily forms of self-care, writing "it is better to cater to yourself than to be sick."[31] Correspondence with María Bautista—a cousin orphaned at the age of five, educated with help from Teresa, and prioress at Valladolid Carmel—was frequently centered on Teresa's concern that María care for her own health.[32]

A letter from Teresa in 1577, to her brother, Lorenzo de Cepeda, typifies her worries about penitential excess. Teresa recommended that her brother take up the practice of wearing a hairshirt but did so with ample warnings and nervousness. She writes:

> For those days when you are unable to be recollected during the time of prayer, or have a desire to do something for the Lord, I am sending you this hairshirt, for it is a great help in awakening love, provided that you don't wear it when fully dressed or when sleeping. . . . I am fearful of doing this, for you are so sanguine that anything could alter your blood. But doing something for God (even a trifle like this) when one has this love brings about so much happiness that I wouldn't want us to neglect trying it.[33]

In her next letter to him she emphasized again the need for moderation in the use of spiritual disciplines, making sure that he paid attention. "Read my letter again, and you will see what I said," she reminded him. She warned, "As for sleep, I tell you and command you that it not be less than six hours. Consider how necessary it is for us who are older to take care of these bodies so that they do not tear down the spirit, which is a terrible trial. . . . this is how you will fulfill your duties to God."[34] In caring for the body appropriately, one fulfills the will of God. "God desires your health more than your penance," she warned her brother in another letter, about two and a half weeks later.[35]

For Teresa, bodily well-being positively contributes to spiritual well-being. Teresa's concern with the dangers of overzealous penitential practices, and a desire to prioritize a moderate approach to the body, speaks to the dangers of prayer that sexually traumatized individuals already know. Spiritual practices recommended carelessly can do more harm than good. Traumatized people can be prone to retraumatization through the practice of prayer, particularly forms of prayer which can be considered "penitential" or deprivation-centered.[36] Teresa's instruction on bodily moderation helps us recognize which forms of prayer can be most beneficial for those who have experienced trauma; those spiritual practices which recognize the body as the sacred vehicle for God.

Teresa offered her own experiences with bodily suffering as a witness to her instruction that all spiritual practices be undertaken with sensitivity to the limits of one's body. She considered it necessary to do all that she was able to within her bodily limits, though she often wished she could do more. As she wrote in a letter to her brother at the end of February, 1577, "to see myself capable of so little is bothersome, for this body of mine has always done me harm and prevented me from good."[37] She modeled a healthy attitude of acceptance of that which was beyond her capabilities.

In a letter to Gaspar de Salazar in December of 1577, after expressing joy that he was in good health, she wrote of herself, "That is not the case with me, but not knowing how, I am at peace and—glory to God—nothing takes it away from me. This noise in my head is distressing to me, for it is constant."[38] Naming the symptoms that plague her and expressing that they cause her distress, Teresa still holds on to the peace of God, knowing that the physical limitations her sickness imposed upon her could not take away the joy of friendship with the divine.

Accepting Bodily Limitations in the Work of Discipleship

While in some of Teresa's writings it appears that her acceptance of her own bodily limitations came easily to her, in other places her internal struggles with self-acceptance are more evident. In her autobiography, Teresa related that her bodily limitations sometimes caused her to think of herself as unduly fragile and helpless. She expressed intense frustration with needing to devote so much of her own time and energy to self-care. She described one extreme instance of feeling "bound" to herself due to chronic pain, nausea, and trouble falling asleep. When she felt this way, she was often overwhelmed with tears of distress and weariness. As she elaborates, "This has happened not only once but, as I say often . . . . It seems to me I became angry with myself in such a way that I truly hated myself."[39]

As she narrates, God appeared to her in these moments, giving her comfort, and explained that even though it was exhausting to devote so much energy to self-care, she must do so out of love for God. Teresa began to understand self-care as a worthy task, committing herself, as she puts it, to "serve this Lord and my comforter with all my strength."[40]

Self-care is a component of faithful discipleship and an exercise of strength for the work of God. Teresa testified to her own growing awareness of the importance of taking care of her body throughout the course of her life. For example, in a 1581 account of the state of her soul to Don Alonzo Velasquez, her confessor and bishop of Osma, she wrote, speaking of herself, "as far as regards her body and health, I think she takes more care of it, and is less mortified in eating; neither has she such desires of doing penance, as she used to have. But in her opinion, all tends to this object, viz., to be able to serve God the more in other things; for she often offers Him, as an agreeable sacrifice, this care she takes of the body."[41]

Throughout Teresa's writings, she spoke rather ambiguously about the body. This ambiguity reflects the very real ambiguity that many sufferers feel about their bodies. Her readers can perceive that the tension between Teresa's tendency to view the body as a wretched guest, and her commitment to care for this body with compassion in service to God, is never fully resolved. As with many chronic sufferers, frustration with her bodily wounds lasted throughout her life. Those wounded by traumatic violence can identify with this kind of frustration. As contemporary sexual violence survivor "Leah" describes it:

> It happens to me, sometimes. I'm listening to the pastor, thinking about God and love, when suddenly I hear or see something, and it's as if a button gets pushed inside of me. In an instant, I'm terrified; I feel like I'm going to die or get hurt very badly. My body tells me to run away, but instead, I just freeze. Last week it was the part about Jesus' blood and body. There was a flash in my head, and I couldn't tell the difference between Jesus and me, and then I saw blood everywhere, and broken body parts, and I got so afraid I just disappeared. I thought the bathroom might be safe, but even it scared and confused me. I forgot my name. I forgot the hot and cold.[42]

In these moments, our bodiliness is not experienced as a gift, but as a disorienting burden. Self-compassion is an arduous, lifelong task that not even the saints among us find easy. Nevertheless, Teresa's witness makes it clear that self-care and patience with oneself are worth struggling for in the work of discipleship.

Integrating Body and Soul

For Teresa, prayer is an embodied practice, since it involves the management of the physical sensory body, and it culminates with bodily integration. Teresa's own understanding of the embodied nature of prayer developed over time, affected by the experiences of her own body over the course of her lifetime—such that the deepest forms of bodily-spiritual integration are only articulated in her most mature writings. The role of the body in the life of prayer is dynamic, in order to keep pace with the embodied developments of the rest of life. That the body has a critical and dynamic role in the life of prayer affirms that the spiritual and the physical can never be fully severed. It is in the interrelationship of the spiritual and the physical that we can discover resources for healing from the comprehensive wounds of trauma.

Gathering the Senses for Union with God

In the earliest stages of the life of prayer, the practitioner needs to put forth significant effort in order to gather their attention to God and to mute other distractions that might engage the senses.[43] Teresa argues that even when we put a lot of effort toward gathering the senses to focus on God in mental prayer, God's presence may not be felt. In her autobiography where she relies on the metaphor of prayer as the work of irrigation, she explains, "if the well is dry, we cannot put water into it. True, we must not become neglectful; when there is water we should draw it out."[44]

Even if there is no water (i.e., no feeling of divine consolation), God sustains the practitioner somehow, illustrating Teresa's expansive hope in the healing, sustaining power of God. She writes, "God is so good that when for reasons His Majesty knows—perhaps for our greater benefit—the well is dry and we, like good gardeners, do what lies in our power, He sustains the garden without water and makes the virtues grow."[45] Teresa realistically addresses the inevitabilities of intermittent (or even life-long) feelings of alienation from God that so many survivors experience. Yet, she does not conclude from this feeling that God is absent.[46] She has eschatological hope that healing grace will be received eventually, even if only outside of the bounds of this life.[47]

If the practitioner progresses to more advanced stages of prayer, she will have the chance to relax her efforts and rest in God, "rejoicing in that holy idleness of Mary."[48] She will be capable of engaging in activities of love and service to the world while maintaining the contemplative gaze.[49] However, multitasking will feel exhausting. As Teresa describes in her autobiography, when the practitioner of prayer is at work in the world tending to labors of loving service and action, she can feel as if "the best part of the soul is [still] somewhere else." She continues, "It's as though we were speaking to someone at our side and from the other side another person were speaking to us, we wouldn't be fully attentive to either the one or the other."[50] As Teresa describes this stage of prayer in the *Interior Castle*, "Everything wearies it, for it has learned through experience that creatures cannot give it rest."[51] Since she is so tired, she wishes to leave this world in order to gain rest.

The challenge for the practitioner of prayer is the need to persist in detachment from the world, coupled with the persistent love of neighbor and engagement in the world (despite disappointment and weariness). By "detachment," common parlance for Christian spiritual writers, Teresa does not mean a dissociative detachment from the body and present experience—a persistent danger for survivors of sexual violence. Instead, Teresa means to suggest a kind of lightness of being that frees her to love.

For survivors of sexual trauma, this kind of freedom necessarily involves the liberation of one's traumatized imagination—the breaking open of the restricted, narrow vision framed by one's past, in order to imagine and, indeed, *expect* a better future. Genuine expectation of a different future may, in fact, cause one to be disappointed and wearied by one's experiences (as Teresa suggests) since an expanded imagination opens one to deeper levels of feeling—both deeper pain and deeper joy. The expectation of another kind of future can release deep wells of disappointment and anger regarding the ways in which life has failed to deliver the safety and joy that befits the survivor's dignity. These waves of negative emotion, however exhausting and painful, are gifts from God since they reveal the genuine worth of the survivor and the depravity of the sins committed against her or him.

In advanced stages of prayer, the individual experiences a greater deal of peace than in previous stages, since the intellect no longer functions as a distraction. Yet the imagination and the memory still run freely here. As Teresa describes it, in the third stage of prayer, the imagination and the memory "torment" and the practitioner should "pay no more attention to the memory than one would to a madman—leave it go its way, for only God can stop it."[52] The trauma survivor may relate to Teresa's account of the disturbing role that memory can play, even in advanced stages of healing work. Judith Herman relates the following dialogue from a group therapy session for incest survivors.

Leila: I have a question about going back. Do other women get to a point where they have gone back enough so it feels completed?

Lindsay: I think you have to keep going back.
Corinne: It does lose its charge, though. Like the first time you remember, the first time you feel the screams in your head, you're real surprised, and all your senses are open. But then after you've done that enough times, somehow it's like, "Yes, that happened," and, "Fuckin' bastard!" And now, there's this. You know, you can leave it after awhile, or maybe you never leave it, but you can get over the grief of it and the anger of it.
Herman: From what I've seen, it's not like it ever goes away, but somehow it loses its gripping quality, its ability to stop you in your tracks and make you feel completely undone. It loses its power.
Leila: Did you feel like it lost its power over you?
Robin: Not a lot! But yeah, I did, a little bit, because once I understood what happened, then I felt a little more in control. Because what was really scaring me was having this incredible fear and not knowing.[53]

It is, as Teresa suggests, some measure of relief to be able to identify traumatic memories as such and to strive to treat oneself with compassion. Yet this does not stop these memories from continuing to function as a source of active torment. Teresa can illuminate the fractured nature of the traumatically wounded person, struggling for holistic healing, who sometimes feels distracted by painful memories and is sometimes unable to uncover memories when they seek to. Teresa prays, "When, my God, will my soul be completely joined together in Your praise and not broken in pieces, unable to make use of itself?"[54] She will, indeed, find herself able to experience something of this wholeness during her lifetime, but she will not document it in writing until (over a decade later) she discusses the final stage of prayer in the *Interior Castle*.

In the fourth stage of prayer—the last in Teresa's autobiography and the penultimate dwelling place in her *Interior Castle*—one experiences such a deep intimacy with God that nothing can distract her.[55] The union between the practitioner and God can be compared to the union of two people who love each other deeply and are able to communicate simply by looking at each other.[56] The bodily senses are completely engaged in prayer and do not compete with the soul in any way.[57] As Teresa describes it, the senses are made heavy; one moves slowly and with a lot of effort. One feels intense spiritual joy but also intense longing for God, causing a feeling of pain throughout the body, even after the encounter is over. As Teresa writes, "The pain is not bodily but spiritual, although the body doesn't fail to share in some of it, and even a great deal."[58] This is the pain of lingering desire following an experience of ecstatic and authentic intimacy. It is not the pain following a violent encounter, though both types of experiences illustrate the very real, and powerful, intercommunication of the physical and the spiritual.

The way that the body participates, intensely, in the life of the spirit blots out any clear demarcation that the reader might assume between the spiritual and bodily realms of Christian life. That which delights or afflicts the spirit, affects the body. And conversely, that which delights or afflicts the body also affects the spirit. Therefore, it is a spiritual matter to exercise great care in preserving one's own and others' bodily safety and integrity. When trauma survivors seek safety for themselves, mourn their past, and aim to reconnect in healthy ways with everyday life, they are doing nothing less than contributing to their own salvation.

Courage for Intimacy

In both Teresa's autobiography and the *Interior Castle*, the fourth stage of prayer and the correlative sixth dwelling place can have a tumultuous character to it: Teresa describes it as involving many torments, ecstasies, spiritual flights, and spiritual lows.[59] But, in the *Interior Castle*, because there is another stage that follows it, Teresa is clearer that the tumultuous character of the sixth dwelling place is preparatory for a deeper and more stable form of union with God in the highest forms of prayer.

In this penultimate stage of prayer, one needs to gain courage for the greatness that is to come. It might sound counterintuitive to build courage for wonderful things (rather than for difficult and trying tasks), but because we are in the habit of thinking too poorly of ourselves, and not in the habit of recognizing our magnificent capacity for God, we need to build up endurance for an encounter with the glory of God within the center of the soul. Teresa explains, "I tell you there is need for more courage than you think. Our nature is very timid and lowly when it comes to something so great, and I am certain that if God were not to give the courage, no matter how much you might see that the favor is good for us, it would be impossible for you to receive that favor."[60]

Courage is needed for friendship with God. It is difficult to acknowledge others' love for us and we need to be purged of malformed self-images that block us from the most intimate forms of union with God. Survivors have experience with the difficult, but necessary, work of purging maladaptive self-perceptions and behaviors.

Active work for recovery is not for the faint of heart: it demands a "tolerance for the state of being ill."[61] The recovery process is executed through rehearsing and examining traumatic memories, sitting with their tumultuous effects.

Yarrow Morgan—poet and survivor of parental sexual abuse from infancy—writes:

> The memory does not come easy;
> it comes with screams that will not stop,
> it comes with tears and terror,
> it comes with shame that I felt this,
> shame that I feel this.[62]

Adrienne, a survivor of brutal gang rape after being drugged and abducted, explains that reviewing old journal entries is integral to her healing process.

> As time passes, I begin to forget. Forgetting might sound like healing, but it's not. I need to be able to acknowledge what has happened in the past in order to make sense of today. Anniversaries are important too. Not only the big ones, like one year or two years after my rape. At first, I acknowledged the 4th and the 5th day of each month as an anniversary. As my rape became a more distant part of my past, the small anniversaries became less important, but I still took note of them. Anniversaries are a time to mourn, to remember, or to do something good for myself. Sometimes they're a celebration of life. Always, they're a time for reflection. Regardless, these days are mine and I allow myself to do what I want with them.[63]

The pain of remembering and mourning—despite the feeling that it might last forever—is not, however, the *telos* or end of recovery. Healthy recovery culminates in a more stable relation to these memories, which is suggested by the stability of the individual in the final stage of prayer described in the *Interior Castle*. The absence of this final stage of prayer in the *Vida* provides the practitioner of prayer with an incomplete vision of the possibilities of healing grace.

Union with God: The Marriage of Friends

The final stage of prayer in the *Interior Castle* has no correlative in her earlier work.[64] This seventh dwelling place is the center of the castle of the soul and "another heaven."[65] The union with God experienced here, which she describes by use of the metaphor of a "marriage," is permanent—meaning that the practitioner experiences perpetual union with God even as she goes about the mundane business of living—and, in keeping with the nuptial metaphor, entails a complete merging of assets. That is, she has a claim to that which belongs to Christ, and he pledges to care for what belongs to her.[66]

It is important to note that the marital imagery that Teresa uses blends erotic desire and philial mutuality. The kind of marriage that Teresa envisions is one in which two friends unite as peers (a critical component of "friendship" as we will discuss below) in erotic longing for one another. Eros and philia are not disjunctive. Therefore, this is not a typical patriarchal marriage agreement in which the husband regards his wife as property. Instead, she is an equal partner. Teresa portrays God as a specific *kind* of erotic partner; in her words, "a true Lover who doesn't leave, the best friend one could imagine."[67] Fluidity of erotic and philial language is perhaps not a coincidence for a female writer trying to express the fullness of being loved authentically. Because so many of women's relationships, especially with men, are characterized by violence and abuse, sexual language begs for specification. Teresa is clear: this is not a violent marriage, but rather a meeting of true friends and equals. Just as Teresa has taken Jesus's name as her own—Teresa of Jesus—she has a vision of Jesus in which he has taken her name, calling himself "Jesus of Teresa."[68]

Intense union with God, in the final stage of prayer, produces two fruits. First, the practitioner experiences "forgetfulness of self," a liberation from fear over her future. Teresa is careful to note that forgetfulness of self does *not* mean forgetting to take care of oneself—especially in matters of eating and sleeping.[69] Rather, forgetfulness of self entails relinquishment of interior fretfulness—an obsession with oneself as an object to be controlled, rather than as a subject oriented toward God.[70]

Second, the practitioner experiences a great desire to accomplish the will of God, despite the threat of suffering.[71] The suffering to which Teresa refers is not the suffering of careless penitential regulation of the body or of lack of love for oneself, but rather the suffering that can result from a deep commitment to bringing about God's transformation of the world. For survivors, this can mean a commitment to the good of personal recovery, despite the suffering that comes from confronting the horrific reality of what one has experienced. It might also include pursuing justice for oneself in the face of the threat of public humiliation, slander, threat to one's life, and any other manner of reactivating their perpetrators' wrath. In some cases, a commitment to recovery can also expand beyond personal recovery to involve a commitment to, what Judith Herman calls, a "survivor mission": engaging in public action in pursuit of social justice.[72]

Because sexual violence is always social and political, the fullness of healing from sexual trauma is not complete until rape culture has been thoroughly eradicated. As poet Ellen Bass puts it:

I was not sexually abused. Yet I was sexually abused. We were all sexually abused. The images and attitudes, the reality we breathe in like air, it reaches us all. It shapes and distorts us, prunes some of our most tender, trusting, lovely and loving branches. We learn that this is who a woman is. This is what men think of women. This is what we are taught to think about ourselves. We all, women and men, live our lives in an environment that fouls one of the magnificent, holy aspects of our natural world. Creation, love, fertility, the union of two becoming one, joining in body and in ecstasy—this possibility, which should be our birthright, has been fouled. We are all wounded. We all need healing.[73]

Yet, it is also true that authentic healing, however partial, is possible for individual survivors short of this comprehensive refashioning.

When the practitioner reaches union with God, she experiences quiet rest and joy in God even in the midst of conflict and injury. The practitioner experiences neither spiritual dryness, nor raptures in this stage—simply the persistent companionship of God.[74] This sense of "stability" deepens one's determination for courageous works of love (of self, of truth, of others, of justice, etc.).[75] It is precisely the inner stability of union with God, in this final stage of prayer, that makes virtuous activity possible.[76]

Teresa compares the seventh dwelling place to a wine cellar in which God gives the soul strong drink,[77] and to the arms of God the Mother who breastfeeds her child, nourishing him and giving him strength.[78] Through prayer, the practitioner gains the "strength to serve" those in one's community through "the birth always of good works, good works."[79]

Fully unified within herself, body and soul, the practitioner no longer experiences matters of action at odds with the practice of contemplation. Rather than struggling with whiplash as one turns from one direction to the other (as she describes in earlier stages of prayer[80]), the practitioner experiences complete, embodied integration such that she arrives at "union *through* action."[81]

Bodily Integration as the Fruit of Union with God

The deep intimacy attained here, through God's grace, is not liberation from the body, the "wretched guest,"[82] as some of Teresa's ambiguous language about the body might suggest. Instead, the practitioner is fully (and joyfully) embodied, delighting in the bodily experience of God, and acting from that delight to embody love in the world.[83]

Teresa offers the generative, cooperative friendship of Mary and Martha as an image of the fullness of the union of work and contemplative prayer that now characterizes the practitioner's life.[84] Teresa argues, "Martha and Mary must join together in order to show hospitality to the Lord and have Him always present and not host Him badly by failing to give Him something to eat. How would Mary, always seated at His feet, provide Him with food if her sister did not help her?"[85] The work of providing food for Jesus must be, Teresa tells her sisters, virtuous action in the world. She encourages them to concentrate their efforts on those in proximate need, never falling into despair over the great need in the world, since God will transform their good faith efforts. Any virtuous action performed by practitioners is done in eschatological hope in God, trusting that we participate in God's transformation of the world through our small efforts. As Teresa writes, "if we do what we can, His Majesty will enable us each day to do more and more."[86] Thus, even limited and failing actions of love have an enduring significance, since they embody God's salvific love for the whole world.

The Embodied Human Person: United within, United with God

Teresa can provide us with a dynamic account of union with God from the perspective of one who has experienced significant suffering over the course of her life. Because the human person is created in the image of God, she is capable (through grace) of fully embodied union—within and without. This fullness of union of body and soul is patterned after the unity of the two natures in the one person of Christ and the unity of the three persons in one Godhead.[87] Helpfully, the textured and uneven nature of her descriptions of the divine-human relationship can frame the pulsing character of engagement with traumatic memories, as well as struggles with self-frustration within the broader arc of God's saving activity of the traumatized person. The way that Teresa understands patient care for the body as part of fidelity to God and fidelity to others can frame survivors' recovery efforts as participation in God's saving work. Teresa is able to help us insist on the importance of the body as that which mediates God to the self and to others—highlighting the ways in which bodily well-being can positively condition spiritual well-being, and thus witness the ways in which bodily *harm* is not simply a secular problem but also creates spiritual wounds. Yet, Teresa also firmly insists that illness and injury do not pose insurmountable barriers to union with God, ensuring that there is space for significantly ill and injured survivors to defy their perpetrators' attempts to make totalizing claims over their lives.

To the extent, that Teresa's honesty about her frustrations with chronic illness can, at times, veer into a denigration of embodied life as an unfortunate but temporary purgation, intended to prepare us for a more perfect life in heaven, free from this "wretched guest," she fails to be incarnational enough for a posttraumatic theology of healing.

Teresa suggested at times that suffering can present an opportunity to grow in intimacy with God. This tendency in her thought can risk valorizing suffering itself as bringing about divine-human friendship and suggests that somehow suffering is desired by God for salvation. In a context of sexual violence, this is a risk that carries too high a price for survivors, potentially jeopardizing both victims' safety and well-being, as well as any notion of a God who is worthy of worship. To a large extent, her later writings mitigate against these early shortfalls concerning the body, yet her misguided theology of bodily suffering fails to reach a resolution. Teresa's framework, therefore, requires (in some places) clarification that the fullness of healing for which we await is not a liberation from the body, but instead a liberation of the body for loving friendship. In Chapters 5 and 6, Edward Schillebeeckx can assist us with that task. But for now, we still have a little more to learn from Teresa. In the next chapter, I will detail Teresa's understanding that the human person is made in the image of God and oriented toward friendship. These will be critical components in the construction of a posttraumatic theology of healing, especially as so many survivors struggle with feelings of shame and defilement.

4
The Survivor as *Imago Dei*: Created for Friendship

For Teresa, every human person, no matter what they have done or have had done to them, is capacious of God. All individuals have been created to love and be loved by God and can participate in the life of God as cocreators of love in the world. If the human person is created in the image of God, then violence and systematic forms of gendered and religious oppression cannot destroy their magnificent beauty.

In the last chapter we learned that Teresa offers survivors of sexual violence a vision of union with God as a patient, lifelong process of coming home to one's body and receiving God there. Here, we will fill out that vision with an analysis of Teresa's ideas that we are created in the image of God and oriented toward friendship. Picking up Teresa's notion that the seventh dwelling place is the union with God as a union of two friends, we will dive deeper into our own identities as magnificent beauties who radiate divine light from within. To know that we have been created beautifully in God's image is to know that we have not been created as an object to be manipulated or consumed. We have been created as subjects, to love and be loved freely. We have been created for friendship.

For Teresa, God is the Friend who, despite God's inherent inequality with humanity, invites us into an egalitarian relationship. Because God is unconcerned with distinctions of honor, God desires us to be free *from* concern over social distinctions and to be free *for* true friendship with ourselves and others. Since the primary site of woundedness from sexual violence is one's capacity for relationality, this kind of freedom is truly healing. For Teresa, to be saved (or made whole) is to be set free for authentic friendship.

Knowing Oneself as Created in the Image of God

In Teresa's autobiography, she uses gardening metaphors to describe the ways in which human beings are called by God to labor with God for union with God as our goal. According to her writings, God creates the garden by planting desirable seedlings and helps to maintain the garden by pulling weeds, but our role in maintaining the garden is to provide irrigation.

The metaphor of watering a garden would have felt poignant to the sisters living in her monastery. Spain's arid climate and uneven landscape make water a precious commodity. The monastery's garden was a particularly contested, though beautiful, portion of the monastery property—but the irrigation metaphor has other advantages. One cannot manufacture water. Water itself is a gift that cannot be summoned. The waterer labors to gather the water and to redirect it to the plants that she wishes to cultivate. But she cannot conjure water if there is none to be found. So it is with grace. The contemplative does not manufacture grace. Grace is God's gratuitous self-offer. The contemplative labors to open herself to God's self-offer, realizing after all that even her own labor does not conjure God's gifts.

For Teresa, there are four ways of watering the garden. Four ways to encounter God's transformative grace in the life of prayer: by means of well, by means of a waterwheel, by means of a river, and by means of heavy rain.[1] The first degree of prayer—by means of a well—requires the most effort, while the last—by means of heavy rain—requires virtually none; receptivity is all that is needed.[2] Yet, for Teresa (and indeed, for much of the Christian tradition), human agency and divine agency are non-competitive. Even when the contemplative labors to be open to union with God, God labors to animate and sustain the contemplative in her effort.[3] God has created the contemplative for union with God and sustains her as the *Imago Dei* as she cultivates this union alongside of God. Our relatedness to God precedes any meritorious effort. God has planted a beautiful garden of the soul, and God sustains us in our relatedness to God by weeding that garden. We play a role in cultivation of this relationship by watering the garden.

More than a decade after penning her autobiography, in her most mature work, the *Interior Castle*, Teresa uses a different set of metaphors to describe the human person and her intimacy with God—an expansive castle. The human soul is like a many-roomed castle in which God dwells at the center. The objective of the life of prayer is to spend time exploring this "plentiful, spacious, and large" structure[4] with at least "a million" rooms.[5] She urges the reader, "It is very important for any soul that practices prayer, whether little or much, not to hold itself back and stay in one corner. Let it walk through these dwelling places which are up above, down below, and to the sides, since God has given it such great dignity. Don't force it to stay a long time in one room alone."[6]

Teresa organizes the many rooms of the castle into seven sets of "dwelling places." She locates the seventh dwelling place in the center of the castle, where God interacts with human persons most intimately.[7] The walls of the castle of the soul are constructed from "diamond or a very clear crystal"[8] such that some of the light from the center, where God resides, can emanate throughout the transparent structure.[9] Teresa takes a classical, doctrinal concept and creatively expands upon it, describing the human person as created by God, to house God, and to discover God within. Teresa's insistence that God dwells within the soul is particularly appropriate for survivors of sexual violence.

Trauma theologian Pamela Cooper-White argues that the context of sexual violence calls for "enthusiastic" incarnational theologies, which emphasize God within the victim-survivor. She writes, "Theology that values power-within is joyfully incarnational, celebrating the inherent goodness or 'original blessing' implanted in the human being, not preoccupied with human sinfulness but, rather, with human goodness and inspiration. It is an *enthusiastic* theology, in the etymological sense of the word: *en-theos*, 'God within.'"[10]

To use another of Teresa's metaphors, the human person created in the image of God is like a tree that is planted near water—a source of life that can stably sustain the soul even through drought. Both metaphors—the self as castle and as a tree—preserve the human person's fundamental relatedness to God while carving out a space to describe the alienation that arises from sin; those who are marked by sin remain related to God, but experience distance in that relationship. The human person who falls into sin still has God as her center and "the shining sun that is in the center of the soul, does not lose its beauty and splendor,"[11] but the soul of the sinful person is unable to enjoy the "brilliance and beauty" of its center in God.[12] It is as if the tree has withdrawn from its source of water and cannot produce fruit.[13]

The architectural imagery Teresa uses in the *Interior Castle* allows her to explain that different people dwell in different parts of the castle of the soul. Because the beginning stages of prayer require the highest degrees of human effort, only those who are determined will enter the first dwelling places of the castle of the soul. Many only dwell within the outer courtyards of their castle, while some have explored the beauty of the rooms, and few have been able to reach the very center, where God dwells, and from where God illuminates the entire castle.[14]

It is only through a deep commitment to knowing oneself that one can come to the realization that one is made in the image of God. And many do not know

God as their origin and identity. Teresa explains, "through our own fault we don't understand ourselves or know who we are. Wouldn't it show great ignorance, my daughters, if someone when asked who he was didn't know, and didn't know his father or mother or from what country he came?"[15] The life of prayer is, in a way, self-exploration. To know oneself truly is to know oneself as one in whom God dwells. To know oneself is hard work, but it is necessary for the trauma survivor who has often been told so many false things about herself: that she is weak, that she is defiled, that she cannot survive apart from dependence on her abuser.

Into Account, a sexual violence survivor advocacy group, reports that after David Haas (the Roman Catholic liturgical music composer), raped a thirteen-year-old in the woods during her confirmation retreat in Minnesota, both the child and a chaperone reported the event to Rev. Michael Korf (an archdiocesan advisor). Rev. Korf responded by telling the child that she should feel shame since "it takes two to tango." Later, at the child's confirmation, Archbishop John Roach singled out the victim to repeat Korf's message, using eerily similar words: "Yes, I know who you are. You should be ashamed. It takes two to tango."[16] Another victim of David Haas later reports:

> Once, he cornered me in a back hallway of a hotel, pinned me in by placing his hands on either side of me, and began kissing me and pushing himself against me. I kept turning my head to try to avoid the kissing, and he became angry, saying how he knew I had a thing for him since we first met, and he was tired of waiting. He said things about how upset he was at my wedding, thinking that it should have been him. I heard that more than once over the years. During this particular incident, he became more irate as he pressed against me, but I still remember thinking that I could not yell or even speak up loudly, because I would be to blame for having accompanied him to this back hallway.[17]

To place shame on the shoulders of victims, rather than on perpetrators, is overwhelmingly common. One incest survivor describes herself in these words:

> I am filled with black slime. If I open my mouth, it will pour out.[18]

In these instances, to know oneself authentically is to know oneself as undeserving of shame and radiant with beauty; despite whatever blame others place on us. Perhaps Teresa does not get it wholly right. It might not be "through our own fault" that we fail to see ourselves truly. Nevertheless, her insistence that nothing can damage our inherent beauty, even our inability to recognize it, is helpful.

Teresa is clear that there are many creatures who try to distract us from knowing our beauty. The first dwelling places are located along the exterior walls of the castle, and many repugnant creatures enter along with the practitioner of prayer as she moves inside. These creatures prevent her from achieving a deep sense of calm or from thoroughly observing the beauty of the rooms which she occupies. These first dwelling places appear dark to her, not because of the construction of the rooms themselves, but rather because of the proliferation of "snakes and vipers and poisonous creatures" present.[19] These noxious creatures represent the things of the world—possessions, business affairs, status indicators, etc.—that can distract one from the path of prayer. Individuals who wish to progress in the life of prayer must learn to limit exposure to these distractions. No matter how well one might learn to steel oneself against these creatures, one cannot live with so many of them without being bitten once and a while.[20] Those who remain in the outer areas of the castle, spending so much time with these snakes and vermin, are at great risk of believing that they are one of these nasty creatures themselves! Survivors of sexual trauma, who often struggle so acutely with feelings of shame and self-disgust in response to what has been done to them, can perhaps understand the dangers of this kind of mistaken solidarity with filth. Joan Miller (a pseudonym), survivor of rape while studying abroad in Italy, testifies:

> When the rape first happened, I felt I was a victim of violence. Over time this morphed into something that I slowly and quietly came to believe I had somehow deserved. The rape, along with the lack of support from family and friends, made me feel indescribable shame. I became disconnected from the world—from my parents, my friends and from God. I went through my final year of college like an empty shell. I had no one who could meet me where I was. I felt I had no place where this new me would be accepted and loved. I was afraid to open up to others for fear of being judged. I tried praying and turning to God, but it seemed like a waste of time. I felt God had left me just like everyone else—that he had let this happen to me.[21]

Teresa argues that those who dwell exclusively in the external portions of the castle have difficulty understanding themselves as wealthy persons, capable of dwelling within the luxury of the inner castle and conversing with God face-to-face, as one might with a lover or a friend.[22] She compares those who do not practice prayer to those who do not care for their bodies, allowing themselves to become weak after an injury from lack of rehabilitative exercise. They do not nurture their own full functionality and health.[23] As we have seen, this is no mere metaphor for Teresa; she believes that bodily self-care is an important component of fidelity to God.

To regularly contemplate the grandeur of God is to learn something about oneself: namely to grow in humility. Likening the work of humility to a bee, busily gathering nectar from flowers,[24] Teresa argues that the work of humility should never be relaxed.[25] Those who attain some knowledge of the self as the image of God will discover themselves as "magnificent" and possessing a "marvelous capacity" for the divine.[26]

Understanding oneself as beautiful is of critical importance for survivors of sexual trauma. Survivor and trauma theologian Hilary Jerome Scarsella explains:

> When victims believe ourselves to be innately corrupt, we tend to believe the violence we experience is our fault, and we aren't able to see ourselves as worthy of protection. But when people who are victimized become open to the parts of ourselves that are worthy and good and dearly beloved, we cultivate strength that is necessary for finding safety and doing the difficult work of trauma recovery.[27]

Self-knowledge is not identical with high self-esteem. While we acknowledge ourselves as beautiful and capacious, we also realize that our beauty comes from another. Therefore, it can be just as accurate to describe ourselves in terms of our "lowliness"[28] and our vulnerability to sin.[29] We are fearful, fainthearted, cowardly, marked by the effects of selfishness, and dependent upon God for everything. Our own merits do not make us beautiful. It is our relatedness to God that gives us our beauty and goodness.[30]

The Dangers of False Humility

For Teresa, true self-knowledge is humility. To know oneself as you are, is to know that you are of the *humus*—the rich soil which births new life and collects life that has been spent. Echoing the second creation narrative in Genesis that describes God as breathing the divine spirit into the soil to create our bodies, and promising that we will be given back to the soil when our lives are over (Gen. 2:7, 3:19), the disposition of "humility" etymologically recalls consciousness of both our dusty origins and our final destination.[31]

Humility might appear, at first glance, to be an unhelpful concept for those struggling with posttraumatic healing. It can suggest an image of a woman who is unsure of herself, who keeps her eyes on the ground and does not look at others directly. It can connote one who does not think that she is worthy of love or success (and therefore does not pursue it), or one who does not resist when she is violated. In a global context, in which racism, nationalism, xenophobia, and wealth consolidation are used to keep power in the hands of a few, those who are most vulnerable to sexual violence (i.e., the poor, the non-White, and the undocumented) are hardly at risk of an overinflated sense of self-worth. Furthermore, if secular culture presents more than enough opportunities to question the beauty and worth of our bodies as they are, then the Christian tradition is of little help when it proclaims (as some churches do, though certainly not all) that women cannot act *in persona Christi* or *in persona ecclesiae*, or that queer sexual expression is a perversion of the natural order. Yet Teresa of Avila's interpretation of the importance of humility in the Christian life can function as a surprising antidote to these oppressive conditions.[32]

For Teresa, the more that we look to God's grandeur, the more we can understand ourselves in humility. The more that we understand ourselves as we truly and humbly are, the more capable we are of transforming ourselves and our world.[33] True self-knowledge makes one strong and perceptive, not cowardly. As moral theologian Lisa Fullam puts it, "humility is part and parcel of the freedom in her unity with God that permits, empowers, even impels her in her mission of reform and teaching. Far from disempowering her, humility set her free."[34] Because self-knowledge consists in humility, true self-knowledge will never lead someone to think that she is entitled to the favors given to her by God. Yet because God is good, God does grant us gifts. If we do not receive God's gifts because we deserve them, we also cannot reject the abundant gifts of God because we believe we are unworthy. Teresa calls this "false humility." False humility denies God's omnipotence, suggesting that God cannot or should not bestow favors to any human being whom God wishes.[35]

Recognizing that women and other socially non-dominant people, are prone to self-punishment and self-debasement, Teresa speaks just as sharply (if not more so) about the dangers of false humility—a kind of self-minimizing behavior—than the dangers of pride—self-maximizing behavior. Hilary Jerome Scarsella notes:

> sin is not necessarily self-prioritizing behavior. In fact, the concept of sin is not confined to wrong behavior at all. It is, rather, *anything*—personal or systemic—that keeps a person from the full embrace of divine love. While it would be quite appropriate for one who is in a position of power over others to be led in worship to confess excessively prioritizing self over others as sin, this is not at all appropriate for a victim of abuse. What keeps a victim of sexual abuse from receiving the full embrace of God's love within the immediate context of abuse

is likely the opposite: an excessive priority of others over self. For a person experiencing abuse, sin (and I speak of sin here in a systemic sense, not in any way that could put personal blame on such a person for this behavior) most often manifests as lack of pride, giving away too much of oneself, excessive care for others, inappropriate tolerance, self-denial, and self-sacrifice.[36]

In Teresa's view, there are ample opportunities for her sisters to misinterpret humility by thinking that it consists of making oneself less than one is and, ultimately, frustrating the actions that God has commanded one to take. False humility can produce fear,[37] overzealous penitential practices,[38] and cowardliness. Teresa explains in her autobiography:

> I believe the devil harms people who practice prayer and prevents them from advancing by causing them to misunderstand humility. He makes it appear to us that it is pride to have great desires and want to imitate the saints and long to be martyrs. Then he tells us or causes us to think that since we are sinners the deeds of the saints are for our admiration, not our imitation.[39]

Teresa acknowledges that she made the mistake of thinking that to refrain from mental prayer was a sign of true humility.[40] She was "waiting to be very purified of sin" before engaging in mental prayer,[41] but instead, the life of prayer and the pursuit of holiness is for those seeking healing.

This is relevant for all those who experience themselves as broken, especially survivors of sexual abuse; one does not have to be whole in order to relate intimately to God. Caroline, a survivor of date rape, even though she has experienced some measure of healing, testifies to her relationship with God, even as she is still wounded by the violence committed against her. Imagining that she is addressing her rapist directly, Caroline writes:

> I took a walk not long ago and thought about how far I have come. Although I feel more guarded and less carefree than I did before it happened, I also feel more aware. I place more value on friendship. I am more in tune with myself. I am better able to recognize when others are hurting. I still get excited about the little things in life, like I did before you hurt me. I am increasingly confident. The consequences of your actions—the pain you caused—challenged me to find and understand myself. I am now closer to my friends and family. I've discovered an inner strength I never knew I had. I've realized that it's okay to not be okay. My faith was rocked, but I'm discovering a new relationship with God.[42]

The practitioner of prayer is conscious of her acute brokenness, or as Jane Grovijahn puts it, her "body-need" of God. The survivor-practitioner is in search of liberation from the "ravaging and distorting" effects of violence on the violated body.[43] In contrast to false humility's tendency to encourage distancing oneself from God by refraining from prayer or by thinking of great deeds as something only other people can do, true humility engenders holy endurance and courageous action. True humility leads one to accept God's blessings and courageously take up the work of healing.

Pastor Rebecca Ann Parker tells the story of Lucia, a woman who came to her for counseling after struggling to follow the advice of a priest who instructed her to accept physical abuse from her husband as a way to imitate Jesus on the cross. Parker tells her:

> "It isn't true . . . God does not want you to accept being beaten by your husband. God wants you to have your life, not to give it up. God wants you to protect your life and your children's lives." Lucia's eyes danced. "I knew I was right!" she said. "But it helps to hear you say it. Now I know that I should do what I have been thinking about doing." She planned to take courses at the community college until she had a marketable skill. Then she would get a job and move herself and her children to a new home.[44]

Lucia's actions required courage and the sacrifice of hard work and persistence. True humility—that is, an honest assessment of oneself as dependent on God—motivates one to seek safety, even when that might require the courageous and difficult work of love for oneself and one's children. True humility leads one to action rather than to paralysis.

Humility also repositions the common tendency to shoulder the burden of transformative change from the actor alone, to understanding the actor as working alongside God and the community of God's people to bring about the fullness of healing. In this way, humility can allow one to persist without falling into frustration at the lack of results.[45] Humility redirects the assumption that we strive for greatness through our own efforts and can comfort us when others disappoint us or when we disappoint ourselves. Humility understands that "this strength does not come from ourselves."[46] Our strength comes from God, who is a friend to the humble and courageous.[47]

True Self-Knowledge

True self-knowledge holds two concepts in tension: as one created in the image of God, the human person is both lowly and magnificently beautiful. A balanced awareness of oneself as created in the image of God is a primary aim of the life of prayer.

On the one hand, to think too highly of oneself can lead to the illusion that one does not need God. This tends to produce both an overly critical attitude toward oneself when one fails to meet one's own (very high) expectations, and an overly critical perception of one's neighbors, interfering with appropriate forms of love between friends. But meaningful, healthy, and moderate forms of attachment (accompanied by realistic expectations) to others is necessary for recovery from trauma.[48] As Judith Herman explains:

> The survivor oscillates between intense attachment and terrified withdrawal. She approaches all relationships as though questions of life and death are at stake. She may cling desperately to a person who she perceives as a rescuer, flee suddenly from a person she suspects to be a perpetrator or accomplice, show great loyalty and devotion to a person she perceives to be an ally, and heap wrath and scorn on a person who appears to be a complacent bystander. The roles she assigns to others may change suddenly, as the result of small lapses or disappointments, for no internal representation of another person is any longer secure. Once again, there is no room for mistakes. Over time, as most people fail the survivor's exacting tests of trustworthiness, she tends to withdraw from relationships. The isolation of the survivor thus persists even after she is free.[49]

On the other hand, one must not emphasize one's lowliness to such an extent that it interferes with the work that God is accomplishing within us. A hyper-self-consciousness of one's unworthiness of God can stand in the way of service to God through acts of love of neighbor and transformation of the world. Teresa advises the practitioner of prayer to be aware of one's lowliness, but not to dwell there, because one has so much to accomplish beyond this—so much to do, so much to create, and so much to love on behalf of God. As Teresa explains:

> Once a soul sees that it is now submissive and understands clearly that it has nothing good of itself and is aware both of being ashamed before so great a King and of repaying so little of the great amount it owes Him—what need is there to waste time here? We must go on to other things that the Lord places before us; and there is no reason to leave them aside, for His Majesty knows better than we what is fitting for us to eat.[50]

False humility only presents our wretchedness to us and leads, as Rowan Williams puts it, to "self-indulgent and self-excusing despair."[51]

Self-knowledge is critical to the exercise of true love, but it is not an end in itself.[52] Self-knowledge does not consist of interest in yourself, but rather of being familiar with your creatureliness and, therefore, your dependence on God.[53] Relation to God gives our lowliness beauty.[54] True self-knowledge grants inner stability and serves as the foundation for acts of love.

True self-knowledge—as one who is simultaneously wounded by sin and yet capacious of God—is not to be taken for granted in a posttraumatic context. This tensive self-understanding can only be held together after significant healing has taken place. For Christians, encountering God in prayer reveals us to ourselves, both as we are and as God has created us to be. This awareness, however, is not the sum of healing. As trauma researchers, such as Judith Herman, insist, so does Teresa. For Herman, traumatic healing extends beyond the personal, culminating in social transformation; for Teresa, the Christian life, propelled by the practice of prayer, culminates in love for one's sisters and the common good.

The aim of self-knowledge is interior tranquility, finding peace with all aspects of ourselves. Using the metaphor of the self as one's dwelling place, Teresa writes:

> Can there be an evil greater than that of being ill at ease in our own house? What hope can we have of finding rest outside of ourselves if we cannot be at rest within. We have so many great and true friends and relatives (which are our faculties) with whom we must always live, even though we may not want to. But from what we feel, these seem to be warring against us because of what our vices have done to them. Peace, peace, the Lord said, my Sisters; and He urged His apostle so many times. Well, believe me, if we don't obtain and have peace in our own house we'll not find it outside. Let this war be ended.[55]

Teresa's description of the challenge of contemplative prayer resonates powerfully with the challenges of healing for victims of sexual abuse. Sexual trauma disturbs the victim at her core, producing a feeling of dis-ease in her body, her soul, and in all of her relationships. The victim cannot flee from these sites of violation. For the duration of her life, she is bound to this violated body and soul, and she cannot experience relations apart from their mediations. Recovery, therefore, is nothing if it does not include a restoration of interior peace within the embodied soul. Even after escaping violence, survivor Lydia explains how a lack of interior peace continued to harm her.

> If you came into my house you could have really eaten your dinner off the kitchen floor. It was immaculate. I was obsessively immaculate. I wore myself out keeping it clean and during ministry, the Holy Spirit revealed that I only had peace if I felt clean, and of course I'd felt very dirty—but I had my whiteness, virginity, cleanness restored to me, and now [if] anybody who knew me then, and hasn't seen me for many years, came into my house they wouldn't believe it. We've got four dogs and it doesn't bother me. I don't have to clean anything now.[56]

The peace that Lydia has found within now allows her to have a healthy, non-obsessive approach to maintaining outer order.

The reality that so many victims of sexual violence are assaulted within their own families and/or within the context of other trusted communities (e.g., churches, schools, at the hands of medical professionals or law enforcement) makes Teresa's metaphor of "our own house" even more poignant. Teresa asks the question that traumatized individuals pose so urgently; if we cannot be safe in our own homes, where can we be safe? The first step of recovery is to seek a safe home and a safe community of support. Once external safety is secured, seeking interior tranquility becomes critical. Importantly, interior peace is not found in naively "counting your blessings," but through remembering and mourning what has been lost. The practitioner of prayer explores the rooms of her soul, gathering together all of her thoughts and memories, and turns them over to God. This can produce the kind of peace that arises between friends after many years of intimacy. The practitioner begins to feel peace with herself as a familiar friend, and with God the Friend, who has created her as vulnerable and beautiful. Without some measure of interior peace, it is difficult for the trauma survivor to connect with others in meaningful ways (the third stage of traumatic recovery).

The Survivor as *Imago Dei*

Teresa's insistence on the human person as the *Imago Dei* offers critical resources for those struggling to recover from sexual trauma. She is neither the first nor the last Christian writer to describe the human person as created in the image of God, but her writings offer the beauty of this classic theological doctrine in unique ways. The *Imago Dei* does not remain an abstract theoretical concept in Teresa's writings, but rather she gives it life in rich horticultural and architectural imagery. In her *Vida*, the soul is a lush garden, planted and weeded by God. In the *Interior Castle*, the soul is a sparkling, fortified structure of ineffable beauty. The soul is ever more spacious, more beautiful, and more precious to God than she can ever name.⁵⁷ Teresa's theological anthropology is able to hold in delicate balance the very real scars of sin, while at the same time, preserves a notion of deep human integrity. The effect of maintaining the beauty of the soul in the context of extreme suffering and defilement can point powerfully to the ever-present possibility of posttraumatic healing.

When survivor language is used to describe those who have been traumatized by sexual violence, it can sometimes mistakenly imply a completed action (as if someone has *survived* trauma), obscuring the enduring nature of traumatic wounding. Survivors are not done surviving—existence continues to challenge one's being. The way that Teresa is able to describe the human person as both damaged by sin and yet also created in the image of God brings a textured approach to the survivor's identity: I am vulnerable; I am hurting; I am powerful; I am loved and loving.

Roxane Gay, writer, and survivor of gang-rape as a child, talks about the ways in which the title "survivor" alone can sometimes miss important aspects of her relationship with violence. She writes:

> I am marked, in so many ways, by what I went through. I survived it, but that isn't the whole of the story. Over the years, I have learned the importance of survival and claiming the label of 'survivor,' but I don't mind the label of 'victim.' I also don't think there's any shame in saying that when I was raped, I became a victim, and to this day, while I am also many other things, I am still a victim. It took me a long time, but I prefer 'victim' to 'survivor' now. I don't want to diminish the gravity of what happened. I don't want to pretend I'm on some triumphant, uplifting journey. I don't want to pretend that everything is okay. I'm living with what happened, moving forward without forgetting, moving forward without pretending I am unscarred.⁵⁸

Similarly, Donna Freitas, feminist scholar and survivor of stalking by a Roman Catholic priest and mentor, writes:

> I am fierce, *and* I am polite. I am strong, *and* I am vulnerable. I want things, *and* sometimes I don't want things. I am a good judge of people, *and* sometimes I am too trusting. I am an ardent, insightful, committed feminist, *and* I let the patriarchy walk all over me. *And* I still blame myself when I look for the reason for what happened to me. I still search for that reason by looking within myself. . . . I am both a survivor *and* still a victim, and somehow I will always and forever be both.⁵⁹

As much as Teresa is able to offer a posttraumatic theology of healing, she also has limitations. When she names sin as that which damages the human person, however, Teresa tends to highlight the effects of personal sins. She is clear that withdrawal from God has harmful effects upon the human person, since it is one's relatedness to God that gives one its beauty.[60] But Teresa does not explicitly acknowledge the ways in which alienation from God can be brought about by another, or as Jane Grovijahn puts it, "God [can be] ripped out of a woman's body."[61] Teresa discusses withdrawal from God as vulnerability to the devils that wage war in every room of the castle, but in the absence of a direct treatment of interpersonal and structural sins, one can get the impression that this withdrawal from God is ultimately one's "own fault."[62] She does not discuss the human person as one who suffers from being "sinned-against."[63] Survivors of sexual violence suffer from the egregious sins of others, not their own free choices. Their bodies have been used as weapons against themselves to fulfill the desires of their perpetrators. These sins, however profoundly they have marked their lives, are not properly their own.

Teresa herself suffered from these kinds of sins—as both a woman and one with a *converso* heritage—yet she did not write directly about herself as sinned-against. While her reform of the Carmelite order pushed back against some of the structural forms of oppression against women and *conversos*, she never questioned the ethics of religiously motivated violence (either through the office of the Inquisition or through holy wars) and especially, the violence of Spain's colonial expansion. She understood colonization and rooting out heresy to be, in themselves, holy endeavors,[64] even if she expanded upon Catholic Spain's notion of who should be safe from harm.[65]

A contemporary theology of healing cannot name sin as only personal culpability but must necessarily acknowledge the personal suffering of being sinned against, as well as the harm inflicted by structural and social sins. In this regard, Teresa's anthropology misses the mark. We will need to turn to resources from twentieth- and twenty-first century theologians, philosophers, and other trauma theorists in order to expand upon this reality of sin. But we are not yet finished with the wealth of Teresa's thought. Despite her limitations, she still has more to offer a posttraumatic theology of healing—namely, a dynamic portrait of humanity as finding its deepest vocation in friendship with God and others.

The Human Person as Oriented toward Friendship

A natural, yet innovative, outgrowth of Teresa's understanding of the human person as created in the image of God is her consistent insistence that the human person is oriented toward friendship. Practical theologian Tara Soughers catalogues, "the word *amigo* appears more than 450 times in [Teresa's] writings and *amistad* appears 128 times. Likewise, companion and companionship appear frequently. *Compañero* appears 85 times and *compañia* (when not used in reference to Jesuits, *Compañia de Jesús*) appears 100 times."[66] We are oriented toward friendship with God and others.[67] It is this orientation that is exploited in sexual violence, but this orientation also contains pathways for healing.

God as Friend

Teresa's dominant metaphor for God is that of Friend. Although friendship is a particular kind of relational intimacy that can only be experienced by equals, God's gratuitous self-offer to humanity makes friendship with God possible. As Rowan Williams explains:

> To make us friends of God, God wholly abandons dignity and status: it is not that God simply brings us up to an acceptable standard and then deigns to treat us as friends. In the incarnation, the Son renounces all claim to 'special' status and comes to be identified with suffering men and women, and this renunciation expresses the desire of the whole of the trinitarian godhead to be present to the human world without reserve or condition. Friendship with God begins with God's refusal even to introduce the question of status, with God's longing for companionship, or rather, longing to share the companionship of mutual self-gift that constitutes the divine life. God initiates this friendship by resolving to have no interest at heart but ours, and we appropriately respond by resolving to have no interest but God's.[68]

As we will see (and may already anticipate), God's refusal to hold us at a distance, despite our comparative lack of honor, opens us up to imitate God's lavishness in friendship with others. Teresa believes we have been created to enjoy this friendship with God and we experience friendship with God most intensely in the practice of prayer. Prayer is the "intimate sharing between friends . . . taking time frequently to be alone with Him who we know loves us."[69]

Friendship Disrupts Hierarchy and Difference

It is in prayer that we learn that God desires friendship with us and we come to experience what friendship with someone so different than us is like.[70] Despite the acute, relational intimacy with God experienced in prayer, God remains radically "other." This is analogous to the way in which friends always recognize the otherness of each other. In friendship, we do not experience the other as an extension of ourselves, but rather as fundamentally a mystery, which we witness and reverence. The otherness of the friend is all the more heightened in philial relationship with God, who radically transcends the created order. To enter into friendship—a relationship of equality—with one who is so radically other, upsets all other socially constructed hierarchies and divisions by extension.[71]

Understanding Oneself as God's Friend

Teresa's theology of prayer is rooted in her rich anthropology; prayer involves authentic self-knowledge. To understand oneself truly is to know oneself as befriended by God. The practitioner of prayer is encouraged to explore her inner resources and learn to acknowledge herself in love as God sees her—both magnificently beautiful and wounded by sin. She is encouraged to take a long look at the reality of herself, to become comfortable in it, and to love herself enough to admit both her gifts and her challenges. In a way then, the one who sees herself as friend of God comes to befriend herself.[72]

The practitioner of prayer is encouraged to befriend oneself in humility, neither placing oneself on a pedestal nor discarding oneself as unimportant. Out of fidelity to God, we care for ourselves materially (nurturing our physical health) and spiritually (nurturing union with God).

For Teresa, friendship with God and friendship with oneself are intrinsically related. In order to draw near to God in friendship, one has to come to an authentic understanding of oneself as God's beloved and an object of God's desire. For survivors of sexual violence, befriending oneself will often involve offering oneself compassion and forgiveness. Survivors tend to struggle with blaming themselves for what has happened to them, painstakingly analyzing whether they had done enough to avoid or resist violence. For some survivors, they may need to come to terms with actions they committed in a state of high stress, which would otherwise conflict with their conscience. For example, anthropologist Cathy Winkler, in the middle of an hours-long attack by a home intruder, told her rapist that he was beautiful and must be desired by many women.[73] In these instances, forgiveness involves acknowledging that these were genuinely wise actions, helpful for enabling survival in impossible situations.

In some instances, survivors have committed genuinely sinful actions or, at the very least, morally ambiguous actions, following their trauma. For example, a survivor might have overlooked, or even participated in violence against their own children or pressured another person in a position of vulnerability to violence.[74] In these instances, forgiveness involves acknowledging the extent of one's culpability, making amends as much as possible, and aiming to move forward, free from cycles of perpetuating abuse. Teresa's anthropology is spacious enough to allow for an acknowledgement of personal sin, as well as self-compassion and enduring dignity.

Friendship with Others

Friendship with oneself and friendship with God ultimately leads one to the possibility of loving friendships with others. The stability that self-knowledge and love of God provides equips the practitioner of prayer to love those in her community and to work for the common good. Because she knows who she is as God's beloved friend, the practitioner of prayer can reach out in friendship to those around her, both giving and receiving acts of love and support, without regard for social standing.[75] As Rowan Williams describes Teresa's vision, "God can only be honoured as we should honour God if we allow God's friendship to override all social divisions."[76] Thus, against her own culture's obsession with *honra* and stratified class structures, friendship—i.e., a relationship between equals—becomes the "primary form of social connectedness."[77] As Teresa puts it, in her community "all must be friends, all must be loved, all must be held dear, all must be helped."[78] Her vision of Carmel is a "community of friends."[79] For Teresa, love is not a positive feeling, but instead the concrete work of being a good community member.[80]

Healthy Boundaries

As we have seen, relationships of mutual love and vulnerability are critical for posttraumatic healing. However, Teresa's anthropology has built-in brakes against unhealthy and inappropriate forms of relationality. In situating God as "both the real object of true friendship as well as the perfect model,"[81] Teresa is clear that some relationships can be damaging or destructive.

Christian love does not entail an unqualified openness to all—some relationships need narrow boundaries, and some individuals are not healthy to have relationships with at all, especially those who exercise power unjustly.[82] Teresa's model of the self as a castle is again useful here—one is capable of defending oneself from invaders, reptiles, and other vermin, while still opening oneself in friendship, appropriately, to trusted others. As philosopher Susan Brison explains, "In order to reestablish that connection in the aftermath of trauma, one must first feel able to protect oneself against invasion. The autonomous self and the relational self are thus shown to be interdependent, even constitutive of one another."[83]

Teresa's autobiography, itself written for self-protection from the threat of the Inquisition, used defensive writing tactics to instruct her readers in ways of being resistant to religious authorities who wished to silence or condemn them. To this point, in her *Vida*, she instructed her readers to choose a confessor wisely and to ensure that this confessor keeps the details of her interior life confidential, in order to minimize opportunities for his own confusion. Teresa counseled her female readers that, "because our weakness is great," confessors need to help them to keep their experiences secret to avoid being falsely accused of delusion by the devil.[84] Teresa skillfully couched her advice to women on how to maintain spiritual autonomy and wholeness in language targeting the supposed "weakness" of women. This would appease the Inquisitors who might be suspicious of the unabashed encouragement of women.

Defending Oneself from Discreditors

Teresa provides many cautionary examples from her own life in which she failed to follow this advice, describing the harm that she suffered at the hands of confessors who falsely believed that she was deluded by the devil.[85] As she describes it, she tried very hard to agree with her confessors that she was under demonic influence, but it only made her feel confused, "completely agitated and wearied without knowing what to do," and "terrified," until God appeared to her in a vision to tell her: "Do not fear, daughter; for I am, and I will not abandon you; do not fear."[86] These divine words instantly calmed her and gave her strength and courage,[87] generating the confidence that nothing could harm her. She lost the fears that plagued her and, in an amazing reversal, began to believe that evil should be afraid of *her*, proclaiming, "Why shouldn't I have the fortitude to engage in combat with all of hell?"[88] Observing the way that God had given her power over all devils, she explained, "I pay no more attention to them than to flies. I think they're such cowards that when they observe they are esteemed but little, their strength leaves them."[89]

Those who have perpetrated sexual violence are purveyors of evil, and we can take Teresa's leveling of evil to heart; it is no match for the power of one fortified by the divine. The power of God is evident in survivors of sexual violence when they draw boundaries with those who do not respect their right to safety and when they refuse to be scared into silence about the reality of evil in the world.

Selective Vulnerability

For Teresa, personal vulnerability (when able to be controlled) should only be directed toward those who can be trusted. Teresa opened herself up in vulnerability to God, but she guarded herself against the devils (in the *Vida*) and against the vermin of the castle (in the *Interior Castle*), making sure to let as few of them into the rooms as possible[90] —bringing the political weight of her metaphor of the castle as a defensive, protective structure into clearer focus. Trauma survivors, as they progress in healing, find that they must practice regulating vulnerability: they limit their exposure to dangerous individuals and relationships (e.g., those who have abused them before, those who they know have perpetrated violence against others, etc.), but simultaneously work to relearn gradations of appropriate powerlessness and passivity in planned encounters with danger or risk (e.g., wilderness trips, martial arts training, prayer, etc.).[91] As trauma psychologist Judith Herman explains:

> By the third stage of recovery, the survivor has regained some capacity for appropriate trust. She can once again feel trust in others when that trust is warranted, she can withhold her trust when it is not warranted, and she knows how to distinguish between the two situations. She has also regained the ability to feel autonomous while remaining connected to others; she can maintain her own point of view and her own boundaries while respecting others. She has begun to take more initiative in her life and is in the process of creating a new identity. With others, she is now ready to risk deepening her relationships. With peers, she can now seek mutual friendships that are not based on performance, image, or maintenance of a false self. With lovers and family, she is now ready for greater intimacy.[92]

If the life of prayer involves vulnerability to God and resistance to some others—particularly those who exercise unjust power, it also involves loving service to different others—particularly those who are powerless and in need. This is a model of relationality according to the pattern of the *Magnificat*: the powerful are to be brought down from their thrones, the lowly are lifted up, the hungry are filled with good things, and the rich are sent away empty (Lk 1:52–53). Prayer is an imaginative practice that helps the practitioner to relearn trust in herself and in a relational other (God); to see herself as capable of resistance and aggression toward others, as well as to see herself as possessing gifts of love and healing to share with others. It is this full and creative range of relationality that is lost with trauma (as one is reduced to a powerless victim), and that must be restored in order to experience healing.

A Teresian Approach to Posttraumatic Healing

Teresa of Avila, the sixteenth-century Spanish mystic whose vision of the embodied human person as the *Imago Dei* and friend of God, carried a strong political critique of her society's obsession with honor and class distinction. From these resources, she can offer us a generative starting point for a mystical-political theology of posttraumatic healing. Teresa's understanding of the human person as the *Imago Dei* names the human person as possessive of an inherent beauty that, on the one hand, should be preserved and held sacred through precious care, yet, on the other hand, cannot be destroyed by maltreatment. Because the human person is fully embodied, and union with God represents the fullness of bodily integration (rather than transcendence of the body), care for bodies (one's own and vulnerable others') is integral to sacred fidelity to God. If it is true, as Rowan Williams argues, that "It is a fatal error to think that we have to leave ourselves and journey somewhere distant in order to find God,"[93] it is even truer for survivors of sexual violence.

Teresa offers survivors of sexual violence a vision of union with God as a patient, lifelong process of coming home to one's body and receiving God there. For Teresa, God is the Friend who, despite God's inherent inequality with humanity, invites us into an egalitarian relationship. Because God is unconcerned with distinctions of honor, God desires our freedom from concern over social distinctions, opening the path for true friendship with ourselves and others. Since the primary site of woundedness from sexual violence is one's capacity for relationality, this kind of freedom is truly healing. For Teresa, to be saved (or made whole) is to be set free for authentic friendship. For those who have survived grave harm at the hands of another, friendship with God, oneself, and others, requires both courage to persist in the *arduum bonum* and, at root, a fundamental hope that evil does not have the final word. I will return to these themes and develop them further in the final chapters of this book. For now, however, let us remind ourselves, honestly, of the ways in which Teresa's theology, despite its gifts, falls short of a fully incarnational theology of healing.

Teresa's impatience with her own body, influenced by her experiences with chronic illness, can, at times, suggest that the freedom which God desires for us is a freedom from the "wretched" body, rather than a freedom for full bodily integration. To the extent that Teresa can fall into denigration of the body (especially in her earlier writings), she fails to consistently carry out her incarnational impulses.

Furthermore, Teresa's theology of suffering needs nuance. She helpfully guides the practitioner of prayer away from excessive penitential practices and encourages her to care for the body as faithful service to God. But, to the extent that Teresa thought that suffering presents the opportunity to serve God if one suffers courageously and patiently, she risks suggesting that God desires human suffering. In the context of sexual violence, no suggestion could be more damaging to survivors. Rape is senseless suffering—never desired by God or productive of any good in the human person. God does not desire any person to suffer rape in order to "learn a lesson," avoid a greater suffering, or grow closer to God. Rape is pointless evil. For Teresa's thought to positively contribute to a contemporary theology of healing, it needs the correction of contemporary theologians who have thought carefully about the absurdity of evil. In the next chapter, Edward Schillebeeckx's notion of "senseless suffering" can assist us with this.

5
Edward Schillebeeckx's Theology of Suffering

Given the limitations of Teresa of Avila's theological anthropology—most critically, her tendency to valorize suffering—we need to turn to another source that can help us speak more clearly to the reality that some forms of suffering (all forms of sexual violence) do not produce any good in victims. Rape does not happen for a divine reason. God does not desire some people to suffer from sexual abuse in order to bring about any greater good (including dependency on God). Sexual violence is senseless. It afflicts people for no good reason.

This does not mean that we should not analyze the psychological, political, and economic factors that contribute to perpetrators' actions. Instead, it means that, theologically, we cannot ascribe a divine reason to perpetrators' actions. In other words, God does not want anyone, for any reason at all, to suffer from sexual violence. Teresa's theology of suffering does not sufficiently deal with senseless suffering and, therefore, her framework is inadequate (on its own) to address the theological reality of rape.

Over the course of the twentieth century, theologians, by and large, have recognized that theology needs to seriously engage with the challenges of radical human suffering in order to be credible. An initial push for Christian reflection on senseless suffering was generated in the wake of the Holocaust. As Christians reflected on the failures of their own tradition to resist serious cooperation in moral evil, it has grown over time to reflect on the horrific legacy of the transatlantic slave trade,[1] as well as on European colonization and Christian mission efforts that set up structural injustices, jeopardizing the poor throughout the Americas, Asia, and Africa.[2] Many contemporary theologians have problematized the identification of suffering with fidelity to God, and argue that excessive human suffering in history demands clear political-theological responses; namely, that God does not will the suffering of humankind. In particular, feminist and womanist theologians have warned us that, as long as "[p]owerlessness is equated with faithfulness," the suffering of powerless persons in society will be given meaning through sanctification of the injustices committed against them.[3] If Christian images function as an idealization of victimhood, Christian theology risks permission, if not prescription, for violent and oppressive social structures and interpersonal relationships. The challenge, as contemporary political theologians have framed it, is "how can we give meaning to suffering without sanctioning it?"[4]

The twentieth-century Flemish Catholic political theologian Edward Schillebeeckx can provide a framework for articulating the shape of human salvation in the context of senseless suffering. Schillebeeckx's understanding of experiences of suffering as "negative contrast experiences" allows us to proclaim God as present to the sufferer, without sanctifying her abuse; to name experience as a trustworthy source of divine revelation; and to claim sufferers' agency in experiences of extreme violation. Although Schillebeeckx never discusses sexual trauma himself, we can reposition his understanding of radical suffering in the context of sexual violence. In doing this, we will discover that God is "for" humanity, desiring holistic human good, including, but not limited to, bodily-material healing, interpersonal healing, and political-institutional posttraumatic healing. Human beings are commissioned to participate in bringing about human salvation through posttraumatic healing work, yet the healing that we can expect from God transcends that which we are able to accomplish through our own efforts.

God Does Not Want Human Beings to Suffer

Edward Schillebeeckx's ideas are similar to Teresa's. Like Teresa, he argues that salvation concerns the whole human person, and that authentic mystical prayer involves engagement in the world with acts of love. Even though both thinkers could be seen to carve out a mystical-political shape for salvation, Schillebeeckx is even clearer than Teresa about the need for politically engaged Christian mysticism. He sees his work as contributing to the twentieth century turn to "political theology." Political theology is committed to attention to power dynamics and that, in response, calls for a kind of Christian discipleship that embraces more than mere personal attitudinal shifts or transformation of interpersonal relationships alone, but also broad social change.

A self-consciously mystical-political approach is necessary for a theological treatment of healing from sexual violence since sexual trauma affects the whole person. The theological response to trauma must call for a full range of healing—of the mind, body, social relationships, sexual relationships, familial relationships, social structures, and political institutions. A mystical approach which excludes the political would fail to restore the individual in the context of her external world. Conversely, a merely political approach would overlook the depth of interior healing that is necessary following trauma. To the extent that Schillebeeckx resonates with Teresa's ideas, sharpening their political edge, he develops Teresa's impulses toward a holistic Christian anthropology for a contemporary context, with necessary attention paid to power and political transformation.

I bring Schillebeeckx to this conversation, not merely to riff on Teresa's insights, but also to correct them using his theology of suffering. Through his development of experiences of suffering as "negative contrast experiences," Schillebeeckx argues that God does not desire human suffering and, more to the point, God does not use suffering as a tool to bring about salvation. Acknowledging the persistent and excessive reality of suffering in human life, God is present to the sufferer in absence. Schillebeeckx's theology of suffering is a necessary intervention to correct Teresa's tendency to sanctify suffering and clearly delineates the importance of human cooperation with God to deny evil the opportunity to flourish in human history.

Schillebeeckx's emphasis on human agency and cooperation with God is critical for healing from sexual trauma. Yet it is often underemphasized by some trauma theologians, to the detriment of survivors. A clear understanding of Schillebeeckx's corrective theology of suffering will allow for a more precise understanding of the mystical-political shape of human salvation. Salvation is human wholeness and is in no way complete while humans still experience senseless suffering. Both Teresa and Schillebeeckx agree that mystical union with God is oriented toward human freedom. But only if we can be clear that God does not want human beings to suffer can we trust that this freedom is not simply another opportunity to painfully experience being overpowered for (supposedly) "our own good," but is, rather, an authentic experience of expansion, joy, and greater well-being.

Edward Schillebeeckx's Corrective Theology of Suffering

Each semester, I teach a new batch of undergraduates, approximately one hundred new faces in the fall and another one hundred in the spring—the majority of whom are in their first year of studies. When I ask these students to talk about the Christian understanding of God, the most prominent theme that students return to repeatedly is divine power. God can do anything and is in control of all things. Everything happens for a reason. There are no coincidences. Faith in God consists of assenting to God's power over the world and, in particular, the individual's life. Very few students, if any, talk about God as goodness or God as concerned with our authentic well-being. Instead, God seems to be most concerned with fidelity to Him (here, I use the masculine pronoun intentionally since most of my undergraduates have male images of God) and, specifically, deference to Him. Although (hopefully) most adult Christians mature beyond an eighteen-year-old's experience of God, it seems that divine omnipotence remains a foundational organizing principle for most American Christians.[5]

This vision of God can be particularly harmful for survivors of sexual violence. When an all-powerful God, who can protect them from violence, has failed to do so, there are only two options: either God is a sadistic abuser who uses violence to accomplish His aims, or belief in the existence of God is an illusion that needs to be let go in order to be free to experience reality as it truly is.[6] Many believe that Christian spirituality necessitates fidelity to an overwhelming power who "injures and belittles people."[7]

Certainly, all human concepts must be purged of sinful distortions in order to be applied to God, but the word "power" presents unique opportunities for manipulation and distortion.[8] Many Christians encounter forms of "power" in their everyday lives that subjugate them, dehumanize them, and take away their own sense of power and agency. Power as "power over" is, if not the most dominant, then the most visible, kind of power in people's lives. This is especially true for survivors of sexual violence, many of whom are economically or socially vulnerable relative to their abusers. For example, attendants at a high-end hotel in Santa Monica, which caters to celebrities and other extremely wealthy individuals, report sexual assault as a routine element of their work. One hotel worker reports:

> "'They feel like they can hug you and touch you and grab you and squeeze you and tell you how good they think your legs look in that uniform,' she said, describing guests at the Peninsula. 'You laugh, you smile and you stand on your back foot and never let them get between you and a door.'"[9]

If God's "power" means the power to inflict suffering, or to use any form of evil to bring about goodness, then this kind of God is not holy.[10] This Being is not worthy of worship.

Edward Schillebeeckx builds his understanding of God not from divine omnipotence, but from divine love and goodness. For Schillebeeckx, God is "the Mystery that has a passion for the 'whole-ness' of nature"[11] and the primary task of any talk about God is to shore up belief in a God who loves human beings.[12] As Schillebeeckx puts it, "only a 'God of life', not a God of life and death; only a living God—a God of living and dead, who still know a future in him—can be worshipped, revered and celebrated by men and women; not a God who diminishes men and women and hurts them or keeps them under and deprives them of their joys."[13] Only a good God is worthy of worship.

Women, children, disabled people, people of color, undocumented people, and queer people are most vulnerable to sexual violence. Instead of defending these vulnerable groups, Christian churches have historically contributed to these vulnerabilities by teaching that, for example, Africans are less than fully rational,[14] men image God while women merely image men,[15] or that queer sexual relationships are intrinsically disordered.[16] It is not surprising that despite outward identification with the publicly abused Jesus, Christians are no less likely to perpetrate violent abuse than those who are not Christian.[17] And, when Christians commit violence against others they often proclaim to act in accordance with the (violent) power of God.[18] The only way that we can talk about divine power, if at all, is to talk about God's power to save us—God's power to bring about human good and to judge, resist, and defeat human evil.

The word "salvation" derives from *salus*, meaning "health," "being whole," "integrity,"[19] and thus, to be saved, must mean to be healed and made whole, not to be violated or broken apart. Sexual violence is never a mere *apparent* human violation that can somehow be used by God for a greater making-whole of the human person. Sexual violence is *authentic* human violation. Rape is an authentic breaking apart of the human person and is never willed by God. Rape is senseless suffering.

Senseless Suffering

Schillebeeckx notes that some experiences of suffering have a purpose or meaning. For example, suffering can be meaningful and desirous in the form of loving compassion. It is painful—yet good and holy—to desire another's well-being, especially when you cannot keep your loved ones free from suffering and hardship. Similarly, the suffering entailed in pursuing a good and holy cause can be inherently meaningful—think, for example, of the suffering that civil disobedience entails. Even in this instance, however, Schillebeeckx is careful to note that it is not suffering itself that is holy, but rather the common good to which the actor holds dear while she works on behalf of social change. These types of suffering can have a transformative effect upon us, uniting us more closely with God, and with each other.[20]

Yet much of human life is characterized by suffering of another kind—senseless suffering. Senseless suffering has no purpose or meaning. Too much of human life and human history has been characterized by a kind of suffering that has *no point at all*. Senseless suffering is so ubiquitous that Schillebeeckx argues it is "the alpha and omega of the whole history of [hu]mankind; it is the scarlet thread by which this historical fragment is recognizable as human history."[21] Despite its pervasiveness, we cannot give this kind of suffering a "specific structural place in the divine plan."[22] We cannot justify it as having some divine purpose. If we could, then any God who might direct these purposes would not be worthy of human worship.[23] Schillebeeckx warns, "we cannot look for the *ground* of suffering in God"[24] since "God is pure positivity" and "the opponent of evil."[25] Evil cannot be explained away by any divine purpose. Instead, "suffering remains impenetrable and incomprehensible."

This is not to say that people cannot and should not use their rational powers to analyze evil acts in order to try to figure out ways to prevent them. There is good and important work that is done by psychologists to give us insight into the psyches of perpetrators of sexual violence. Perpetrators often lack empathy, value hypermasculinity, and are socially located in contexts that excuse or even encourage sexually violent behavior.[26] Yet, even if we could have a perfect view into what makes an individual turn into a perpetrator, these reasons do not, and cannot, rationalize his behavior. No amount of insight provides a level of understanding that can excuse the perpetrator's actions or, as Schillebeeckx puts it, "harmoniz[e] it with God's Goodness or our positive humanity."[27] We can never get to a clarity of analysis where we should say, "Oh, yes! It makes perfect sense why he did this. Any rational person would do the same thing." While empathy for the perpetrator's own hardships is possible, there is no legitimate, moral possibility of rationalization.

Negative Contrast Experiences

God has created us as autonomous. Our God-given autonomy does not necessitate evil actions, but it is possible to use our autonomy to commit evil acts. This is a risk that the creator God took in creating autonomous creatures. But the creative activity of God is not yet complete, and God does not allow evil to have the last word. Evil cannot "checkmate" the creative God: in the resurrection of Jesus, "God transcends these negative aspects in our history, not so much by allowing them as *by overcoming them*."[28] The memory of the resurrection presents us with the reality that God is a god who opposes evil in history. God is still opposing evil in history. And God will finally defeat evil with the eschatological consummation of creation and the final judgment of the world— the fulfillment of God's creative purposes already begun. While we await the eschatological completion of creation, in which evil will finally be defeated by goodness, Schillebeeckx argues that we have access to tools that enable the perception of what God desires for us and what God opposes. Experience can reveal God to us.

The revelatory nature of experience is a critical starting point for survivors of sexual violence. When so many survivors struggle for basic recognition that what they experienced really did happen to them, it is imperative to affirm that human experience reflects reality. Experiences of suffering are profound revelations about the nature of reality—namely, that something is seriously wrong. We must veto the world as it is.[29] Survivors' experiences of dis-ease can be trusted. These experiences of violence and abuse are not from God (that is, God does not dole out suffering), yet the spontaneous reaction of the sufferer—anger, disgust, discomfort, sadness—can be from the God who is also angered whenever human beings are violated.

We come to know God's opposition to human suffering through graced experiences of negative contrast. Schillebeeckx's concept of "negative contrast experiences" describes human experiences of suffering as provoking a spontaneous reaction of indignation. If not explicitly, then at least implicitly, the sufferer protests that which happens to her, feeling as if, "No! It can't go on like this; we won't stand for it any longer!"[30] This response to suffering is a "pre-religious," "spontaneous," and "pre-reflexive,"[31] naturally critical-prophetic impulse that arises in no particular way from Christian revelation, but rather is fundamental to all human experience. Juliette, a survivor of a violent attack by a date at the end of the night, writes about her intuitive feeling of violation, despite being unsure how to name what happened to her.

> When he finally left that evening, I did not feel much of anything, not even the developing bruises I had on my chest, legs and arms. I sat on my bed feeling numb. When my roommate came back, I began to tell her what had happened and she cried, telling me that I had just been raped. Strangely, I did not believe her—that could never happen to me, I thought to myself. I am a strong-minded woman who would never fall for a guy's game. However, I did not feel right in any sense of the word. I felt that my mind and body had been completely violated.[32]

Another survivor testifies to the intuitive feeling that she had of violation as a very young child. Again, without knowing exactly what to call it or whether she should rely on her own interpretation of her experience.

> The first time I was forced I was about five. It was a man who lived next door. He used to babysit for my mother while she worked. I couldn't understand it but I knew it was bad. I knew I was bad. I told

my mother, but she wouldn't believe me. She said I was making it up. I thought maybe I was. So when my uncle started doing it when I was eight, I didn't even tell her. I just let him. When he stopped it was the man my mother was living with. It never stopped until I was grown.[33]

An incipient hope, and an intuitive knowledge of human well-being, animates this instinctive response of indignation.[34] The fundamental human experience of a "'no' to the world as it is" reveals a deeper, "unfulfilled . . . 'open yes' [which] is the basis of that opposition and makes it possible."[35] Schillebeeckx explains, "Protest is possible only where there is hope. A negative experience would not be a contrast-experience, nor could it excite protest, if it did not somehow contain an element of positive hope in the real possibility of a better future."[36] Hope allows the sufferer to experience injustice in *contrast* to an (however vaguely felt) intuition of human wholeness, even when one has never experienced wholeness. Schillebeeckx thinks that most of us have had some fragmentary experiences of love and happiness which "revitalize the open 'yes,' affirming it and keeping it alive"[37] in a violent world. These positive experiences give us tastes of salvation—healed and whole humanity.

Yet even these fragmentary experiences of goodness, Schillebeeckx thinks, are "constantly being contradicted and crushed by evil and hatred, by manifest and muted suffering, by abuses of power and terrorism."[38] Without some fragmentary experiences of love or human goodness, it is difficult to imagine how one might develop the intuition that experiences of violence demean us. Positive experiences do not make suffering *more* palatable (against the saccharine advice to "Look on the bright side!" or "Count your blessings!"), but rather *less* palatable. Positive experiences sharpen mourning, anger, and moral resistance in the face of suffering.[39]

In experiences of negative contrast, the sufferer senses pre-reflexively in a "vague, yet real" way, what ought to be.[40] Although complete salvation exceeds that which we are able to conceptualize, we are able to experience in the midst of suffering an *authentic* "anticipation of 'total sense' or 'hale-ness', being whole." We are privileged to *genuine* hints of what salvation will look like.[41] Suffering has an epistemological power to reveal an intuition of the good, sensed indirectly in its absence. This indirect vision of human good fuels a response of resistance and reveals to us that God is not identified with that which befalls the victim. Survivor Joanna describes the process of realization that her abuser was not an instrument of God's will.

> I was just screaming at God, saying—I don't want you in my life; I don't want you anywhere near me. You're supposed to look after me. I'm told you're my father. If you were my father you wouldn't stand

there and watch somebody rape me and I was really, really angry with
God. That happened, I think for the rest of the day. But by that evening
I was just in floods of tears, asking and pleading with God to come back
in my life. I didn't want to be without him, and then I realized that it
wasn't God's fault, it was this man and not God.[42]

We glimpse eventual, universal meaning by means of negative contrast
experiences, piecing together these glimmers in parables and stories. Experiences of negative contrast equip one with a dimly-perceived sense of directionality, a kind of parabolic hope, which aims toward the good without knowing, or being able to explain, exactly, what this good is and will be.[43] It is only through a realization of what ought not to be, that one is able to experience some kind of positive (though indirect) vision of human meaning.[44] It is through these experiences that one is able to then "demand a future and open it up."[45] These basic feelings of both protest and hope are a "preliminary stage" for further reflection (scientific, theological, moral, etc.) on what to do, what to create, and how to act on one's intuitions.[46]

Because of the reality of sin, our experience of human life falls short of the fullness of humanity as it was created to be. Therefore, we do not have any direct experience of the fullness of created humanity. Sexual violence wounds the human person in all of her created dimensions. Salvation is comprehensive physical, interpersonal, social-political, and spiritual post-traumatic healing. We cannot imagine the human person fully healed from traumatic sexual violence, because we have no direct experience of life free from the effects of violence. But we can intuit the shape of the healed human person, partially and in contrast. We know what healed humanity is *not* like; we know the ways (or at least some of the ways) in which we fall short of the fullness of healing.[47] We know we are currently missing the mark: our bodies are wounded, our relationships are filled with threats, and our communities are minefields of violence.

Anthropological Constants: What Human Well-Being Is Not

Instead of detailing a positivistic description of human salvation, Schillebeeckx offers seven "co-ordinates" of human salvation; "anthropological constants."[48] These are not positive norms but rather negative limits. They function to point out that which *cannot* be the fullness of human well-being or, in other words, that which cannot represent eschatological salvation. On their own, these anthropological constants are "hollow and formal,"[49] but insofar as they can point out what the fullness of humanity is *not*, they can indicate that humanity is in need of eschatological healing. Schillebeeckx understands these anthropological constants of "true humanity" as pointing toward the shape of eschatological salvation, indirectly perceived by means of negative contrast. Because these constants are not known positively, but only in their lack, they can point us toward dimensions of human life in need of present healing. It is worthwhile to enumerate each of Schillebeeckx's seven anthropological constants below in order to indicate the relevance they may have for delineating posttraumatic healing.

1. **Human well-being cannot exclude material well-being** (meaning, both the materiality of the human body as well as the material realities of the non-human natural world). It is an illusion to believe that true human freedom consists in rule over nature. Instead, freedom cannot exist outside of the limits of the bodily-material.[50] We can never be free of our bodies, especially insofar as our bodies place limits upon our ability to work without rest or live without pain, but there are ways in which we can imagine our bodies as a source of joy and connection with others (in all their limitations), rather than as weapons to be used against each other and as storehouses of the shame and secrecy of sexual violation.

2. **Human well-being cannot exclude interpersonal well-being.** Personal identity is not possible outside of acknowledgement of one's relationships with others. Rather, we flourish relationally—finding joy, belonging, and love *with* others—just as we harm each other relationally, limiting each other's capacity to experience joy, true community, and God's love.[51]

3. **Human well-being cannot exclude the transformation of social and institutional structures.** Human freedom cannot be secured without the aid of institutional structures to support it. Healing from sexual trauma must be supported by institutional and social structures (e.g., ecclesial, familial, governmental, educational, economic, etc.) if it is to be accomplished at all.[52]

4. **Human well-being cannot exclude expression and embodiment in history.** Schillebeeckx warns, "the presumption of adopting a standpoint outside *historical* action and thought is a danger to true humanity."[53] Thus, the fullness of human well-being cannot be the culmination of a process of historical amnesia—"getting over it" and moving on—but rather consists of accounting for, and transforming, historical traumas.[54]

5. **Human well-being cannot be achieved in the separation of theory from practice.** Human meaning and well-being can only be found in real, historical time and in robust cultural expression.[55] Human well-being must be practically and concretely expressed—not merely an agreed upon state of mind or acceptance of unjust human life as it is.

6. **Human well-being cannot exclude the religious and "para-religious" dimensions of humanity.** A fundamental trust is basic to human experience. This trust, this "form of faith," is "the ground for [human] hope" and makes action in pursuit of the good possible.[56] Therefore, "any liberation which by-passes a *religious redemption* is only a partial liberation, and furthermore, if it claims to be the *total* liberation of man by nature, destroys a real dimension of humanity and in the last resort uproots man instead of liberating him."[57] Human well-being involves the reparation of alienation from God—the source of human freedom and happiness. For survivors, this can be an especially difficult relationship to repair if they have inherited abusive images of God, or if their abusers professed religious belief.[58]

7. **These co-ordinates form a synthesis that "cannot be reduced either idealistically or materialistically" to any one of these alone.**[59] An example which Schillebeeckx himself points to as particularly problematic is the tendency to elevate humanity's spiritual needs (the sixth anthropological constant) over its material needs (the first anthropological constant). Christian salvation refers to the wholeness of humanity according to all these levels; it cannot mean one to the exclusion of others. Healing from sexual trauma is a comprehensive process that restores all aspects of human life, wounded by sinful violence.

Human freedom is a "situated and thematic freedom, not a free initiative in a vacuum or an airless room."[60] "True humanity" is an eschatological reality that we experience now only in hints and half-visions.[61] We live a "borderline" existence, experiencing salvation only in fragments and looking forward to a future in which we will be able to experience it more fully.[62] Thus, while we strive for healing now, we will not experience the fullness of healing on this side of the eschaton.

Some might be suspicious of Schillebeeckx's optimistic view of human agency in the face of suffering. It is possible to get the impression, when reading Schillebeeckx's writings, that experiences of suffering reveal an intuition of the good which then empowers the patient to automatically work toward realizing this good or, at the very least, to resist the evil of suffering. This would fail to acknowledge that the disorientation of contrast can function as much as a burden to action and resistance as an impulse to action and resistance. Keeping the dynamics of trauma in mind, we can remind ourselves that experiences of contrast can fuel resistance only if the experience of contrast itself does not annihilate the sufferer in the process. Experiences of contrast are indeed the condition for the possibility of resistance, but their overwhelming nature can also cause paralysis and death. But a Schillebeeckxian frame can, in turn, remind trauma thinkers that the experience of pain is itself a protest and a refusal to resign oneself to dehumanization (and, therefore, a sign of hope).

Schillebeeckx's Incarnational Mysticism

Schillebeeckx's language of negative contrast experience can help us to speak more clearly about the effect of traumatic violence upon the human person. Trauma is absolutely negative and yet, at the same time, can also function as a site of revelation. The revelation of trauma is negative in nature. It is precisely in our *resistance* to traumatic violence or in our experience of trauma *as pain*, or as that which *should not be*, that the truth of God and of our potential as human beings is revealed. The language of negative contrast experience allows us to identify traumatic violence as revelatory, without in any way sanctifying the violent act itself.

While Schillebeeckx maintains a clear condemnation of suffering as absolutely negative, he simultaneously opens up a discussion about the productivity of suffering. Negative contrast describes the way in which suffering can produce knowledge in the victim—suffering generates a spontaneous resistance to evil, which underlies an inchoate sense of human good. We perceive this human good only in contrast, in faint glimmers of light shining through the cracks of our woolly world. Schillebeeckx's description of this response as spontaneous, locates the movement of grace, at least partially, with*in* the victim rather than wholly with*out*, as some trauma theologians tend to do.[63] Edward Schillebeeckx's insistence on the reliability of experience as a starting point for discerning the contours of a fully redeemed humanity preserves an important sense of the victim's co-participation with God in bringing healing about.

Although he does not use this term himself, the theology of Edward Schillebeeckx can be understood as an "incarnational mysticism" which values the input of the body, and its spontaneous reactions to the world.[64] It values how the body is treated; its health, and well-being. It takes the automatic responses of the body to protect and preserve itself seriously, something that has not always been emphasized in mystical traditions which focus on purgation of one's desires. There is, indeed, a sense of purgation, or conversion, with Schillebeeckx, but it is not a conversion away from the flesh or from the goodness of the body and its powers of perception. Rather, it is a conversion toward the integration of the body into a life of virtue, with a particular emphasis on the virtues of hope and endurance in the face of suffering.

The experience of suffering reveals God as pure positivity, as one who is against evil and for the good of humanity. This is the kind of God about whom the world needs to hear in the midst of experiences of evil. As Schillebeeckx argues, "We certainly need no divine grandfather, a kind soul to whitewash and make light of our mistakes and our cowardice. We need deep concern for humanity and thus 'need' a God who is pure freedom, unmerited, generously given grace."[65] Because it is better to not believe in God at all than to believe in a God who wills human suffering, we desperately need an understanding of God as one who is concerned with the good of humanity.[66] The good news of Christianity is precisely this: that "these three, God, Jesus Christ and humanity, are one in the sense that they can never be set over against one another or in competition with one another."[67]

6
The Story of Jesus and the Mystical-Political Shape of Salvation

The story of Jesus helps us to understand God as one who opposes evil. The death of Jesus—the public, brutal torture of a human being—was meaningless suffering. It had no reason. The violence of the cross accomplished no good; its only purpose was to terrorize those who witnessed it and to remind the Jewish people that they did not have ultimate control over their own bodies. Jesus died because of the actions of sinful and violent political actors and God never wanted that to happen. Therefore, we must say that we are saved "despite the death of Jesus."[1]

Yet because of the resurrection—God's opposition to the evil that happened to Jesus, God's conquering of the evil of Jesus's unwarranted suffering—"this 'despite' is so transcended by God."[2] The resurrection resists Jesus's death and overcomes it. The death of Jesus, at the end of the day, can play a role in salvation history, but only indirectly. Schillebeeckx makes clear, "Only *in the overcoming of it* can we say that the negative aspects in our history have an indirect role in God's plan of salvation: *God is the Lord of history.*"[3] Rape is meaningless suffering and never desired by God. Sexual violence is never part of God's plan, and God rejects and resists the demeaning violence of rape in our lives. Our history of sexual violence can be part of our story of being saved by God *only* insofar as it marks the evil committed by human beings that God is overcoming—not that which God has given to us as a test or refiner's fire.

Teresa of Avila's sixteenth-century presuppositions about suffering do not clearly suggest that rape is senseless suffering that God does not desire. Teresa treats suffering as an opportunity, given by God to the sufferer, to practice patience and, ultimately, draw the sufferer closer to Godself. I argue, however, that a God who uses violence as a tool to accomplish salvation is not worthy of worship. This lack of clarity about the meaninglessness of suffering, however, is not only a mistake of past theologians.

Some contemporary trauma theologians can ascribe dangerous meaning to meaningless suffering. For example, Serene Jones privileges the cross as a site of God's disclosure. She argues that Jesus's torture on the cross can give public testimony to the otherwise invisible torture of which we cannot speak in our own lives, mirroring our stories of suffering back to us.[4] Before the cross of Christ we are "utterly vulnerable to its mysteries and laid bare by its witness."[5] In this way, the cross redeems us[6] as "God takes . . . death into the depths of Godself."[7]

However, if God is present to us primarily in suffering and its aftermath, without a robustly dialectical description of revelation such as that which "negative contrast experiences" can provide, this risks privileging human brokenness over health and well-being. God is not disclosed in the cross, but rather beside the cross. We feel God's presence negatively: in the resistance that we feel toward our suffering, in our intuition that suffering is not what should be, and in our desire for something better for ourselves and for those whom we love.

In this chapter, I use Edward Schillebeeckx's telling of the story of Jesus as a starting point for imagining the mystical-political shape of Christian salvation. The story of Jesus reveals to us that God is one who is always opposed to evil. The cross of Jesus is meaningless, except as that which has been opposed and resisted by God. Analogously, our own violations have no structural place in salvation history, except as that to which God says, "No!" As Schillebeeckx puts it, the only way that God can reveal Godself in suffering is as "veto or as judgment."[8]

The cross is not enough. We have nothing to see there except protest. We need resurrection. We need a glimpse of liberation for God's revelation. The cross is not cherished in itself, and it is not given by God "as an essential part of redemption."[9] Some may object by saying that the cross was necessary in order for God to share in human suffering, but salvation—healing—does not consist in increasing the number of those who suffer pain by insisting that God suffers too. Schillebeeckx argues that to emphasize that God shares in our suffering is not sufficient: "it does not make clear *to what extent, how* and above all *whether* God is still a redeeming and liberating God. A God who only shares our suffering leaves the last and definitive word to evil and suffering. In that case, not God but evil is the definitive omnipotence."[10] God's opposition to evil and human suffering, however, cannot be adequately articulated propositionally in philosophical-theoretical reflection. It can only be told in the story of Jesus—the story of a person in history.

Jesus: A Sacrament of God's Opposition to Evil

God's response to human suffering is best known not through a theoretical reflection on the nature of God, but rather in remembering the story of a concrete person in history. Jesus's story does not blot out, or relativize, the particularities of our own stories of suffering and communication with God. It animates and energizes our own story, shaping our lives into a fifth gospel—a continuation of the disclosure of God to human beings in flesh and history.[11]

Jesus's Experience of God

Although it is not possible to make definitive claims about Jesus's psychology, Schillebeeckx argues that we can gather some clues about Jesus's self-understanding through a careful examination of what he said and did during his lifetime.[12] Schillebeeckx hypothesizes that Jesus was empowered in his preaching and healing ministry by an experience of God as "Abba." Jesus used this familial term to address God in the Gospels[13] and it indicates, most fundamentally, that Jesus perceived himself as having an intimate relationship with God.[14] At the root of Jesus's Abba experience was a kind of contrast experience: Jesus's experience of the God who cherishes and frees humanity contrasted with the profound human suffering he encountered in the world around him.[15] In the end, God is "for" humanity, meaning that God champions human good and does not desire human suffering.[16] Jesus's teaching and ministry were a proclamation of the approaching rule of God in which God, who stands against suffering and evil, will offer a positive future to human beings.[17]

The contrast that Jesus sensed throughout the whole of his life intensified with his perception of his impending arrest and torture. Sensing the imminence of his violent death, the potential collapse of the community which he had formed, and the failure of his mission of reconciliation and fellowship, it would be natural to wonder why a God who desires human good would allow such unjust evil. At the Last Supper, however, Jesus placed his trust in God as one who is "for" humanity.[18] In what was, most likely, an intentional farewell meal with his closest friends, Schillebeeckx hypothesizes that Jesus might have talked to them about his impending death for the purpose of guarding them against despair. At this meal he announced both the end of "earthly fellowship" and an "offer [of] . . . the prospect of fellowship renewed in the kingdom of God."[19]

Despite his torture and death, Jesus trusted that his life's work would not amount to nothing.[20] He instructed his disciples to carry out his mission, remembering him as often as they gathered for the "breaking of the bread" and the "cup of fellowship," in a move which effectively integrated his death into his overall surrender to God throughout his life.[21] Jesus anticipated total salvation, even though his finite attempts at liberation had apparently failed, for he trusted that God would complete that which he had already begun. The contrast between Jesus's understanding of God as "for" humanity, and the suffering that he endured, prompted Jesus to trust in his experience of the love of God in the face of great human evil, and to anticipate that the coming of God's kingdom would bring about an end to human evil.[22]

Jesus's Death: The Absurdity of Violence

This description of Jesus's death as meaningless may differ dramatically from how many victim-survivors hear about Jesus in Christian settings. Many Christian survivors relate that they were taught (directly or indirectly) that God sent Jesus to earth in order to die for our sins, in some form of substitutionary atonement. As a result, the *telos*—the real point—of Jesus's life was to suffer a violent death. Many Christian survivors have gotten the impression, in religious settings, that when we experience suffering, we are drawn closer to Jesus—the ultimate sufferer—whose torture outpaces our own, either because it was more intense than our suffering and/or because he is less deserving than we are. Survivor Priscilla testifies:

> I think over the years, I've struggled with the idea that some Christians have that God allows things to happen to make you a better person. I actually find that quite insulting to God really. I cannot imagine that any loving father would allow a child to go through what I went through in order for them to be something when they grew up. I can't get my head around that. That's not my Father. He wouldn't do that. The fact that he's used it, that it hasn't been wasted, that's a different thing, but you do hear this kind of talk that oh, well, it's part of God's plan. I don't believe it was ever part of God's plan. I don't think it's part of his plan for anybody to hurt, or to go through that kind of pain, whether it's physical abuse or mental abuse or sexual or whatever it is. I don't believe that that's part of his plan at all.[23]

Similarly, theologian and activist Rita Nakashima Brock describes her experiences working with young activists at summer workshops in Los Angeles. Many of the young people have experienced violence and abuse firsthand.

> I counsel some of the religious kids, and the more attached they are to traditional ideas about Jesus, the more likely they are to think of their

abuse as "good" for them, as a trial designed for a reason, as pain that makes them like Jesus. They are often in denial about the amount of pain they live with. It amazes me that they survive and appear so "normal." They are wounded, but they have an astonishing passion to be whole. They reach out to others despite abuse, neglect, and hate. We try to help them see the forces that destroy relationships. Finding others who have experienced abuse helps them face their pain more directly and begin to find strategies to resist it. They go back home and do amazing work in their families, schools, and communities.[24]

When Christians talk about Jesus's death as willed by God as a form of substitutionary atonement, there are at least two damaging consequences: first, God is portrayed as one who wants suffering; and, second, the suffering of our own lives is relativized as insignificant because it pales in comparison to Jesus's. Even further, this narrative fails to be adequately substitutionary because Jesus suffers, *and* we suffer. Jesus does not end up functioning as a substitute for our suffering at all, but instead sanctifies our suffering, providing both a model for and a minimization of it. Even though I do not favor substitutionary soteriology, this form of substitutionary atonement fails, even according to its own aims. In contrast, Schillebeeckx resists the idea that Jesus's death was the point of the incarnation. He argues the opposite, "Jesus' whole life is the hermeneusis of his death."[25] In other words, the meaning of Jesus's death can only be understood by shifting one's gaze back to the way that Jesus lived his life.

Jesus disrupted conventional power relationships throughout his life.[26] He did not think of his mission from God as *inevitably* leading to death, but rather as a possibility that he only saw coming at the end, as his earthly failures piled up on top of each other.[27] Jesus's death is a consequence of the way he lived, but it is not a strict or necessary consequence. This is an important distinction to make in order to resist rationalizing violence. The impulse to resist a rationalization of the crucifixion is critical for all who suffer from traumatic violence, especially sexual abuse: one has not been "chosen" to suffer for a reason. There is no logic inherent in victimization. Survivor Barb describes how difficult it is to let go of the idea that she either deserved to be raped or was chosen to suffer for some cosmic reason.

> We are women who have endured one of the most degrading acts that can be perpetrated against us. Even worse, these acts are usually committed by our boyfriends, husbands, male family members, male friends, or acquaintances. Yet, here we stand, our spirits intact. Being raped by a stranger is horrific, but when we are raped by someone we know, someone we trust, someone whom we thought knew and

respected us, we face an overwhelming sense of betrayal. It is highly personalized. Self-blame runs deep. I've learned through my own experience and from listening to other women that self-blame is the last thing we give up. While it may sound off, I've come to realize that remorse is a coping mechanism. As long as I felt I was to blame for being raped, I felt I had control over what had happened to me. Believing that I may have had some role in the assault gave me an illusion of power at the time when I felt I had none. The hardest thing for me to do was to admit, 'No matter what I did, no matter what I said, no matter how hard I tried, I couldn't stop him from doing what he did to me. I couldn't stop him from saying what he said to me. I couldn't stop him. I was powerless.' That was humiliating for me. But more difficult was the point in the healing process when I was ready to admit that I was not to blame. That was very frightening. At that moment, I was truly stripped of my sense of power, even though that sense had been only an illusion all along. Suddenly, I was faced with my own vulnerability; there was no way to deny that the same man or some other man could do this to me again.[28]

Jesus did not think about his death as having a salvific meaning. Jesus would have known that the Romans had the power to crucify—every Jew would have known that. He also had the recent memory of the state-ordered death of John the Baptist.[29] He did not will his own death, nor did he know from the beginning of his public life that his crucifixion would befall him.[30] Jesus accepted death, but only after he realized that a violent death was unavoidable. At that point, Jesus actively and creatively incorporated his death into his mission of salvation by entrusting his friends with the project of carrying out his unfinished work.[31] And yet, even with Jesus's acceptance of violent death, he refused to accept it as willed by God, who remains "Abba," the one who wills human good and opposes evil.[32]

During Jesus's death God remains with Jesus, yet God is silent.[33] If God is pure positivity, if God is passionate love for humanity, how could God possibly speak through an experience of torture and hatred? The cross is not from God—it cannot reveal God—except to reveal the absence of God, to say this evil is *not* God.[34] God is something else. God is not present to Jesus in the cross itself, but beside the cross as an indignant witness.

God does not intervene in the horrors of history, not even for his own son.[35] God cannot intervene to stop this violence from occurring, since God has already voluntarily renounced this kind of power over creatures through the act of creating them as autonomous.[36] God is defenseless. But, God is not yet done creating. God responds to the horror of violence with a new creative act; God resurrects Jesus and overcomes the finality of his senseless death. God is not forever silent. With the resurrection of Jesus, God also promises future justice and exaltation to all others who have been tortured and abused.[37]

The Resurrection: God's Response to the Absurdity of Evil

In this new act of creation—the resurrection—God affirms Jesus's life and corrects the negativity of his death. By affirming Jesus's life, I mean two things: God affirms Jesus's work of proclaiming and bringing about the kingdom of God through his practices of healing and table fellowship; and God affirms Jesus's experience of communion with God that he enjoyed throughout his life.

By affirming Jesus's proclamation and praxis of the kingdom of God, the resurrection insists that any good done to advance the kingdom has permanent validity. Jesus's work to heal and extend the table to the alienated is not destroyed with his death. Although it was cut short, his work was not meaningless. It seems as though anyone who acts in this way will inevitably become a target of retaliation but, nevertheless, Jesus's work will have an enduring significance. Some survivors adopt a similar attitude; resistance to violence is worthwhile even with lethal consequences. Karen, whose husband has been released from prison after serving seven years for brutally beating and raping her at knife point, explains that she refuses to move to another city and give up her advocacy work and relationships, even if that means risking another attack.

> Because he is free, I am often asked why I choose to remain in the same house in the same city. I do so because I have resolved not to give him any more power over my life. My friends and family are here. My life is here and I love my job. He will not make me flee. The rape and its aftermath gave me the will, strength, and ability to become an advocate for other survivors. As a result of my [negative] experience at the hospital [being examined after the rape], I became trained as a Forensic Nurse Examiner and I now coordinate the local Sexual Assault Nurse (SANE) Program. . . . In addition to seeing patients in a clinical setting, I work for a non-profit, community-based organization that provides a wide range of services to victims of crime, including community outreach and Rape Awareness Education.[38]

Susan Estrich, legal scholar, and survivor of an attack by a stranger in a parking lot, similarly speaks and writes about the realities of rape, despite personal risks to her own safety. She explains:

> Once in a while—say, at two o'clock in the morning when someone claiming to be a student of mine calls and threatens to rape me—I think that I talk too much. But most of the time, it isn't so bad. When my students are raped (and they have been), they know they can talk to me. When my friends are raped, they know I survived.[39]

Affirming Jesus's communion with God insists (for all of us) that unity with God cannot be destroyed by death.[40] When violence is committed, it cannot separate the victim from God's love, even as her body is broken. The closeness with God that Jesus enjoyed could not be destroyed by the violence of his death. God does not abandon the sufferer in her moments of deepest pain and alienation. The resurrection reveals that, what may have appeared to be the absence of God, was instead the silence of God. Theologian Helen Bergin explains:

> God's silence as Jesus dies abandoned is not a silence of rejection or withdrawal, but a silence that is allowing human freedom to act out its freedom to the limit. At the termination of the human activity, God's totally confounding action of raising Jesus, over-rules the defeat of human deviance and of sin and of death.[41]

God's presence remains unbroken. The resurrection ratifies Jesus's life's work and his relationship with God, *continuing* that which had already begun during Jesus's life.

Yet the resurrection is also the beginning of something *new*; in the resurrection, the negativity of suffering and death is defeated. The resurrection replaces what appears to be the failure of Jesus's mission with the beginning of the "installation of the kingdom of God"—the beginning of God's judgment of the world's evils and the rupture of all oppressive relationships. And it replaces Jesus's public humiliation with "exaltation and glorification" as one who could not be broken or defeated.[42] The cross is transformed into "the symbol of total protest (to the death) against the alienation of our human history of suffering, and is a consequence of the message of God concerned for mankind, so that Jesus' resurrection makes it clear to us that suffering does not have the last word."[43] The resurrection bears the first fruits of a more glorious harvest in which God will judge all evil and all victims of violence will be restored and delivered justice. The resurrection is not only a corrective to Jesus's suffering, but the beginning of a corrective to *our* suffering as well.[44] Since suffering and evil "cannot have a cause or motive in God," the death of Jesus itself is not salvific.[45] Evil and suffering, which are humanly initiated through the freedom granted to finite creation, are resisted by God. God transcends suffering by overcoming it.

Because Jesus's own ministry and teachings were shaped by the deep conviction that evil does not have the last word, these two ways in which the resurrection functions—affirming Jesus's life and correcting his death—are intimately connected. Jesus anticipated that God would correct the negativity of evil in his own life and in the world writ large. The corrective function of the resurrection does not erase the reality of suffering and death, as if it never happened to Jesus: "Suffering and death then remain absurd and may not be mystified, even in Jesus' case."[46] The negativity of death, because it is not given meaning or explained away, remains, but something else, something more significant remains as well—the enduring validity of the good. Through the resurrection, God fills Jesus's death with meaning, without stripping death of its absolute negativity. As Schillebeeckx explains, "there is no situation in which God cannot be near to us and in which we cannot find him. The believer can even make sense of situations in which he or she truly experiences meaninglessness and absurdity, whereas the absurd remains absurd. That is in no way to say that the circumstances in which we may find ourselves in one way or another are 'the will of God'."[47]

Through her resistance and protest to violation—experienced, perhaps, as subtly as the feeling of *pain* in response to this event—the trauma survivor experiences a kernel of the salvific power of the resurrection. Jesus's resurrection affirms that violence does not disrupt the presence of God to the survivor (although God's presence may not be felt), and that something more enduring and powerful than the violence itself remains: a desire for wholeness and an intuition about what this wholeness entails. This desire and intuition make the survivor's spontaneous responses of pain, anger, and disappointment possible. These negative emotions are holy and reflect what God does not want for us.

The Christian Response to Suffering: A Narrative-Practical Response of Remembrance and Resistance

The Christian answer to suffering can only be a "narrative-practical" response of remembrance and resistance, not a rationalization of evil. Christians remember and resist suffering through the lens of the memory of Jesus's suffering. This *memoria passionis* is fundamentally a memory of God as one who protests human suffering by refusing any enduring meaning to the cross, except as an instrument of evil which has been broken and discarded. The memory of the cross, in the end, is a memory of one who was raised. The Christian community is the living *memoria passionis Christi*—preserving the presence of the Spirit who resists evil amidst believers.[48]

The church is responsible for remembering and maintaining an active *memoria passionis*.[49] Communal, liturgical celebrations are one way, though certainly not the only way, in which ecclesial communities can give life to the process of remembering the suffering of Jesus in a narrative-practical fashion, and to inspire practical forms of resistance in the lives of community members. At their best, liturgies can reinforce an awareness of the distance between contemporary experience and a prophetic vision of God's rule. Liturgical practice can indicate that our history of suffering is not necessary and it can be changed.[50] For example, bringing concerns about sexual violence to prayer in an ecclesial community can affect a conscious shift in the priorities given to each other's safety and the degree to which survivors take their own sexual integrity within the community seriously. In turn, the degree to which a community is characterized by an attentiveness to the sexual integrity of its members (via transparency, accountability, prompt response to sexual violations, etc.) can influence the prayer life of its members—encouraging images of God as one who desires genuine human safety and freedom.

Liturgy can enact, embody, and encourage different attitudes and levels of healthiness within a community. Liturgical prayer can embody transparency, equality, truth-telling, prophecy, and accountability. Christian communities that wish to combat sexual violence can interrogate their communal prayer practices. Is a community's practice of prayer multivocal? Does the community engage in practices that encourage listening to each other? In community life, are there limits to inclusion—i.e., clear boundaries about what kind of behaviors are inappropriate, and open and ongoing conversations about what constitutes breaking these boundaries? In ecclesial cultures that tend to emphasize the separation of clergy and lay people more than transparent leadership and open debate about matters of faith and morality, sexual abuse (when it happens) often remains unchallenged and undiscussed. Philosopher Theresa Tobin argues that a doctrinal emphasis on exclusivity additionally contributes to a lack of sexual safety. If victim-survivors believe that religious communities lack the fullness of truth, they can feel trapped in violent communities.[51] Rebecca Ann Parker, theologian and survivor of repeated childhood rape by a neighbor, explains the ways in which her ecclesial community negatively shaped her own and her parents' ability to see and name sexual violation.

> Had my parents been able to see and understand what was happening to me, I know that in their love for me they would have come to my rescue. But as my mother said to me later, "It is so terrible that we didn't see what was happening to you. In those days nobody talked about sexual abuse of children. We didn't imagine that such a thing

really happened." The internal silences I created replicated the public silences. What my community could not name it could not see. And what the community could not see, I could not integrate. My religious community, most of all, could not see violence against children because it could not name clearly the violence that happened to Jesus.[52]

Parker later narrates an experience of liturgical prayer in which she felt seen and held as a survivor of violence. This communal prayer, experienced as an adult, started to heal some of her childhood wounds.

> I knew the worship leader and trusted her. We were sitting in the round in a small chapel. We could see one another's faces in the candlelight. Words were spoken that told of Jesus' crucifixion. It was a narrative of lamentation and grief, not praise and thanksgiving. Prayers were offered for victims of violence and abuse, all those who suffer in body, mind, and spirit. Then bread and wine were offered to any who wished, as a sign that there is nourishment for the suffering, comfort for the grieving, and hope that someday all people will gather at one table in peace. . . . Somewhere deep inside me a noise that had been roaring for years became silent. An old ache, like a stone, began to fall.[53]

Sadly, survivors do not often find Christian communities to be places of sexual safety or frank discussion of violence. As Schillebeeckx puts it, "The church is—that is, it *ought to be*—a free and liberating environment in which Christian personal identity can flourish."[54] Many contemporary believers leave when they find that the church fails to be a space of love and freedom. One survivor of incest describes her image of God, when her perpetrator professed to be a representative of God:

> My father was a fundamentalist preacher. He would preach all Sunday about the sins of the flesh, then he'd come home and molest me and my sister. I hate God. I hate the church. I hate all men. God isn't about love. He's about violence and hate.[55]

Another survivor, Louise—an Australian mother of five—lived in a long-term abusive marriage. Rape and other forms of physical violence were a part of her everyday life. With each pregnancy, the abuse intensified. An ABC news report describes how, when her situation was at a breaking point and she was convinced that her husband would kill her, she sought help from her pastor. Her pastor responded by interviewing her daughter, in order to see "if Louise was telling the truth." He concluded that her husband "just had a bad temper."

Representatives from the church visited Louise at home and either left before coming inside for fear of intimidation by Louise's husband or simply communicated to Louise that "God doesn't like divorce." Louise's marriage eventually ended, but even fourteen years later, after her escape, she reports enduring isolation, depression, and barriers to relationships—especially relationships in an ecclesial context.

> Sometimes she gets up on a Sunday morning and gets dressed for church, but just sits on the end of her bed. 'I am a bit too scared of pastors, of people,' she says.[56]

We need to call ecclesial communities that perpetrate or maintain sexual violence what they are—purveyors of religious violence.[57] As Schillebeeckx writes:

> A church that does not permit human rights in its own ranks, and thereby mutilates the human face in the name of God allegedly transcending all humanity, has reached the end of its road in a culture gasping for genuine humanity: in that respect at any rate it is not a church, and is also not true to the gospel of Jesus Christ in his human manifestation that is the revealed form of the living God.[58]

At a minimum, ecclesial communities must maintain cultures in which human rights flourish—namely, with clear reporting guidelines, clear disciplinary measures for offenders, accountability for all levels of church leadership (especially at the highest levels), and open access to positions of leadership and decision-making for all members. These measures merely establish human rights. They are the *beginnings* of love, but certainly not its fullness. The fullness of love consists of nothing less than robust freedom for all human beings.[59] To leave a church community that fails to establish these minimum measures is not an act of cowardice or moral failing, but rather an act of hope. It is a refusal to accept that which demeans humanity and a genuine expectation that a more humane community is possible (even if it must be somewhere else).

The Christian story of Jesus is still unfinished. Therefore, the full story of our sufferings is also unfinished. We are awaiting God's overcoming of all evil. Through faith, we know that the story of salvation, which has already begun, will open up into an even greater future in which God transforms our partial efforts toward healing and wholeness. For now, our efforts anticipate full healing, not only when they fall short, but even when they utterly fail.[60] Redemption is not entirely in our hands. Even failed attempts at healing have enduring validity, because God takes our fragmentary accomplishments and opens them up to a greater future.[61] The eschatological future *requires* our action, aiming toward full healing,[62] though cannot be *reduced* to it.[63]

However, the success of our actions is not what brings eschatological healing about, for God still gives us a future even when our efforts fail.[64] Human beings participate in their own salvation by working toward human liberation, with the faith that God transforms our efforts and gives them a graced future. Schillebeeckx writes, "That is the paradox of Christianity—we tread in the footsteps of the God who is to come to us from the future and, in so doing, it is still we who make history."[65]

Survivors and their allies participate in the process of the reception of healing grace through their attempts to restore victims' agency, reestablishing healthy interpersonal boundaries and forms of intimacy, and transforming social and political structures to support sexual equity and a culture of consent. Even when these efforts remain partial (as they always do), or even when they radically fail (as they often do), God gives us a graced future through these efforts, transforming these "fragments of salvation" into the fullness of freedom for all of us who are wounded.

Salvation Is Human Wholeness

Schillebeeckx warns the reader, "human salvation is not salvation of souls, as some spiritual gurus keep insisting."[66] Salvation is not just a spiritual and personal process, promising an other-worldly reward. Salvation is the restoration of the *whole* human person as she was created to be, in her "full spiritual corporeality or embodied spirit."[67] Salvation concerns the whole person in all her created dimensions: physical-material, interpersonal, social-political, and spiritual.

Christian salvation involves the healing of the whole person. The comprehensive meaning of salvation can be garnered etymologically: "the root of the word *salus* or salvation is connected with *sanitas*, health; with being whole or with integrity."[68] Christian salvation concerns the broad health of the individual person in her social context. The trauma victim is in need of salvific healing not only spiritually, but also physically, relationally, and politically. As Schillebeeckx puts it:

> Christian salvation cannot be simply the 'salvation of souls'; it must be healing, the making whole of the whole man and woman, the person in all his or her aspects and the society in which the person lives. Thus Christian salvation includes ecological, social, and political aspects,

though it is not exhausted by them. Although Christian salvation is more than that, it is at least that.[69]

Christian salvation must include "community denunciation" of sexual violence,[70] clear reporting guidelines, limits on perpetrators' freedom of action for the purpose of incapacitation,[71] extensions of statutes of limitations to open up prosecution of past crimes, and free psychological resources for victim-survivors. The sum of these measures clearly does not constitute the fullness of Christian salvation, but salvation is "at least" these measures. The work of Christian salvation must involve concrete measures of human action toward healing. Eschatological salvation must be embodied and actualized in our human structures of existence in the form of real healing and freedom.[72]

The kingdom of God is a theological metaphor that Jesus used to anticipate the salvific social and political healing of human beings. Schillebeeckx explains, "The kingdom of God is a new world of suffering removed, a world of completely whole or healed men and women in a society where master-servant relationships no longer prevail."[73] It represents a vision of the future in which healed individuals will live with each other in the freedom of egalitarian relationships.[74] Schillebeeckx argues that Jesus was an "eschatological prophet,"[75] who initiated his eschatological vision of salvation by embodying it in his manner of life. Jesus's life was characterized by his "caring and abiding presence among people experienced as salvation coming from God."[76] His very presence was experienced as facilitating the individual and social flourishing that he promised was part of the kingdom of God. As one who healed and ate with others who were otherwise socially alienated, his presence brought others freedom and deep joy.[77]

Jesus's table fellowship and healing activities were directed toward those who were normally considered beyond God's hospitality and nurturing care—gentiles, sex workers, those working in collaboration with Roman imperial authorities to oppress the Jews, etc.—and, thus, symbolized God's own openness to friendship with all of humanity.[78] Jesus did not just talk about the kingdom of God as an abstract intellectual idea, but rather *enacted* his vision of the kingdom of God in his ministry. As a healer, Jesus ushered in a new social order where those who were weak, socially isolated, and impoverished (either because of oppressive class structures or the economic demands of caring for oneself and one's dependents[79]), might be enveloped and restored by God's loving care. As host, Jesus practiced open eating, initiating fellowship meals at which all might eat freely, nourished by God's own hospitality.[80]

Powerfully, Schillebeeckx points to Jesus's interaction with Zacchaeus— the tax collector who climbed a tree to see Jesus in the Gospel of Luke

(Lk 19:1–10)—as an example of how Jesus enacted his vision of the kingdom of God in his ministry. Jesus did not tell Zacchaeus that God loves him, but rather demonstrated God's love to Zacchaeus by eating with him in his home.[81] By doing this, Jesus confronted Zacchaeus with God's hospitable love, and Zacchaeus converted from his predatory economic practices to make amends to all those whom he had failed to treat hospitably. The fellowship meal is not simply an icon of the kingdom of God, but it is a real symbol of the kingdom of God, a sign that brings about that which it signifies.[82] Jesus's fellowship meals brought about the egalitarian community he proclaimed was on its way. Eating together brought about the communal healing that Jesus insisted was necessary for the full reign of God.

The resurrection of the body is an image of healing on a personal level—"connot[ing] individual, personal participation of all people in God's kingdom."[83] These two images—the kingdom of God, as a social and political image, and the resurrection of the body, as a personal image, are a unified theological whole indicating that all of human life—the personal, the interpersonal, and the social—is thoroughly marred by sin and requires restorative healing.[84] Not only are our families, churches, and schools thoroughly wounded by sexual violence, but so also are the very legal systems that we have in place to address misconduct in those spaces. These legal systems favor perpetrators' rights over the needs of victims.[85] Yet alternative models of justice-seeking outside of the legal system are often even less effective at meeting victim-survivors' needs.[86]

Even further, legal scholar Catherine MacKinnon argues that, at the most basic level, to experience and express oneself as a woman is to be socially constituted as an object (rather than a subject), acted upon through sex.[87] The idea of womanhood *itself* is thoroughly conditioned by rape culture.[88] There are no aspects of human life unharmed by the sins of sexual violence.

When the two Christian images of salvation—the kingdom of God and the resurrection of the body—are taken together, they reveal that Christian salvation is not just the salvation of disembodied and individualized souls, but it is thoroughly mystical-political.[89] The task of the Christian, therefore, is to participate in the work of mystical-political healing wherever brokenness can be found. In the case of sexual violence, the survivor who experiences enduring trauma is compelled to commit herself to her own healing out of fidelity to the Christian mission. And those who live in community with her are commissioned to support her and contribute to this task. Theological ethicist Megan K. McCabe argues that restorative healing must include the very transformation of the category "woman" as conditioned by rape culture.[90] This work of healing is a mystical-political practice because it is the work of the community on behalf of the common good. It is motivated by a faith commitment to the task of bringing about the kingdom of God (on a political-structural and relational level) and the resurrection of the body (on a personal level).

Authentic Mysticism

Many survivors report that they learned that union with God is accomplished through the acceptance of suffering and that this primed them for acquiescence to abuse.[91] Some survivors have heard from the pulpit that Christian discipleship involves submitting to domestic abuse,[92] and others, in turning to clergy for pastoral care, have been told, "God has permitted this, and we only find true peace in God's will."[93] Jennie, a survivor of marital abuse, reports that turning to several Catholic, pastoral resources provided a consistent message that prayer was a tool that would enable her to stay in her violent marriage. As journalist Simcha Fisher reports, "One priest gave her Jacques Phillippe's spiritual classic, *Interior Freedom*, encouraging her to cultivate internal calm. A Catholic therapist taught her to dissociate, so that she could endure abuse patiently."[94] But, for Schillebeeckx, mysticism does not imply acceptance of what is as God's will.

Schillebeeckx argues that authentic mysticism is never simply a "flight to inwardness" and certainly is never a "flight into the status quo."[95] Consequently, it is dangerous to talk about the life of prayer as a flight from the world. The life of prayer issues a summons to "flee *with* the world to the kingdom of God."[96] To participate in political transformation through the cultivation of "political love"—"the historically urgent form of contemporary holiness, the historical imperative of the moment, or in Christian terms, the present *kairos* or moment of grace."[97] This kind of love—political love—is supported by other loves, namely love of God. Mysticism, "an intensive form of experience of God," and politics, "an intensive form of social commitment,"[98] are "two forms of one and the same theologal attitude."[99] Thus, "Recollection of the life and execution of Jesus and belief in his resurrection is therefore not just a liturgical action but at the same time a political action."[100]

Mystical practices are spiritual practices which reach toward human wholeness, freedom, and well-being over the course of a lifetime.[101] The mystical life is one of enacted virtue, rather than an exclusively abstract and inward encounter with God. Against a common tendency to associate "the mystical" with the personal realm and "the political" with the social and structural, Schillebeeckx maintains that the mystical is inherently political. Because the individual person can never exist in an isolated fashion, unaffected *by* and unaffecting her context, the personal is never wholly divorced from the political. Mystical life is not to be found in the realm of the merely theoretical and rational, it is also not to be found in the realm of the extraordinarily paranormal (speaking in tongues, dreams, and levitations). The mystical life is the quite ordinary struggle for liberation in which experiences of pain, joy, boredom, frustration, quiet contentment, loving, and feeling loved mingle freely. It is rooted in the everyday, mundane realities of the virtuous Christian life.[102] For the survivor of sexual violence, the mystical life will involve the basic (and often repetitive) tasks of seeking safety, reconnecting with everyday life, repairing one's relationship with God and others, and envisioning and working toward new social and political structures that can promote sexual safety.

When the sins of sexual violence have damaged our bodies, our communities, and our imaginations, we cannot say for certain everything that human healing entails, without risking an overly narrow or premature sense of false satisfaction. We cannot offer a positivistic definition of human good wholly free from the myopic hold of rape culture. Rape culture restricts our imaginations, making it difficult to envision little more than that which we have already experienced. But the fullness of human life is certainly more expansive than what we can currently imagine.

Religious belief need not pacify human beings into acceptance of injustice. Religious experiences can put us in touch more deeply with the ways in which we fall short of the fullness of human salvation—personally and collectively.[103] Prayer has a "critical and productive force" of its own, opening up deeper wells of joy in response to positive disclosures of God, and indignation in response to experiences of negative contrast. As Schillebeeckx argues:

> Mysticism in no way means "God and only God." Francis's Hymn to the Sun makes this clear, when Francis says, "Be praised, my Lord, with all your creatures!" The mystic will, however, first let everything go, give up everything, including himself or herself, restored a hundredfold. Authentic mysticism is never flight from the world but, on the basis of a first disintegrating source-experience, an integrating and reconciling mercy with all things. It is approach, not flight.[104]

As a model of this politically-engaged mysticism, Schillebeeckx offers the biblical Martha of Bethany, described in the Gospels of Luke and John as an early leader of a house-church and provider of hospitality, "whose concern for God makes her solicitous for human beings."[105] While this may be a surprising model of the mystical life, since many in the Christian tradition pit Martha's action-orientation against her sister Mary's contemplative-orientation to argue that "Mary has chosen the better part" (Lk 10:42),[106] readers will remember that Teresa of Avila also prioritized Martha in her description of the mystical prayer offering the loving, cooperative coupling of Martha and Mary as a model for the most mature stages of union with God through ethical action.[107] For both Teresa and Schillebeeckx, social-political action and mystical union with God mutually support one another.

A Posttraumatic Theology of Healing

In contrast to Teresa of Avila's tendency to exalt suffering as a tool that God uses to draw us closer in friendship and—perhaps, more surprisingly—against the tendency of some contemporary trauma theologians to privilege the cross as a site of divine disclosure, I argue that God is not disclosed in the cross, but rather *beside* the cross, as indignant witness. The only way that we can say that suffering can reveal God—if at all—is if we can be clear that experiences of suffering are negative contrast experiences. In these experiences, we feel God's presence negatively, in the resistance that we feel toward our suffering, and in our desire for something better for ourselves and for those we love. Suffering can have an epistemological power to reveal intuitions of what human well-being might be like. Indirect visions of human good fuel responses of resistance, and reveal God as not identified with that which befalls the victim. But we must be clear: God is pure positivity—God is neither behind the abuse, animating it, nor is God above the abuse, indifferent to it. Rather, God is closely present to the survivor in absence, making the absence of God (and, consequently, of human good) known.

Christian salvation involves the fullness of human well-being—complete posttraumatic healing. And salvation, according to Edward Schillebeeckx, has a distinctively mystical-political shape. Posttraumatic healing is *mystical* insofar as it impacts unity with God, and it is *political* insofar as it must involve the transformation of structures of power that constrain and facilitate human life. Healing from sexual trauma is not merely a cognitive and individual enterprise, but involves material restoration, as well as relational and social elements. Salvation cannot be reduced to human efforts, aimed toward healing, but healing is a key component of eschatological salvation. Salvation implies healing and goes beyond it.

The eschatological salvation for which we await includes personal healing of our material wounds and illnesses brought on by traumatic violence,[108] psychological healing from the grip of obtrusive memories; interpersonal healing within our broken families and friendships, social and political healing of our religious and secular communities, and spiritual healing of our relationship with God. We cooperate with God in bringing this healing about, remembering and celebrating the ways in which God has already saved us, and mourning and longing for the ways in which our salvation is not yet complete. With the fullness of salvation, the tortured and abused Jesus will proclaim judgment on the world and bring justice to all tortured and abused victims.[109] For victim-survivors living in the painful tension of the already and the not yet, divine judgment cannot come too soon. In the remaining chapters, I will lay out some resources within the Christian tradition to help strengthen us as we wait—courage and hope.

7
Courage in the Work of Posttraumatic Healing

In a Christian context, posttraumatic healing is a mystical-political practice. Posttraumatic healing is a *mystical* practice because it involves the restoration of right relationship with God. This includes restoring our spiritual senses to perceive God where God is present in ourselves, and in our world, and to notice where God is revealed in absence. Posttraumatic healing is a *political* practice because it involves the transformation of the social and institutional contexts which enable sexual violence. The mystical-political shape of posttraumatic healing reflects the mystical-political shape of Christian salvation on the whole, reminding us that if salvation is to have any meaning at all for ourselves and our broken communities, it must involve communal healing from sexual trauma. And, most fundamentally, posttraumatic healing is a *practice* because it is a disciplined, comprehensive, long, and arduous process.

This life-long process of transformation is filled with both moments of disappointment and moments of unexpected beauty. But for those who believe in God, these moments are revelatory. Moments of beauty are positive disclosures, partial visions of the healed and whole future we are promised, and moments of pain and disappointment, especially insofar as they produce indignation in us, dialectally illuminate what should not be. Positive experiences help us to form a more pointed resistance to negative ones, "nurturing, establishing and sustaining" the "open yes" to wholeness and well-being that makes a strong and clear "no" to all that demeans us possible.[1]

Healing from sexual trauma is a task that involves restoration on many different levels—personal, spiritual, interpersonal, and socio-political. The sheer breadth of all that is in need of repair can be overwhelming. Survivors are faced with the task of learning to become comfortable in their own body again, and to recognize the sensory body as a reliable and worthwhile vehicle through which to experience the world. We must learn to manage intrusive memories and to experience time as it happens. We must repair our relationship with God—that which is "Not-God"[2] needs to be identified as such, idolatries need to be shed, and an authentic encounter with God needs to be cultivated (gradually and with God's assistance). We must learn to set appropriate boundaries with human others and open intimacies with those who can be trusted. Yet because "[a]buse does not occur on a blank canvas, but in a social context that allows for and encourages it,"[3] full posttraumatic healing can never be limited to a series of personal-individual or interpersonal tasks.[4]

The fullness of posttraumatic healing calls for a transformation of the social context that enables violence in the first instance. Until communities can dismantle rape culture, transform social and institutional structures, and establish a culture of free consent and healthy sexual expression, individuals will continue to be victimized. Those who support victims will always have more to do, and comprehensive healing will remain out of reach. In other words, as long as women experience rape and the threat of rape as a deterrent to walking outside alone, as long as parents have legitimate fears of the sexual violation of their children in schools and in religious communities, and as long as sexual violence functions as a common expression of relational dominance, in areas of political conflict and in the family homes of those living in "politically stable" areas,[5] posttraumatic healing is not objectively complete for any of us. Healing must be universal if it is to be complete anywhere.[6]

Considering the apparently ever-receding horizon of posttraumatic wholeness, how can we think theologically about healing? How can we give a description, however inadequate, to the ways in which God's healing grace can operate in those who have been marked by sexual violence? We can take a cue from non-theological trauma researchers. Because of the long, comprehensive, and arduous nature of posttraumatic healing, many trauma psychologists have noted the importance of courage in the work of posttraumatic recovery.

Psychologist Judith Herman argues that recovery requires a "tolerance for the state of being ill." This tolerance, or "holding on," is a kind of strength to persist in the good work of recovery despite hardships. For Herman, this ability to hold on is empowered by a hope that wholeness is still possible, despite the very real gravity of the evil endured and the damage suffered. As Herman puts it, traumatic recovery does not rest "on the illusion that evil has been overcome, but rather on the knowledge that it *has not entirely prevailed* and on the hope that restorative love may still be found in the world."[7]

Secular trauma theorists recognize that healing relies, in part, upon courageous action taken by victims to pursue healing, empowered by a hope for the future. Yet, non-theological trauma theorists also recognize the ways in which misguided optimism can be just as damaging and prohibitive to the healing process of survivors as despair can be.[8] Christian hope can provide a language to empower courageous activity, undertaken toward healing, that authentically expects something new, but is also grounded in a realistic understanding of human capacities. The language of Christian eschatological hope is able to hold in tension what we can accomplish (with God) with an awareness that the fullness of healing has always *still not yet arrived.*

God's healing grace, in a posttraumatic context, has an eschatological shape. Healing is characterized by two moments: the "already," that which we can experience now, and the "not yet," that for which we still hope. In those of us marked by sexual violence, God empowers healing now, this side of the eschaton, through the gift of courage. In this chapter, we will explore the function of courage in the work of posttraumatic healing. Courage is persistence in the *arduum bonum*, that which is good, but difficult. Jesus is a model of resistive courage for survivors who hold on to the good but difficult. Courage is animated by a hope for the future. For survivors of sexual violence, the object of hope is the fullness of healing—personally, interpersonally, and socio-politically. Courage is a critical component of the posttraumatic healing process, and the foundation for hope. Christian eschatological language can make the particular dynamics of posttraumatic healing explicit—namely, that authentic healing is possible, and involves the positive exercise of human agency, yet at the same time our need for healing surpasses our ability to bring this healing about.

Courage in a Posttraumatic Context

When people talk about "courage" in the context of sexual violence, especially the form of courage that can be practiced in situations when there are no apparent modes of agency—namely, "endurance"—many survivors and their allies may rightfully begin to feel nervous. One gets the impression that the victim must "endure" whatever happens to her with patient acceptance and not try to change her situation. These fears are well-grounded since victims of sexual violence, particularly those who live in ongoing abusive relationships, are often told to try to make the violent relationship work. Especially in Christian contexts, where the model of Jesus as a willing, suffering servant is misappropriated, victims are often told that it is their responsibility to love and forgive their abusers "seventy times seven" (Mt 18:21–22).[9]

Victims are frequently given the impression that their forgiveness, offered before real repentance and transformation is displayed by the perpetrator,[10] has the capacity to transform the abuser into a healthy and loving human being.[11] The harm of this kind of advice cannot be overstated.[12] It dangerously confirms the victim's own deepest fears and the abuser's rationalizations. It is the victim who is culpable for the violence, not the abuser—if she can only try harder, she will be able to sidestep the perpetrator's wrath.

In instances where a Christian who is suffering from ongoing sexual violence does not receive any explicit Christian counseling, a Christian interpretive framework can still negatively shape her response to her abuse and suggest that Jesus models silent acceptance of whatever suffering may come one's way out of fidelity to God. As one survivor recounts:

> During the time when I was being abused, I always walked into the sanctuary silently pleading for guidance. While almost nothing of the average Sunday service was useful to me, communion became strikingly relevant. Here was the story of an innocent person, Jesus, who decided to silently *endure* bodily mutilation as well as emotional and spiritual anguish in order to demonstrate love for his enemies. Rather than retaliate or strive to protect himself, he let himself be murdered for the sake of the unjust. This, the liturgy said, was love, the kind of love Christian followers who take the bread and the cup are instructed to emulate. Taking communion was described as a recommitment to following the way of Jesus' suffering love, and so it became a ritual of accepting the pain I was taking into my body from my abusers. It provided me with strength and resolve to *keep quiet and endure*. In retrospect, I see that it was a powerful part of all that prevented my escape.[13]

In contexts where violence has ended, but the victim remains traumatized, the advice to survivors to put the past behind them and get on with their lives is common and counterproductive.[14] As Ann Cahill argues, "The exhortation to 'buck up,' to pack the experience away neatly and forever, fails so spectacularly because it assumes that there is a self that exists independently of the traumatic experience, a self that can voluntarily choose to interpret and take up that experience in a variety of ways, the best of which is simply to ignore it."[15]

In these situations, the language of "forgiveness" is often used as another tool to rush the victim's healing along as quickly as possible. However well-intentioned forgiveness advice might be, it can give the victim the impression that she can bring about forgiveness through the force of her own will, and if she is not able to do this, she has failed in some way.[16] This advice can be just as coercive, and violently intrusive, as the action(s) that the victim is being instructed to forgive.[17] "Forgiveness" is not synonymous with healing. While forgiveness of the perpetrator(s) might play a role in some survivors' healing journey, it is not a constitutive element of posttraumatic healing.[18]

Endurance: Strength When Agency Is Limited

To practice endurance in the face of suffering is to practice strength when one's agency is limited. It is not to "forgive and forget," or to simply accept whatever suffering may come one's way. To misidentify endurance as a commitment to accept suffering and, in particular, to portray Jesus as the model of this kind of endurance, is to strip endurance from its traditional, political framework of courageous action.

Traditionally, courage is the moderation of fear and daring in the pursuit of a good that is difficult to obtain, and in the Christian tradition, Jesus has functioned as the paradigmatic courageous actor.[19] Courageous action is typically divided into two types—aggression and endurance. Aggressive courageous acts are possible when one perceives approaching danger. Courageous acts of endurance are possible when danger has already arrived and harm cannot be avoided.[20] Endurance is a mode of courageous action when agency is limited. To practice endurance does not mean to do nothing and hold on, but rather to resist present evil in an authentic and creative way.[21]

The context of posttraumatic healing, in particular, demands that we ask ourselves how one can display personal integrity and agency (the necessary conditions for posttraumatic healing) when, by all outward accounts, one has been stripped of agency and integrity. In a posttraumatic context, courageous action is required in the pursuit of healing despite the inevitable pain that comes from confronting traumatic memories, from encountering lack of support from those who doubt what has happened to the victim-survivor (or those who think that it does not demand attention), and from facing the wrath of her abuser(s). When it is possible to act from a place of *aggression*—e.g., to pursue legal action against one's abuser(s), to seek a divorce (in the case of spousal abuse), or to leave one's place of residence (in any case of domestic abuse)—to act aggressively is to act courageously. Yet, when it is not possible to take any external, offensive action—either in cases of victims who are dependents, without social power, or when the immediate external threat has passed (for example, the adult survivor of childhood sexual abuse who continues to experience internal threats to her or his life, but who is no longer under the external power of the abuser)—acts of courage are available to the individual in the form of acts of *endurance*. Courage is the moderation of fear and daring in the pursuit of a "good" that is difficult to obtain. For the survivor of sexual abuse, the good for which endurance strives is her own safety and healing, and (eventually, by extension) the safety and healing of others.

Continued suffering is a component of the healthy process of healing. However, there is a critical difference between suffering endured for the sake of the good of healing, and the suffering undertaken in the hope of paying for past sins (committed either by or against the victim). Courage in a posttraumatic context, especially courage in the form of endurance, does not require staying put in an unsafe situation out of a desire to "forgive." Neither does it consist of pushing through pain and anger as quickly as possible, so as to return to the life that one had before violence intruded. Courage is always the pursuit of the good, despite whatever suffering might come from this pursuit. In the context of sexual violence, courage is a commitment to healing, however long, comprehensive, and arduous this process might become. Jesus models this kind of courage not as a willing suffering servant, but as one who resists the violence of the Roman Empire and assigns his own meaning to his life and work.

Violence Against Jesus: "A Sign of Tragedy," Not Divinely Orchestrated

In a posttraumatic context, the death of Jesus must be interpreted as "a sign of tragedy."[22] God does not will the death of Jesus. Jesus's death is the consequence of sinful human structures that allow the death of vulnerable individuals as a means to bolster imperial control and inspire terror among the occupied. Similarly, God does not desire anyone to be a victim of sexual violence. Rape is never a part of God's plan. Rape is the result of the perpetrator's sinful actions and the social-political structures that enable (and encourage) these sinful actions. Jesus was likely chosen as a victim of state-sanctioned violence because of his habit of disrupting power relationships. It is important to remember, however, that the Romans did not need permission to crucify anyone. Even though many victims wonder whether there is a "special purpose" for which they have been "chosen," or a specific fault which has isolated them for abuse, violence is often random and without rational order. The particular case of Jesus need not be any different. Jesus did not know that he would die by crucifixion at the beginning of his public ministry, and he did not seek this kind of death. Jesus acted courageously throughout his life by choosing not to allow the threat of Roman violence to scare him into the curtailment of his vision and values (Mt 16:25).[23] He continued to preach the politically charged vision of the kingdom of God even when it became apparent to him that the authorities would see this as a threat to their own power and control. Once it became clear that death by crucifixion was unavoidable, Jesus creatively worked to incorporate his death into what he understood to be his mission.

Jesus's Courage in the Face of Death: Resistive Endurance

As Jesus drew closer to his own death, he was forced to make sense of his circumstances. He had to try to make sense of how this kind of tragedy could happen to him, and how it threatened the community that he had created with his friends and followers.[24] In this community, they had experienced the kingdom of God as already present—they ate together as equals, they celebrated a new social order in which God would reign, and injustice would be abolished. Even more, they had a radical faith that this was only the beginning. As Jesus's death approached, they heard the threats against Jesus's life, and they sensed that authorities were not happy about the movement that they had built. It seemed as though this would be the end. Their faith seemed at odds with the historical circumstances. Jesus needed to come to terms with this dissonance as much as anyone else. He sensed that this was just the beginning of God's renewal of the Earth and yet, by any rational accounting, it looked as though this renewal would end prematurely. What now?

As a way of making sense of this for himself and his vulnerable community, Jesus made a creative and courageous decision to return to a familiar activity; he gathered his friends together for a meal. Throughout his public ministry, Jesus ate with his friends and followers as equals. It was at the table that Jesus could communicate a vision of the kingdom of God and God's desire for human communities. Jesus used the image of a table feast in his own preaching and parable-telling, comparing the kingdom of God to an extravagant wedding feast (Mt 22:1–14, Lk 14:15-24). Jesus's miracles involved feeding more than five thousand people with an initial offering of food that was only able to feed five (Mt 14:13–21, Mk 6:30–44, Lk 9:10–17, Jn 6:1–15, cf. Mk 8:1–21) and turning water into wine, so that the wedding feast at Cana could continue with appropriate extravagance (Jn 2:1–12). Jesus's disciples had a reputation for eating and drinking (Lk 5:33) and Jesus himself had a reputation for dining with those who others in his community would have shunned (Lk 5:27–32). He returned to this practice of gathering his friends and followers together, at a common table, to celebrate Passover the night before he died.

Knowing that soon his body would be publicly violated in the most painful and humiliating ways that the Roman government could imagine, he creatively gave his body away to his friends and followers. He said to them—even to those who would end up disappointing him—"Take, eat; this is my body" (Mt 26:26). He gave his body, and thereby his mission and his story, to those who gathered together in his name to re-member him and eat together as equals. This was a way for Jesus to insist that his body did not belong to those who would try to take control of it the next day. The authorities would not take control of his message and his mission.[25] Imperial authorities intended to scare this community into submission, to scatter them and make it impossible for them to continue to practice the coming kingdom of God. But they were not effective. The community that Jesus and his friends and followers built together could not be killed. This movement would not die.[26]

Jesus did not have the luxury of knowing how his own story would end, but he decided to place his trust in the God who had called him to his mission and to trust that this God would make a way out of no way. This was Jesus's way of avoiding "passively allowing death to overcome him,"[27] and to transform an unavoidable event into an opportunity to extend his vision of the kingdom of God. In this way, Jesus's death was able to function as the service of bringing about the kingdom on earth. This was not because the kingdom of God requires the spilling of blood, but rather, this was due to Jesus's own creative resistance to the violence that was being committed against him. He was able to respond creatively and courageously because he was empowered by the faith that God is capable of redemption in even the most impossible of circumstances. This creative action should not be confused with an acceptance of his death as the will of God. Jesus refused to understand suffering as willed by the Abba, who always and everywhere desires human well-being.[28]

Jesus's own approach to death was not quiet acceptance of whatever might happen to him. Instead, Jesus acted courageously, even when faced with severely limited agency, by resisting the meaning of crucifixion foisted upon him by political authorities and creating meaning out of his death. This is what endurance—courageous action when agency is severely limited—can look like. It consists of refusing to hand over one's body to perpetrators of violence, even if violent wounds cannot be avoided. It consists of finding whatever way possible to preserve a spark of one's integrity, however small. It consists of resistance, even when that resistance might fail to be noticed by the perpetrators. In a traumatic context, resistive endurance consists in seeking justice, seeking autonomy, seeking community, and seeking wisdom.

Resistive Endurance: Seeking Justice, Seeking Autonomy, Seeking Community, Seeking Wisdom

Survivors of sexual violence practice resistive endurance in a variety of ways including (but not limited to) seeking justice, seeking autonomy, seeking community, and seeking wisdom. These are practices of creative courage—creatively pursuing the good of healing when options are limited.

Seeking Justice

For survivors of sexual violence, the resistive practice of seeking justice might involve pursuing accountability within the legal system. For some survivors, this is a healing option. For example, philosopher Susan Brison describes:

> When I was hospitalized after my assault I experienced moments of reprieve from vivid and terrifying flashbacks when giving my account of what had happened—to the police, doctors, a psychiatrist, a lawyer, and a prosecutor. Although others apologized for putting me through what seemed to them a retraumatizing ordeal, I responded that it was therapeutic, even at that early stage, to bear witness in the presence of others who heard and believed what I told them. Two and a half years later, when my assailant was brought to trial, I also found it healing to give my testimony in public and to have it confirmed by the police, prosecutor, my lawyer, and ultimately, the jury, who found my assailant guilty of rape and attempted murder.[29]

This path of seeking justice within the court system is often long and painful but can be worthwhile for some survivors. As Cathy Winkler describes, following her rape by a home intruder,

> His rape attack left me with two choices: not to report the crime and live with the knowledge that he would continue inflicting his hell on other women—a hell that I am now familiar with, or, to spend years as I have in the court system trying to stop his attacks.[30]

For others who suffer from sexual violence, particularly those who habitually experience violence at the hands of the police and court system—people of color, incarcerated people, sex workers, and undocumented people[31]—justice cannot be found in the criminal system. Judith Herman argues that the legal system is inherently biased against all victims *qua* victims, especially female and juvenile victims.

> Efforts to seek justice or redress often involve further traumatization, for the legal system is frankly hostile to rape victims. . . .it is organized as a battlefield in which strategies of aggressive argument and psychological attack replace those of physical force. Women are generally little better prepared for this form of fighting than for physical combat.

Even those who are well prepared are placed at a disadvantage by the systematic legal bias and institutional discrimination against them. . . .It therefore provides strong guarantees for the rights of the accused by essentially no guarantees for the rights of the victim. If one set out by design to devise a system for provoking intrusive post-traumatic symptoms, one could not do better than a court of law. Women who have sought justice in the legal system commonly compare this experience to being raped a second time.[32]

Justice, instead (or in addition), might involve accountability within a faith community or family system. For example, after survivors of sexual abuse by Catholic liturgical music composer David Haas demanded and put substantial pressure on Christian organizations to discontinue using Haas's music, many Catholic dioceses and several Catholic, Lutheran, and Mennonite hymnals permanently suspended the publishing of Haas's work.[33] Often, recognition from just a few people who hear and believe one's story of sexual violence, can significantly contribute to the sufferer's healing and experience of justice.

Seeking Autonomy

Many survivors of sexual violence cultivate resistive courage through the practice of seeking autonomy that reforms and reclaims their bodies. Sexual violence transforms the victim's body into a weapon used against itself. Perpetrators communicate to victims that their bodies are liabilities; they are invitations to abuse and will function as reminders of abuse for the rest of their lives. Victims often feel as if their own bodies cannot be trusted, since they involuntarily freeze or react as if the original traumatic event is ongoing.

The transformation of the victim's body into a weapon to be used by the perpetrator against the victim is a classic strategy of torture. As literary theorist Elaine Scarry argues, in the context of torture, all materiality—particularly, everyday domestic objects—is intentionally converted into instruments of pain to "demonstrate that everything is a weapon [and] the objects themselves, and with them the fact of civilization, are annihilated."[34]

Within the context of the torture of sexual violence, the body of the victim is annihilated by converting it into the very thing that destroys itself—whether through recurrent intrusive memories, depression,[35] gastrointestinal and pelvic floor disorders,[36] and a plethora of self-destructive behaviors, including substance abuse and compulsive self-mutilation.[37]

Survivors of sexual violence employ a diversity of strategies to transform their posttraumatic bodies, including self-defense training (i.e., effectively reshaping their bodies from an offensive weapon used against themselves into a defensive weapon to be used against others)[38] and other forms of body modification and re-representation. For example, Susan Brison describes:

> After my own assault, I wished I could add eyes to the back of my head, but I settled for cutting my hair so short that, when viewed from behind, I might be mistaken for a man.[39]

Donna Freitas, survivor of stalking by a Roman Catholic priest, describes that in the midst of her abuse, she significantly altered the way in which she presented herself in an attempt to protect herself from further abuse.

> I started dressing differently. Gone were the fashionable outfits, the high-heeled boots, the short skirts, the tight tops, replaced by baggy jeans and baggy sweatshirts. Baggy everything. I stopped wearing my hair long and loose and instead put it up in a ponytail or a knot. Sometimes I didn't even shower before school. I wondered if this might help, if somehow he'd gotten the idea that I'd been dressing that way for him. That maybe if he saw me disheveled, he'd realize I wasn't interested in looking good for him. Not at all. Not one bit.[40]

Just as often as reclaiming one's body can be a part of one's process of healing, it can become a resistive practice that goes horribly wrong, becoming damaging to the survivor. Survivor Barb shares:

> My thought process at the time was that food was healthy; food was good for me. But I believed I was not worthy of anything good and I certainly didn't want to nourish my violated body. Anorexia allowed me to prove to myself that I could decide how my body would be treated even if that meant punishing it. But while I may have reclaimed decision-making power over my own body, I was slowly committing suicide;[41] I wanted to die.[42]

Similarly, writer and childhood survivor of gang-rape Roxane Gay describes in her book *Hunger: A Memoir of (My) Body* that she gradually became "super morbidly obese" to protect herself from further violence. She writes:

> I don't know how things got so out of control, or I do. This is my refrain. Losing control of my body was a matter of accretion. I began eating to change my body. I was willful in this. Some boys had destroyed me, and I barely survived it. I knew I wouldn't be able to endure another such violation, and so I ate because I thought that if my body became repulsive, I could keep men away. Even at that young age, I understood that

to be fat was to be undesirable to men, to be beneath their contempt, and I already knew too much about their contempt.[43]

Gay explains further, "I did this to myself. This is my fault and my responsibility. This is what I tell myself, though I should not bear the responsibility for this body alone."[44]

Seeking Community

Survivors of sexual violence practice resistive courage in seeking community. Because sexual violence destroys healthy relationships and propagates shame and mistrust, networks of authentic care and support are healing for survivors. Although survivors risk much by entering into relationships with others, healing is not possible without those relationships. True friendship, practiced with God and with others, can function as an antidote to the isolating dynamics of trauma. Friendship, the most free and open of all relationships, carries the capacity to transform the survivor's interpersonal wounds and serve as the foundation for socio-political action.[45]

The trust cultivated in the relationships between a survivor and her therapist, spiritual director, and/or pastor, can also be a healing kind of relationality where the helping professional accompanies the survivor as she remembers what has happened to her and mourns her loss. Joan Miller, a survivor of rape as a college student studying abroad, writes in *America Magazine* about the healing relationship she experienced with her therapist. This therapeutic relationship allowed her to open herself up to other forms of relationality.

> Prior to my first session, I felt very nervous and unsure of how I would be received. I would not have blamed anyone for not wanting to step inside my world. Instead, my spiritual director poured love and kindness into the darkness and my light started to shine. I felt safe sharing with her. Instead of apathy or disgust, I was met with love, compassion and care. I was finally able to cry over what had happened to me.[46]

Seeking Wisdom

Survivors practice resistive courage in seeking wisdom. Those who have experienced sexual violence frequently develop creative ways to survive in the midst of untrustworthy relationships and unpredictable situations. With limited modes of agency, they have often developed an ingenuity, sensitive to the limits and facilitations of their particular contexts. For example, some women cooperate in their own rapes in order to survive. This requires creative ingenuity, sensing the disposition of the abuser, and what the survivor can do to preserve her own life. American psychotherapist Audrey Savage, survivor of violent attack by a stranger while camping in Wales, cooperated in her own attack, once it had begun, by removing her own clothing, talking to her attacker afterwards, and letting him into her tent. The day after her attack, her perpetrator said to her:

> I'm glad you stopped fighting me last night. You saw how I was.

She narrates:

> He didn't say he would have brutally beaten me if I hadn't cooperated, but I knew he would have. He didn't say he would have done whatever he needed to do to have his way if I hadn't cooperated, but I knew he would have. He didn't say he would have killed me if I hadn't cooperated, but I knew he would have. I knew my cooperation had saved my life.[47]

Savage explains further:

> Somewhere inside of me I was smart enough to save myself by letting him have the power—all the power. I knew he was willing to beat me to a bloody pulp in order to prove his power. I realized I couldn't save myself from this horrible invasion of my rights, nor could I save myself from the psychological aftereffects, but I could save my physical self from further brutality. Therefore, I let him have the power he demanded. I cooperated in every way I knew. I believed then and I believe now, that cooperation was my salvation. He was a brutal man. I knew it. I knew it by his conversation and by his behavior.[48]

And yet, these details were exploited in court by the defense as constituting her consent to sex.

The wisdom of survival is highly context dependent. It is a practical kind of wisdom that sometimes employs modes of action which, in other contexts, would not be liberating or even ethical. For example, as anthropologist Cathy Winkler recalls, during her rape by a home intruder:

> to make myself a valued and alive commodity to him, I treated him like a respected human being of sensibility, and I praised him as a man of handsome beauty, and one loved by women for his lustful prowess.[49]

While praising one's attacker can be a strategic mode of self-preservation in the midst of a rape, it is a psychologically harmful practice to continue after the safety of the survivor has been established. Resistance is multiform and fluid.[50]

Pain and Loss: Sacred Insights

Finally, survivors practice resistance by simply experiencing pain and loss. As Edward Schillebeeckx makes clear, the experience of suffering *as* negative, reveals an intuition that the experience is one that should have never happened. This intuition, that sexual violence is wrong, is a holy insight. It allows the victim a starting point for clearly condemning what has happened to her, mourning what she has lost, and imagining a world free of such violence. This insight itself resists the perpetrator's aims: to strip the victim of agency, to normalize harm, and to kill imaginative hope. This sacred insight reveals a foundation of hope in the very experience of pain *as painful, as negative*—namely, that we are meant for something better. We are meant for love, for freedom, and for wholeness.

Other Scriptural Models of Courageous Action: The Hemorrhaging Woman and Hagar

Scripture attests to creative and resistive courage as integral to friendship with God, witnessing the ways in which God works alongside of the sufferer for her well-being. In three of the four gospels, we hear about the hemorrhaging woman who dared to touch the clothing of Jesus, resourcefully seeking healing for herself (Mt 9:20–21; Mk 5:25-34; Lk 8:43–48). This unnamed woman, who is physically unwell, socially isolated, and economically vulnerable,[51] acts courageously to seek healing, without proper request or permission.[52] She is a model of courageous wisdom. Jesus's response to this woman's bold move is not to reprimand her, but instead to praise her resolve and to address her as a "daughter," thereby affirming his relationship with her and pushing against the social isolation that has categorized her life for the past twelve years. As biblical scholar Susan Calef notes, "rather than claiming credit for the healing—after all, the power that healed her resided in Jesus—he attributes it to her, citing the woman's own faith as its cause."[53] The woman in need of healing cooperates with Jesus in securing wholeness for herself, and Jesus affirms her action as holy and faithful.[54] Although the reader might get the impression that this is a story of a woman who makes a singular, isolated, bold move in search of healing, Mark's inclusion of the detail that she was attended to by many physicians and "had spent all that she had," (Mk 5:26) strongly suggests that she had been pursuing her own healing for many years, however unsuccessfully.[55] Her persistence is even more remarkable given this context.

In an essay titled "Silence," Bella Moon (a pseudonym), survivor of neglect and sexual abuse while in foster care, shares that she had committed to therapy for twenty-five years before ever disclosing her experience of sexual abuse. Now, in her fifties, she writes that her experience of abuse left her feeling "invaded, terrorized, and finally, paralyzed."[56] Bella's experience is not unusual—it typically takes survivors decades to begin to confront their own violent histories fully. Often a lifetime is not enough. But, to the degree that they persist in efforts to heal, they resemble the hemorrhaging woman who spent all she had to seek wholeness.

In Genesis, Hagar—the Egyptian woman enslaved to Sarah and Abraham, who has been cast into the desert with her son Ishmael—finds herself without any water. She puts her son down from her back and walks away, knowing that it would be too painful to watch him die of thirst. She then hears God's voice, and the God whom she has named El-roi (the God of seeing) tells her to pick up her son again and assures her that, through her hands, God will hold Ishmael secure. With the courage to see Ishmael in his suffering and hold him, her eyes are now opened wide to all that is around her. She can see exactly what she and her son need to survive for the moment—water. God empowers Hagar to act for herself and, as the God of seeing, opens her eyes to what she needs to survive, but she must cooperate with God to secure the resources she needs.[57] Hagar is a model of courageous wisdom. She courageously responds to God's call in the desert, and although the author does not explain how they continued to survive without a community in a hostile environment, the reader is prompted to imagine that continued survival proceeds much like this episode, one moment at a time, with no specific vision for the long-term. Trauma survivors can understand this kind of grace. Not knowing whether it is all going to come together in the end but knowing that, just for right now, they are surviving. This is what Delores Williams refers to as a "survival/quality of life" paradigm of salvation.[58] According to this paradigm, God works alongside of human beings as they struggle for their individual and communal well-being, highlighting the importance of the roles of human initiative, intelligence, and responsibility in the long struggle for freedom. God is not a dramatic interventionist, but rather a partner, providing direction and strength.[59]

Endurance: Courage for Long and Slow Things

The kind of courage that is needed in the work of posttraumatic healing is perseverance in long and slow processes. When courage is an explicit topic in the Christian tradition, however, this is not the kind of courage that is often under discussion. Aristotle, whose thought provides a foundation for many Christian virtue theorists, understood death in battle as the paradigm for courageous action.[60] Thomas Aquinas, intentionally building on Aristotle, specifies endurance (rather than aggression) as fortitude's chief act[61]—thus, opening the virtue from a narrow focus on those able-bodied males (i.e., warriors) to those who are in situations of relative powerlessness and are unable to protect themselves from harm through aggressive action (as is often the case for victims of rape)—and identifies martyrdom as the paradigm of endurance.[62] Decentering Aristotle's military paradigm is an important development, especially if one is to consider the role of courage in healing from sexual trauma, since it allows, as philosopher Rebecca Konyndyk DeYoung argues, "[a]nyone who is weak, vulnerable, or unable or unwilling to use force [to be . . .] a candidate for practicing this virtue—including women, children, the elderly, the economically and socially disempowered, and even the disabled."[63]

Furthermore, Aquinas's understanding of courage is important for trauma survivors, since courage in general (and endurance in particular) is characterized by holding fast to the good, despite whatever suffering may arise from pursuit of that good. Aquinas's framework makes it clear that suffering is never to be desired for itself. In the face of a long tradition of the deadly use of martyrdom language in the contexts of sexual trauma (particularly as it has been used to encourage victims to accept passively abusive situations), Aquinas's articulation of courage is critical because, for him, the courageous actor only suffers because, given her commitment to the good, she cannot avoid suffering. As Konyndyk DeYoung writes, "The martyr's evil *will* and *does* become present (inevitably) because she *cannot* keep it at arms' length; the martyr's stronger opponent sets the terms of what will come and when."[64] This makes it apparent that the one who suffers from sexual violence is never to choose to remain in an unsafe situation out of a supposed "love for one's enemies." The courageous person has a love of the good and does not value suffering in itself.

In the case of sexual trauma, the "good" is one's own well-being, the well-being of one's dependents, and right relationality. First seeking safety, and thereafter continuing to prioritize one's own recovery, is the only way to hold steadfast to this good. As any trauma survivor knows, this is no easy work. Recovery itself entails a great amount of suffering, and therefore requires courage to persevere. As Flora Keshgegian argues, "In a seeming contradiction, healing necessitates much pain. Survivors need to be willing to experience frightening pain."[65]

If one can ever, legitimately, say that a path of suffering is salvific, it is in this instance. The pain of healing, for surely healing *is* painful, is a freely chosen kind of suffering and holy work. Suffering itself does not save us, but those who are struggling for their own healing do suffer out of a love of what is good and will not be dissuaded from what trials arise in the pursuit of healing. It is important to remember that the traumatized individual does not have any path available to her that is free of suffering. She does not have the opportunity to accept the pain of recovery as a choice between suffering and not suffering. Rather, choosing to endure the trials of recovery is choosing to face the harm one has experienced head on, to resist the evil of violence, and to hope for the good of comprehensive well-being.

"Unshouted" Courage

Though Aquinas's framework for thinking about courage can be helpful in some ways in a posttraumatic context, Aquinas effectively replaces one heroic action for another without doing much to dismantle the assumption that courage consists in highly visible, peak moments. He trades martial heroism for martyrized heroism without questioning the fundamental identification of heroism with courage.[66] Many survivors might not recognize themselves as martyred heroes. Many do not feel that heroic language fits their experience of courage at all. In a posttraumatic context, healing rarely centers on grand gestures. Healing is usually non-linear, slow, long, frustrating, and boring. Although survivors often wish that they could secure well-being with a dramatic action (however difficult or painful it might be), this is not usually possible. Instead, the courage of healing is usually, as womanist theologian Katie Canon puts it, "unshouted." Canon explains:

> "Unshouted courage" is the quality of steadfastness, akin to fortitude, in the face of formidable oppression. The communal attitude is far more than "grin and bear it." Rather, it involves the ability to "hold on to life" against major oppositions. It is the incentive to facilitate change, to chip away the oppressive structures, bit by bit, to celebrate and rename their experiences in empowering ways.[67]

Therefore, other thinkers in the Christian tradition might be more useful in discussing the kind of courage that is needed in the long and slow process of "hold[ing] on to life."[68]

Teresa of Avila offers a theology of courage suited to the long and slow work of posttraumatic healing. I have already related this anecdote, but it is worth returning to. At the beginning of her autobiography, Teresa tells the story of her plan to run away from home with her brother. They were inspired by the lives of the saints and wanted to imitate their example. As she explains, "When I considered the martyrdoms the saints suffered for God, it seemed to me that the price they paid for going to enjoy God was very cheap, and I greatly desired to die in the same way."[69] Their plan was to "go off to the land of the Moors and beg them, out of love of God, to cut off our heads there"[70] but, alas, "[h]aving parents seemed to us the greatest obstacle" to executing their vision. Teresa relates this story as early evidence in her life of the gift of "courage,"[71] and desire for God. Yet, whatever quality she is describing here is clearly inadequate, and will need to develop into a fuller, more spiritually mature understanding of courage as her life narrative progresses. True courage, as Teresa will demonstrate, is not primarily finding someone to cut off your head so that you will go straight to heaven. Instead, courage is the patient receptivity to the present gifts of God. It is the strength to face the reality of one's life, as well as the internal dangers and beauties that await as one embarks upon the related discoveries of the self and of God. During the course of her life, Teresa demonstrated a more authentic form of courage in her unwavering commitment to a life of prayer (despite the challenges of boredom, busyness, fear, and a malformed sense of self), management of painful chronic illness, and extensive reforming activities (especially in the face of others who undermined her projects and believed that she was under demonic influence).

Prayer Generates and Sustains Courage

For Christians (and for those of many other religious traditions), the courage required for works of resistance is generated in the life of prayer. For individuals not fortified by a religious tradition, creative and courageous works of resistance may be birthed, but they are difficult to maintain without some kind of faith in the primacy of goodness over evil.[72]

For Teresa, courage cultivated in the life of prayer is a source of strength for the whole of life. Prayer is like wine that fortifies the soul, giving one the strength to serve and stand alongside of others.[73]

Yet the life of prayer itself requires extensive labor on the part of the practitioner, especially in the early stages. Consequently, the life of prayer requires endurance on the part of the practitioner. At the same time, the courage that friendship with God requires is ultimately a divine gift, since "the mixture of boring effort and intermittent consolation simply trails on until God interrupts it."[74] As Teresa explains it, we "persevere" and God grants the "courage" (*ánimo*) necessary for us to complete our task, suggesting that humans and God cooperate in friendship.[75]

Because regular and meaningful prayer is a struggle for so many of us, the role of fortitude in the life of prayer is a common theme in the Christian tradition. As Schillebeeckx puts it, mystical prayer itself can be an experience of contrast that calls for the endurance to push through feelings of alienation when consolations are imperceptible.[76] Schillebeeckx argues that experiences of alienation themselves can bring more comfort than frustration to the practitioner, since they signal God's transcendence and, thus, God's capacity to bring about our salvation, especially when wholeness is beyond our natural reach.

It is difficult to pray, to open oneself to truth, and to enter into relationships with anyone, especially the divine. For traumatized people, when relationships have been a source of violation, prayer can be particularly terrifying. The bodily aspects of the life of prayer, and the language that the mystics use to describe the prayer relationship, can amplify this fear.[77] Yet there is no place that the traumatized person can turn that escapes the dangerous realities of bodiliness.

There is no way to have relationships with others (even God) completely free of danger and undemanding of vulnerability, but Teresa can offer us language to articulate the value of *qualified* vulnerability and intimacy. This is critical for the trauma victim who seeks to relearn gradations of fear and vulnerability.[78] Qualified vulnerability and intimacy are difficult and require great courage. This is not the courage of battle, or the resistive death of a martyr, but instead the slow, painful courage of endurance in relationships.

Courage for Qualified Vulnerability and Intimacy

For Teresa, the life of prayer involves varying levels of vulnerability, depending upon the nature of the one with whom one is in a relationship. Relationship with God involves profound vulnerability and transparency, while relationship with "noxious creatures" should involve the cultivation of a high degree of self-protection and defense. Both modes—vulnerability and defense—require courage. In a mode of vulnerability, courage is needed to move toward the center of the self, exploring new rooms, and remaining open to unexpected and untamable beauty. In a mode of self-protection, courage enables one to learn not only to steel oneself against the influence of the noxious creatures residing around the exterior edges of the soul, but also to empower oneself to move away from them and deeper inside the castle.

Courage is also needed in order to refuse to identify with the filth that invades the beauty of the castle.[79] In the interior part of the castle, the influence of noxious creatures may still be felt, yet vermin are no longer capable of disturbing the practitioner of prayer since she is in such close proximity to God, the King. The political weight of the metaphor of self as a castle, a fortified structure, becomes clear; we are strengthened in relationship with God for appropriate relationships with others. The self is a defensive, protective structure, with transparent walls, such that the light of God can illuminate us from within.

Relationship with God does not entail unmitigated openness to all others, and it does not involve acceptance of abuse. Instead, relationship with God involves access to deep forms of power and strength that sometimes manifest in the form of resistive endurance. This God-given power is used appropriately to resist those who would hurt or manipulate us, and to be in the service of love for the vulnerable who need our care. Teresa speaks of God as giving her courage to engage in aggressive resistance to "devils." She writes:

> If this Lord is powerful, as I see that He is and I know that He is, and if the devils are His slaves (and that there is no doubt about this because it's a matter of faith), what evil can they do to me since I am a servant of this Lord and King? Why shouldn't I have the fortitude to engage in combat with all of hell? I took a cross in my hand, and it seemed to me truly that God gave me courage because in a short while I saw that I was another person and that I wouldn't fear bodily combat with them; for I thought that with that cross I would easily conquer all of them.[80]

These devils are agents of deception, purveyors of lies about who God is and who we are. When they speak, they cause anxiety and affliction, unlike the quiet refreshment that God's voice provides.[81]

The conquest of these devils, however, does not guarantee their disappearance. They are still present to Teresa, but she has no reason to fear them. She writes, "There was no doubt, in my opinion, that they were afraid of me, for I remained so calm and so unafraid of them all. All the fears I usually felt left me—even to this day. For although I sometimes saw them, as I shall relate afterward, I no longer had hardly any fear of them; rather it seemed they were afraid of me."[82]

Traumatized people know what it is like to continue to encounter evil even after it seems that evil has been vanquished. Traumatized people, even after healing has begun, will continue to be haunted by memories of their violation(s). Furthermore, the traumatized person has no guarantee that after she has sought safety from one violent environment, she will not encounter another. It is not possible to protect oneself once and for all. Encountering evil is a continued reality for traumatized people. For the sexually traumatized person, traumatic memories, violent people, and sexist and racist structures may remain, but as the survivor begins the healing process, she is able to manage encounters with these elements. The fullness of healing, however, remains incomplete as long as violent behavior and rape culture continue to exist.[83]

Self-Defense

God empowers Teresa to defend herself aggressively via combat when she can, and to steel herself against the devils when she cannot aggressively combat them. Through encounter with God in prayer, Teresa is strengthened. This strength allows her to know to whom she belongs—to God, who desires her well-being, not to those who wish harm for her.

Teresa's language of active, bodily modes of self-defense, and her argument that encounter with God transforms her into "another person" who can confidently battle evil, calls to mind feminist philosophers' arguments, such as those made by Ann Cahill, that self-defense training facilitates the emergence of a "new body that [. . .] perceives dangers as worthy of retaliation and anger."[84] Sexual trauma survivors often struggle to act aggressively, believing that they are unworthy or incapable of self-defense. After her own recovery from an attack by a stranger while on a solitary walk, philosopher Susan Brison experienced subsequent self-defense training as reshaping her body for courageous resistance. She writes:

> I [. . .] learned, after martial arts training, that I was capable, morally as well as physically, of killing in self-defense—an option that made the possibility of another life-threatening attack one that I could live with. [. . .] far from jeopardizing their connections with a community, this newfound ability to defend themselves, and to consider themselves worth fighting for, enables rape survivors to move among others, free of debilitating fears. It was this ability that gave me the courage to bring a child into the world, in spite of the realization that doing so would, far from making me immortal, make me twice as mortal, as Barbara Kingsolver (1989, 59) put it, by doubling my chances of having my life destroyed by a speeding truck.[85]

Self-defense training is one tool for transforming the bodies of women, and other vulnerable people, from weapons to be used against themselves into weapons to be used defensively against violent others.[86] Brison may never employ lethal force. This is not the real power of self-defense training. The transformational capacity of self-defense training rests in the process of the training itself, a process which reconditions the body into a different kind of perception: that I am worthy of safety, that I have the capacity to protect myself if I need to, and that actions harmful to me are deserving of every kind of resistance I can muster. Self-defense instructor Melissa Soalt argues that the group component of training, in particular, can ameliorate the traumatic response to new threats and encourage a healthy, non-traumatic response. Soalt explains:

Just the sense of having fifteen people there for you, cheering for your success—that's a very unusual experience for women in this culture. Those connections are what help reduce the fear or freeze response. People who have had to use their self-defense training later tell us that when they were in danger, they actually heard the voices, the sound of the group cheering them on.[87]

In sexually violent circumstances, the relational body is the site of vulnerability. Therefore, in healing, cultivating (specifically) embodied and relational modes of resistive strength is critical.

Courage in Service to Transformation of the World

While, for Teresa, the life of prayer involves openness or vulnerability to God, and resistance or even defensive combat with others (particularly those who exercise unjust power), it involves loving service to different others (particularly those who are powerless and in need). Teresa's model of relationality follows the pattern of the *Magnificat*: the powerful are to be brought down from their thrones, and the lowly are lifted up, the hungry are filled with good things, and the rich are sent away empty (Lk 1:52–53). In the center of the castle of the soul, the seventh dwelling place, there is a great sense of "stability" and the gifts of increased "determination" for the work of virtuous action.[88] Prayer is like food that fortifies the whole body, providing the "strength to serve"[89] those in one's community through "the birth always of good works, good works."[90] As Teresa explains, "the calm these souls have interiorly is for the sake of their having much less calm exteriorly and much less desire to have exterior calm."[91] Informed by her own experience, she envisions that those who have practiced interior prayer are able to insert themselves into the messy drama of everyday life without becoming overwhelmed by their environments.

Practitioners of prayer are able to witness the pain of others and the realities of structural sin without losing their ability to function. This exterior stability is critical for survivors of trauma. Not only those who see themselves as activists (whether for sexual justice or for any other cause), but also more foundationally, to have full and complete lives, which invariably involve being able to respond in love to others and to experience the fullness of human intimacy (which necessarily involves nurturing service and care). Philosopher Susan Brison describes growing through the love for her son, birthed after her rape, as part of her posttraumatic healing journey.

One hopes for a bearable future, in spite of all the inductive evidence to the contrary. After all, the loss of faith in induction following an

> unpredictable trauma also has a reassuring side: since inferences from the past can no longer be relied upon to predict the future, there's no more reason to think that tomorrow will bring agony than to think that it won't. So one makes a wager, in which nothing is certain and the odds change daily, and sets about 'willing to believe' that life, for all its unfathomable horror, still holds some undiscovered pleasures. And one remakes oneself by finding meaning in a life of caring for and being sustained by others. While I used to have to will myself out of bed each day, I now wake gladly to feed my infant son whose birth, four years after the assault, gives me reason not to have died. He is the embodiment of my life's new narrative and I am more autonomous by virtue of being so intermingled with him. Having him has also enabled me to rebuild my trust in the world around us. He is so trusting that he stands with outstretched arms, wobbling, until he falls, stiff-limbed, forward, backward, certain the universe will catch him. So far, it has, and when I tell myself it always will, the part of me that he's become believes it.[92]

Brison experiences hope as she witnesses the survival of her own capacity to love and to desire goodness, despite the dehumanizing violence to which she has been victim. In the life of her son, she experiences the embodiment of a fundamental reality of her own posttraumatic life; evil has not completely overtaken goodness. Even if nothing in the future can be predicted, especially not our own safety or the safety of the ones we love, she centers her life on loving, interpersonal dependency. This orientation is a functional kind of stability, aware of the instability of the world.

Teresa of Avila commends her sisters to virtuous action in the world, concentrating on those in proximate need and promising that God will transform their partial and inadequate efforts made in good faith.[93] Social action is a necessary component of healing from sexual trauma. Because social structures facilitate the normalcy of rape, rape culture must be dismantled in order for the establishment of full healing to occur. This is not to suggest that the work of cultural transformation is the responsibility of survivors alone, or that survivors of sexual trauma cannot experience full and healthy lives without taking on social activism. Social transformation is necessary for the fullness of the healing of our communities. This transformational work cannot happen completely without active listening to, and learning from, survivors. Those who have suffered from sexual violence have an indispensable role to play in the work of cultural transformation.

The burden of the political transformation of the social order does not rest on the shoulders of any individual victim of sexual violence, or even the collective shoulders of victims. The burden of transformation rests primarily on the perpetrators of sexual violence. Perpetrators' actions, and social policies that support perpetrators' actions, need to change. Unfortunately, perpetrators are unlikely to change their behaviors without some kind of pressure from survivors and their allies. The social change we demand is not for the sake of perpetrators, but rather it is for our own healing and for the well-being of future generations yet unvictimized. Herman tells the story of Sharon, a survivor of rape by her father, to illustrate the connection between the desire for the well-being of future generations and one's own well-being.

> Sharon Simone, who with her three sisters filed suit for damages against her father for the crime of incest, describes the sense of connection with another child victim that spurred her to take action: "I read about a case in the newspaper. A man had admitted he raped a little girl twice. The child was brought to the sentencing hearing because the therapist thought it would be good for her to see the man led away; she would see that crimes do get punished. Instead, the judge allowed a parade of character witnesses. He said there really are two victims in this courtroom. I thought I was going to go berserk with the injustice. . . .That was such a turning point. The rage and the sense of holding someone accountable. I saw that it was a necessary thing. It wasn't that I needed a confession. I needed to do the action of holding someone accountable. I wanted to break the denial and the pretense. So I said, I *will* join that lawsuit. I'll do it for that little girl. I'll do it for my brothers and sisters. And I think a little voice said, 'You should also do it for you.'"[94]

In experiences of captivity, victims may not experience the capacity to imagine a transformed future. Captive individuals, subject to chronic trauma, begin to constrict their sense of the future from years to days, hours, or even minutes,[95] sometimes entering into states of altered consciousness in which reality is timeless.[96] Some victims, through no deficit of their own character, but because of circumstances of their continued bondage, do not survive.

For those who do survive, the process of healing will involve reintegrating a sense of the passage of time, and the capacity to envision a future. This work cannot begin until the bonds of captivity have been broken. During their healing journey, many survivors eventually approach engagement with the next generation and begin to think about what Judith Herman refers to as "survivorship as legacy."[97] For a great many survivors, legacy will be confined to their personal lives. For example, the legacy of passing along an integrated trauma story to their children or to those in their immediate social circles.[98] But for some, this may involve engagement with the wider world.[99]

Sarah Buel, once a battered woman and now a district attorney in charge of domestic violence prosecutions, describes the central importance of her own story as a gift to others: "I want women to have some sense of hope, because I can just remember how terrifying it was to not have any hope—the days I felt there was no way out. I feel very much like that's part of my mission, part of why God didn't allow me to die in that marriage, so that I could talk openly and publicly—and it's taken me so many years to be able to do it—about having been battered."[100]

Regardless of how an individual survivor's path pans out, the fullness of traumatic healing is incomplete in the absence of a transformation of the social-political order. We—as a human community—are not free from the wounds of sexual violence until rape culture has been rooted out and extinguished. This kind of social transformation need not be the sole responsibility of survivors, but it also cannot be done apart from listening to them.

Social action may take many forms, including legislative changes,[101] media advocacy,[102] or church reform,[103] but it is important to remember that it may also take informal shape. Sociologist Nancy Nason-Clark's study of Christians and domestic violence, reveals that women in church settings frequently support abused women in their communities outside of visible and organized church-sponsored channels. For many of those interviewed, they offered what Nason-Clark described as a "friendship model" of support to abused women—inviting women over for coffee to chat and share their stories; offering advice and a perspective on what is "normal;" material support (such as warm clothing or assistance with bills); childcare; a safe place to go if they choose to leave their violent partners; and accompaniment through legal justice processes. Because domestic abuse typically relies so heavily on strategies of captivity—namely, the systematic and deliberate severing of all ties of interdependence outside of the victim-perpetrator relationship[104]—this kind of relational support can be particularly effective. Nason-Clark notes that, often the burden of sororal aid is shared among a group of women within a church community, so that one ally alone does not become overwhelmed. Nason-Clark elaborates:

> While churchwomen never named their collective efforts on behalf of abused women as *social action*, they were acutely aware of the cost of individual friendship. For them, the answer to feeling overwhelmed by the practical and emotional needs of particular victims of abuse was to think about how they as a group of churchwomen could share the responsibility of friendship, which they almost always referred to as a *ministry*.[105]

Friendship and Social Transformation

Whether an informal "friendship model," or a more formal and visible mode of structural support and advocacy[106] is at play in support of those suffering from sexual trauma, friendship retains a critical role in any social healing. This is because all political love is grounded in friendship. As feminist theologian Mary Hunt argues, "friendship is an underlying stance that one takes toward the world, beginning at home and with those closest to home. Loving one's neighbor is the most logical extension of loving oneself and one's family. Friendship is political in its breadth, but personal in its depth."[107]

The social-political work of transforming institutions within rape culture is frequently fueled by the love of friendship. As a case in point, women's consciousness-raising groups formed in the 1970s—where women gathered together to share stories about their lives—prompted the recognition among many participants that violence and abuse were salient features of women's lives. The knowledge gained in these gatherings, and the energy generated by the friendships formed in the groups, spurred large-scale feminist, structural reform of American life—including, for example, the foundation of a rape research center within the National Institute of Mental Health in 1975.[108]

For the non-traumatized person, friendship with those who have suffered from sexual trauma can open one's eyes to the realities of rape culture and provide a stimulus to action grounded in real (non-idealized) love of another. For the sexually traumatized individual, friendship can be a form of intimacy that can facilitate human trust and can often feel safer for survivors than even consensual sexual relationships.[109]

Friendship is a critical component of a full human life. As Aristotle writes in his *Nicomachean Ethics*, "without friends, no one would choose to live, though [s]he had all other goods."[110] Friendships are the freest of all human relationships—implicitly reciprocal[111] and yet also radically open. One can be friends with anyone else. Differences in gender, age, social status, or even species are no ultimate barrier to friendship.[112] Yet, by definition, *philia* is a bond characterized by mutuality. As theologian Elizabeth Johnson explains:

> Friendship is the most free, the least possessive, the most mutual of relationships, able to cross social barriers in genuine reciprocal regard. Like all good relationships friendship is characterized by mutual trust in the reliability of the other(s), but what makes it unique is that friends are fundamentally side-by-side in common interests, common delights, shared responsibilities. Mature friendship is open to the inclusion of others in the circle assuming an essential stance of hospitality.[113]

The freedom of friendship does not imply freedom from obligation, since friends make claims upon each other.[114] Instead, the freedom of friendship implies freedom *from* class and social divisions *for* the opportunity to give of oneself and receive of another in the fullness of mutuality. As Teresa makes clear, we are called, by virtue of the incarnation, into friendship with God—the one who is "so different" from us.[115] Indeed, the experience of God as Friend animates, and makes possible, deep friendship between humans. The ally to the sexually traumatized person struggling for recovery can mediate God to the survivor in, and through, the love of friendship.

Caroline, a survivor of date rape, testifies to the healing role of friendship in her own life in an open letter to her perpetrator.

> I woke up from a nightmare one morning before work. In my dream, I had been raped and I dreamt that immediately afterwards, I was trying to tell someone what had happened. I was on the phone but something was preventing me from talking. It was as if someone were choking me; all the breath was taken from my lungs. I woke up in a panic. I didn't participate much at work that day. After work, my supervisor and a good friend asked if I'd run an errand with her. In the car she asked if something was bothering me. After some hesitation, I told her about my nightmares and what had happened to me. I felt sick to my stomach as I recounted the events and tried my best to distance myself from them. Yet my friend listened and I began to feel that I could safely talk about what you had done. Opening up to friends was the key that unlocked months of suppressed emotion.[116]

In the seventh dwelling place, the stage of prayer in which one is most fully centered on God and centered in oneself, Teresa describes the cooperation of two friends, Mary and Martha, in similar fashion to the friendships that Nason-Clark describes. They join together in mutual support, working together to accomplish what one alone could never do. Teresa asks, "How would Mary, always seated at His feet provide Him with food if her sister did not help her?"[117] They work together out of their own desires to cultivate and maintain a "friendship with the Lord."[118]

The work of friendship is both mystical and political. Friendship between humans has its source in friendship with God, while at the same time human friendship can mediate God's love and God's desire to befriend us. Donna, a survivor of multiple forms of sexual violence including incest, rape by a stranger, and clergy sexual abuse, explains:

> One of my deepest lessons comes from *The Wizard of Oz*. When the evil monkeys attack the scarecrow in the haunted forest, his insides

are ripped away. A leg is over there, an arm is someplace else, but his
friends come and put his stuffing back in. It is my friends who have
helped me put my stuffing back in—stuffing that was ripped out by
incest, by multiple rapes, by predators.[119]

Human friendship is both the source and highest expression of healed and whole social relationships.

True and genuine friendship is the foundation of right political relationships in which freedom is respected, consent is treasured, and bodily integrity is cultivated in encounters between people.[120] As theologian Mary Hunt argues, friendship is always a "political activity,"[121] not simply a "privatized relationship."[122] Friendships are "those voluntary human relationships that are entered into by people who intend one another's well-being and who intend that their love relationship is part of a justice-seeking community."[123]

The pursuit of justice is, in fact, fueled by friendship—where the other is known, loved, and given her due. And, conversely, friendship without justice is no true friendship; true friends do not manipulate or exploit each other.[124] As Hunt describes the work of friends who accompany each other in their posttraumatic healing work:

A Holocaust survivor, married to another Holocaust survivor, tells of
their frequent nightmares. When one of them wakes up screaming
from a nightmare about the most heinous crime in our time, the other
gets up too. They make tea for one another, regardless of the hour.
They have drunk a lot of tea in fierce tenderness.[125]

Friendship helps trauma survivors hold their traumatic memories, to feel "held together."[126] The ritual of waking from sleep, even when one is not in the throes of a traumatic memory, to sit with the other, sharing a warm drink, communicates, "I am here with you in your pain." This accompaniment enables survival.[127] This dramatization of the survival of love[128] functions as nothing less than an experience of resurrection for many traumatized individuals.

The political work needed for healing from sexual trauma, animated by friendship, outpaces that which we are able to accomplish. Often those who strive to do God's work can be discouraged with the realization of all that needs to be done. Teresa is aware of this reality as she addresses her *Interior Castle* to sisters who vow to spend their lives in service and loving friendship with each other. She petitions them to never assume that, since they attend to those who are "in [their] company" (viz., other vowed sisters) that their work is insignificant.[129] Love for one's fellow sisters is "not [. . .] small but very great" and "very pleasing to the Lord."[130]

Teresa recognizes the ways in which those who have a desire for God's goodness can easily become paralyzed in the face of the overwhelming needs of the world. Confrontation with the sheer pervasiveness of sexual violence is often enough to inspire paralysis, let alone an added awareness of the complex, embedded legacies of sexism, racism, ablism, and colonization that support cultures of rape. Yet Teresa argues that human paralysis is a strategy that evil uses to sustain itself. She writes:

> sometimes the devil gives us great desires so that we will avoid setting ourselves to the task at hand, serving our Lord in possible things, and instead be content with having desired the impossible [. . .] You need not be desiring to benefit the whole world but must concentrate on those who are in your company, and thus your deed will be greater since you are more obliged toward them.[131]

Teresa recommends that, "we shouldn't build castles in the air" but instead, we should "do what we can" with a confidence that these limited efforts will be transformed by God.[132] It is possible to act with a healthy self-consciousness of the inadequacy and provisional nature of one's actions. Non-paralyzing self-consciousness can be supported by eschatological faith. When one is aware of the comprehensive nature of full healing and all that it entails, it is easy to become overwhelmed with the work that lies ahead. But activity that is done within a framework of eschatological tension need not fall into despair.

Nason-Clark also describes contemporary churchwomen who support those suffering from domestic abuses as painfully aware of the ways in which their actions fail to meet the breadth and depth of need in their communities. She writes:

> Although some women who were victims of abuse—and beneficiaries of help from other churchwomen—talked about how important that support had been in their own lives, evangelical women themselves were rather critical of their own *inattentiveness* to the needs of those around them. As a group, they were not at all willing to see their individual or collective efforts as laudable, or even satisfactory. Because the *need* of abused women for support outmatched churchwomen's ability to *supply* that need, women in our focus group study were not very satisfied with their ministry performance in this area.[133]

A feeling of inadequacy is a common response to the accompaniment of survivors of sexual violence, especially when supporters aim to transform the social structures that enable violence and abuse. The work of personal, interpersonal, and social healing extends beyond our capacity to bring it about. It is difficult work, requiring great courage to persist, despite the pain of confronting the enormity of one's own and others' suffering.

Endurance for the Work of Healing

Describing the work of a support group, formed by Coastal Community Church in Canada, for women victims and survivors of sexual violence, Nason-Clark explains that the work of healing, paradoxically, is not necessarily directed at *decreasing* the pain of its participants, especially in the early stages of work. She describes:

> Dealing with so much pain pushes both victims and facilitators to the boundaries of their emotional and spiritual resources [. . .] Many times the level of emotional suffering *increases* for victims as they start to share their pain. All group members begin to feel both a sense of personal vulnerability and the weight of another sister's anguish and abuse. Compassion and care is not for the fainthearted.[134]

The struggle for recovery from sexual trauma with (and for) others is a courageous activity of endurance. Those who persist do so because they trust that something good can come from feeling this pain together. Those who persist offer their small, sometimes failing, efforts to each other and to the God who cooperates with us. As Teresa encourages her sisters, who offer their inadequate efforts to God, "if we do what we can, His Majesty will enable us each day to do more and more, provided that we do not quickly tire. But during the little while this life lasts—and perhaps it will last a shorter time than each one thinks—let us offer the Lord interiorly and exteriorly the sacrifice we can. His Majesty will join it with that which He offered on the cross to the Father for us."[135] Our partial and failing work is joined to Jesus's own partial and failing life, cut short by the cross—the ultimate sign of failure—and redeemed and completed by the resurrection.[136] This is a form of eschatological hope in God; with our small efforts, God will bring about the transformation of the world.[137]

8
Recovery and Hope

Survivors of sexual trauma live with the reality of a damaged world, yet pursue comprehensive healing—personally, interpersonally, and socio-politically—with courage. When the goal of comprehensive healing continually remains illusive, what empowers this work? Survivors do not have the privilege of knowing that if they simply gather enough courage to tell their stories, they will be heard. They cannot be sure that if they bring the crimes of perpetrators to light, justice will be served.[1] And, from a broader perspective, there is no clear sense over the course of human history that we have secured a greater degree of safety for children, women, and sexual and gender minorities. The idea of social progress is a beloved illusion. Given these cold realities, how are survivors and their allies able to persevere in the difficult and long work of recovery, especially when progress is imperceptible?

In their struggle for comprehensive healing, survivors and their allies are empowered by hope. Recovery from trauma necessitates a robust hope in order to hold steadfast to the good when difficulties remain constant. Because the word "hope" has been evacuated of meaning in contemporary culture—often standing in for a mere wish or an optimistic feeling—it is critical to unpack what I mean with care. I argue that it is only in the tension between the already and the not yet carved out by eschatological hope that we can adequately speak of posttraumatic healing: there is much that is within our reach, but the fullness of healing still runs out ahead of us.

Courageous acts of healing are animated by hope. They are animated by the hope that the hard work the survivor is doing is worthwhile, and that it will attain something good, even though it does not feel good at all. Acts of courage are animated by the hope that this work will attain something long-lasting, that the survivor will not simply crumble from the weight of her pain, and that she can bear the memories that she has repressed. Survivors are animated by the hope that they are worth healing, that the world is somewhere worth living, and that some people can be trusted. They are also animated by the hope that God is not one who will deceive us.

Hope is a theological disposition. It is a habit of reaching out toward a future good with expectation, particularly when the good is difficult to obtain.[2] It is not merely a good feeling or optimism, but, instead, it is a well-grounded expectation that something which is difficult is indeed possible. Edward Schillebeeckx argues that the deepest foundation of any experience of pain is hope. Hope animates the "No!" that rises within us when we remember the violence we have experienced in our own lives. Hope is the feeling of sickness that one feels when witnessing another's history of violence. It is our active desire for well-being in the world. Our persistent expectation for encountering human goodness is what makes us so sick, sad, and angry when human behavior is evil.

One afternoon while writing this book, I sat down for coffee with a woman from my church community. At this point, I did not know very much about her, simply that she had started a couple of ministries in my city focused on supporting survivors of sexual violence. Because of our shared interests, we began our conversation exchanging the logistical shape of her work and mine in turn. After a little while, the conversation turned to the inevitable.

"How did you get into this work?" she asked.

This is a question I have come to dread.

When it was her turn to answer, she looked me square in the eyes and began, "Well, one night when I was walking home from work . . ."

I drew in my breath sharply to prepare myself.

Anyone could guess where this was going but I silently hoped that I was wrong. Partly because I am a human being living in the world, and partly because I am a researcher in the area of sexual abuse, I have heard and read countless stories of sexual violence and I am infrequently surprised when I learn about another incident. But, every time, I can feel the fear, anger, and sadness rising within me. Every time, I feel indignation. Every time, I hope that I have misinterpreted or incorrectly guessed at what will come next. Every time, I hope for a different ending, even if I have already heard the story before. Although there are times that I wish I could turn off this pain, this dread and unease are gifts from God. They are hope, spilling out and calling for a better future. The foundation of this pain is hope. Because I still want something else, and somewhere deep inside I believe that violence should not exist, I feel pain. Hope is not just an optimistic feeling, but rather it opens us up to pain in response to that which should never have happened.

Schillebeeckx describes the longing for human good and well-being that underlies negative contrast experiences, such as the one I have just described, as common to human experience. One need not be propelled by a specifically Christian faith commitment to experience the suffering of sexual violence as a negative contrast experience. Yet a kind of implicit creation faith is present in experiences of negative contrast.[3] The one who reacts to evil as that which *should not be* exhibits a trust in her own perception of the world, and a confidence that that which *should be* is possible, however difficultly obtained.

The one who experiences negative contrast does not have a definitive image of total salvation or well-being. Nevertheless, the ways in which this future good pulls upon her and shapes her resistance to present evil are genuine. Without necessarily laying bare a clear vision of human wholeness, experiences of sexual violence do reveal some wisdom concerning human good. This is a kind of dialectical wisdom that can spur us to imagine that which does not yet exist and to "demand a future and open it up"[4] in a perpetually self-transcending fashion.

For Schillebeeckx, a universal longing for the impossible and a hope that the impossible can be accomplished is found in the depths of human existence. Hope in the impossible (i.e., hope in an "unfulfilled open yes"[5]) animates the fundamental 'no' to the world as it is. This hope represents a "fundamental trust that the future has meaning on the basis of the unspoken assumption that being [hu]man—the impossible—is nonetheless possible."[6]

Religious believers, as Schillebeeckx puts it, "fill out the one two-sided basic experience" with a "more precise direction."[7] For Christians, specifically, indignation. Per Schillebeeckx, "the fundamental muttering of humanity[,] turns into a well-founded hope. Something of a sigh of mercy, of compassion, is hidden in the deepest depths of reality . . . and in it believers hear the name of God."[8] And thus, a specifically Christian faith interacts with the basic human experience of negative contrast, to encourage endurance in the process of imagining and implementing future possible goods.

Hope Animates Longing for a Different Future

The person of faith cannot articulate, in a positivistic way, what the content of human flourishing (and, indeed, the flourishing of the whole created order) is, any more than one without faith can. Yet, because of faith, the Christian does have an awareness of the eschatological promise of God, and with that awareness comes support for imaginative hope in which the non-believer does not have ready access.⁹ A Christian eschatological faith supports and strengthens the fundamental human longing for future good in at least two ways: (1) It provides a *ground* for hope in the life, death, and resurrection of Jesus and (2) It ensures that our imaginative vision is always *self-consciously provisional* and *perpetually self-transcending*. In other words, eschatological hope is an expectation that has both roots and wings.

Hope Grounds Longing

A Christian eschatological perspective provides solid ground for natural human hope. How can a human community hold on to a common vision of good when it is not clear that human good is possible? What can encourage a community to persist in a critique of the present order without falling prey to exhaustion? Eschatological faith assures us that "it is indeed possible to build up humanity and that this is not a labor of Sisyphus."¹⁰ By interpreting human history as a history of salvation, an eschatological vision provides roots for natural, human hope. It ensures that hope is neither mere optimism nor an untethered form of fantasy. Memories of God's promises, remembered in the past and actualized in the present, ensure that hope for the fulfillment of human flourishing as promised by God can be a genuine expectation. We can know that what should not be, will not be, with the eschatological consummation of creation.¹¹

After a rapid eye movement treatment and guided visualization session with her therapist, Rebecca Ann Parker relates the experience of realizing that her childhood self had felt the steadying presence of God in the midst of her horrific abuse as a child by her neighbor—Frank. Although it was nearly annihilating for her, she had been preserved (however partially) by God's spirit. Parker explains:

> The child left for dead—she is the part of me who has experienced God! She knows there is a power that can stop Frank, and that, even if Frank succeeds, this power is greater than him and will still hold her and preserve her. She is my faith. She is the one who has never given up. She is the one who has been able to preach all these years, when I have been able to say from some place deep inside of me that there was a grace at work in life that would see us through. She has always been with me. Her knowledge has never left me. . . . But, shit, it makes me angry that this is how I came to know God.¹²

This early experience of God functioned as a saving grace, grounding Parker's hope in God's life-long presence. Even though she could not see all of the ways in which she needed healing, or the ways in which healing might be brought about, she was able to hold on to hope that safety and wholeness were worth fighting for and that her experiences of violence were not all there was to life. The experience of God's preserving presence allowed her to not become wholly accustomed to violence and terror. As Parker puts it, "to live is to be haunted by presence, presence that will not let us rest easy with violence, presence that will not let us become numb to pain."[13]

For Christians, Jesus is both the model for and the source of hope. Jesus models hope by trusting in, and expecting assistance from, God, who is "for" humanity. For Jesus, his mystical experience of God as a nurturing parent—his "Abba experience"—fortified him to approach death courageously. Not despairing of God's absence but expecting that God would somehow transform his abuse into exaltation. Although he did not know how this transformation would be brought about, or what it might look like, he "entrusted all his failure to God."[14]

Jesus's actions, empowered by hope, are the seeds of the object of his hope, the survival of his mission beyond death. What appears, at the outset, to be a small and unsuccessful resistance to the powers that claimed his life, in reality contained an ultimate, lasting success. Jesus's conviction that suffering would not have the last word was the beginning of the actualization of this reality. This memory of Jesus's own faith empowers those who follow after Jesus, especially victims of sexual trauma. That even (apparently) failed attempts at healing can have enduring validity, since God has transformed the failure of Jesus's life into the survival of love.

Endurance in prayer brings forth eschatological hope in Jesus's life and in ours. It is hope that enlivens the survivor to begin the process of opening herself to the reception of God in prayer. It is hope that enables her to persevere when she cannot feel divine consolation. And it is hope that steadies her as she encounters God, in what can sometimes be unsettling moments of the loss of possession of self. Finally, it is hope that allows the individual, who is united with God, to act on behalf of the transformation of the world, especially when results are not immediately apparent. This kind of hope is embodied in Jesus at Gethsemane before his arrest, as he addresses God in prayer: "Abba, for you all things are possible" (Mk 14:36).

The Christian expectation for human fulfillment (i.e., the impossible) is "promised in Jesus Christ and becomes real, through grace, in history, and so *possible*."[15] God has established the ultimate validity of the good in the resurrection of Jesus Christ. The resurrection extends Jesus's proclamation and praxis of the kingdom of God beyond his death, ensuring that Jesus's crucifixion will not interrupt Jesus's work. The resurrection demonstrates that God's cause is the well-being of humanity.

Because, in the Christian tradition, resurrection is transformation without destruction[16]—that is, the emergence of something that is genuinely *new*, yet not in such a way that the old or inadequate is discarded—Jesus's life and mission, as well as the way in which he approached his death, have an enduring significance. It is not that his resurrection is the only real or important thing about the story of Jesus (or, more commonly, that the gruesome reality of his death is the most important component of the Jesus story). Rather, the point is that nothing in his story is discarded. All is transformed, all is redeemed. His death cannot cast a shadow over his life's work. None of it is blotted out, even though his suffering can be clearly identified as in, no way, willed by God.

This eschatological and transformative (rather than apocalyptic and interruptive) model of the resurrection is imperative in a posttraumatic context. It is only this model that can fully affirm the reliability of survivors' experience and the enduring sacredness of survivors' bodies. Survivors can fundamentally trust that their pain reveals authentic violation and that their bodies are sites of real encounters with God and, thus, are in need of the fullness of material-spiritual healing. God's confirmation of the life of Jesus through the act of the resurrection, despite the partial nature of Jesus's efforts and even his apparent failures, confirms for Christians God's concern for human good and desire (and, moreover, God's promise) to bring all finite and failing creation to completion.[17] It is only in, and through, the promise of God, that we can know that human flourishing—the fullness of human healing—is possible. This faith in the promise of God has a critical-practical effect on those who hold it to fuel an imaginative vision of the good that transcends that which has already been achieved.[18]

Eschatological Hope Ensures That Our Imaginative Vision Is Self-Consciously Provisional

A Christian eschatological vision expands the grounds for human hope beyond the limits of human achievement. We can affirm the fragmentary and partial achievements of personal, interpersonal, and socio-political healing as mediations of God's promise of salvation for creation, without restricting our imaginative vision to what appears possible through human ends.

Hope does not assure us that "things aren't that bad" or, "everything is actually working for our good." Rather, hope opens us to feel our pain deeply, to notice what is less than human in our lives, and to expect more. Many times, the "more" that survivors can imagine is not necessarily the eradication of evil in a definitive way, but something more modest: that evil will not be able to stamp out goodness entirely. It is a kind of hope in which goodness and beauty exist alongside evil and horror and cannot be overcome by them. Struggling to thrive under the weight of a history of childhood sexual abuse, and the more recent dissolution of her marriage and an unwanted abortion, Rebecca Ann Parker testifies to this kind of hope in an anecdote about her plan to drown herself in a lake near her home on a cold spring night. When she arrived at the lake, ready to execute her plan, she was surprised to find the Seattle Astronomy Club gathered around telescopes looking at Jupiter. They invited her to view the beauty of the sky with them. When she did, she was overwhelmed by wonder. She felt that she could not die that night. She decided to stay alive and experience the full breadth of pain, joy, beauty, and horror of the human experience. As she explains:

> It would be wrong to think of this moment as one in which joy triumphed over despair, or love of life defeated desire for death. . . . I did not defeat negative feelings of anguish and despair because I saw something more lovely and good. Rather, I became able to feel more. My feeling broadened. Pain, sadness, and despair were not eliminated or overcome. I embraced them within a larger heart. All the feelings and memories I had couldn't be held by a decision to die. I could only hold everything with a decision to live.[19]

But, sometimes, hope can transcend these modest visions and allow us to imagine a future without evil. This is eschatological hope.

Eschatological hope allows us to lift up small successes as participation in bringing about God's desire for the world. For example, extending the statute of limitations for prosecuting sexual abuse crimes against minors, while still holding onto far-flung visions of a world in which rape is unthinkable and never need prosecution at all (i.e., to imagine a world in which any child could be left alone with any adult without fear of violence).

A vision of the future promise of comprehensive healing in its fullness escapes even the most perceptive critics of our culture. In some ways, the lack of a wholly clear and comprehensive, positive vision of this future is a gift, since it forces us to never rest in our imaginative process or grow unresponsive to the ways in which reality presses upon us and challenges us to alter our assessments. Consequently, Christians can firmly root themselves in a confidence in the ability of God to bring humanity to its fulfillment, avoid the temptation to delineate what this end is in a narrow fashion, and also encourage human co-participation in bringing about human fulfillment.

Comprehensive salvation—the transformation of human existence such that "there shall be no more death or mourning, wailing or pain" (Rev. 21:4)—represents a future promise of well-being. This promise, granted to humanity by God and secured by God's faithfulness, is still accomplished through the graced resources of humanity itself.[20]

A Christian eschatological perspective generates an expansive kind of creativity that makes room for divine-human cooperation. This kind of expansive creativity breaks open the narrow imagination of the traumatized individual or the traumatized community that replays the act of violence again and again. As one trauma survivor tells Serene Jones, "I can't control my own imagination—it does weird things to me. It freaks out. Gets all shattered and chaotic and plays out scenes I don't want."[21] In response, Jones talks about posttraumatic healing as the opening up of a closed, truncated system,[22] offering "stories of new imaginings"[23] (i.e., new "thought stories") with which to live and through which to interpret the world. Christian theologian Pamela Cooper-White similarly portrays posttraumatic healing as a process of creative, imaginative expansion.[24]

The specifically *eschatological* Christian imagination offers a vision of the world, and us, as already met by God's grace, but not yet fully redeemed. It is an imagination uniquely inflected by expectation: it is shaped by trust in a God who is present in absence, a God who approaches but who is still ultimately to come, and who, upon arrival, promises the eradication of all evil. This God who is already in the process of saving us, but not yet finished, does so not by overtaking us, but rather, as a creative source that non-competitively and collaboratively animates human creativity.

In rape culture, the human imagination is limited, in tragic ways, to encourage us to accept realities that fail to meet the fullness of our dignity. In this climate, it is easy for the human imagination to become imprisoned by the "impotency of dull satisfaction,"[25] or to be restricted by false preconceptions about the limits of human freedom and respect. A Christian eschatological vision, especially insofar as it always maintains a *proviso*, creates a dynamic of "permanent criticism" and "constant improvement," motivated by the "firm conviction that this building up of a more human world is genuinely possible."[26] An eschatological vision provides the stimulus for imaginative action, especially when despair or malaise threaten those working toward comprehensive healing.[27] A specifically Christian eschatological hope never allows one to proclaim, definitively, within history: "[T]his is the promised future."[28]

We cannot realize the fullness of our own healing in a complete process of emancipation.[29] Yet, as the Council of Trent suggests, we do not do nothing for our salvation.[30] The eschatological future *requires* Christian praxis to aim toward human liberation.[31] At the same time, the eschatological future cannot be *reduced* to what we are able to achieve through their liberating efforts.[32] This gap between what we are able to accomplish through our own efforts, and that for which we hope, cannot be closed without forsaking fertile ground for a dynamic human imagination.

On the one hand, communities cannot imagine new possibilities of sexual justice if the tyranny of rape culture limits their vision. On the other hand, if there is no connection between one's imaginative vision and the current order, there are hardly any ways to begin engaging in transformational work. Christian eschatological hope can function to support a fragile balance between an expansive vision of the future and realistic expectation, positioning hope as inclusive of human effort, while refusing to be limited by human achievement.

Eschatological Hope Engenders Participation in God's Transformation of the World

The eschatological promise of salvation is a gratuitous gift from God to all creation. However, this is not a gift given to passive recipients. Instead, it is an invitation to take part in the consummation of the created order. Eschatological hope is not participation in bringing about a kingdom of God prefabricated, but somehow hidden from view. Instead, it is active and cooperative effort, together with God, to build the promised kingdom.[33]

Eschatological hope is an expectation that human beings can and will achieve comprehensive posttraumatic healing in and through the promise of God despite all apparent failures.[34] Eschatological hope consists in a confidence that all human striving for the good of healing is given "permanent validity" in God and works to participate in God's salvific transformation of the world.[35] Christian hope is fueled by the faith that "good must have the last word."[36] Human action empowered by Christian hope is neither timid (since the Christian is confident that her activity is a necessary part of salvation) nor hubristic (since she does not mistakenly believe she can bring about the fullness of healing on her own). Instead, efforts toward posttraumatic healing, empowered by Christian hope, are both courageous and self-consciously provisional. To blunt the provisional nature of these efforts is, paradoxically, to limit the possibilities of human good. Without the permanent criticism that eschatological hope affords, we fall into the trap of ideologically limiting the possibilities of healing.[37] Eschatological hope functions in a critically negative way to ensure both a perpetual discontent with the world *and* a perpetual commitment to its good. Eschatological hope commissions Christians to transform, in imaginative ways, what *is* into what *should be*, converting the basic human impulse to imagine and expect into a responsibility to resist and create. Eschatological hope empowers resistance to sexual violence and the creative dismantling of rape culture.

False Hope and Authentic Hope

The process of healing from sexual violence personally, interpersonally, and socio-politically exceeds that which human activity can accomplish on its own. Judith Herman argues that to confront the realities of psychological trauma is always to bear witness to the possibility of human vulnerability. When traumatic events are not simply accidents or "acts of God" (e.g., natural disasters), but rather evil actions, perpetrated by human beings toward other humans (as in the case of sexual trauma), Herman argues that, "those who bear witness are caught in the conflict between victim and perpetrator."[38] The act of witnessing (whether one's own pain or someone else's) takes on a moral dimension—an imperative not just to feel pain or sorrow, but also to name culpability and strive for accountability. Herman writes:

> It is morally impossible to remain neutral in the conflict. The bystander is forced to take sides. It is very tempting to take the side of the perpetrator. All the perpetrator asks is that the bystander do nothing. He appeals to the universal desire to see, hear, and speak no evil. The victim, on the contrary, asks the bystander to share the burden of pain. The victim demands action, engagement, and remembering.[39]

To choose to open oneself to the pain of traumatic memories, and to act on behalf of comprehensive healing, is no ordinary task, especially when "ordinary" human life is characterized by "social processes of silencing and denial."[40] Healing requires strength and endurance that exceeds what any individual is capable of alone. It requires the courage of a community—a community grounded not only in the present, but firmly rooted in a tradition of courageous resistance and liberating hope. As Herman argues:

> To hold traumatic reality in consciousness requires a social context that affirms and protects the victim and that joins victim and witness in a common alliance. For the individual victim, this social context is created by relationships with friends, lovers, and family. For the larger society, the social context is created by political movements that give voice to the disempowered.[41]

One can get the impression, when reading these words from Herman and similar statements from other social activists, that where individual action is inadequate, collective action can save us. While this might be true, the nature of collective action needs to be specified. Collective action is more than the multiplication of individual, isolated actors. It requires shared belief, coordinated effort, and—most importantly—a communal sense of purpose.[42] Collective action (in contrast to many individual actions) rests on a shared imagination of what does not exist.

The pervasive nature of sexual violence and the failure of the majority of institutions to provide accountability should, by most rational accounting, make this kind of imagining and yearning for a future that has never existed impossible.[43] Or, if not impossible, perhaps we can say that the effort required in continuing to protest injustice, to imagine a better future, and to work to bring about that future, would leave most of us utterly exhausted and drained of all resources.

Healing requires reserves deeper than those which can be articulated by the secular field of psychology alone. Healing requires hope solidly grounded in the genuine expectation that transformation is possible through God's creative work and our free, creative, and courageous cooperation. Hope sustains survivors and their allies in imagining the impossible. Hope gives them the energy they need to hold on during the long and slow work of personal, interpersonal, and socio-political recovery.

But not just any optimistic attitude can function this way. Psychological researchers are clear that a *false* sense of hope, animated by unrealistic expectations, is paralyzing over time.[44] In order to manage unrealistic expectations, some sexual trauma clinicians eschew the term "healing" all together, in favor of the term "recovery."[45] They argue that while healing can connote for patients a "progressive trajectory,"[46] culminating in being "cured,"[47] "recovery" can more clearly connote the ongoing and messy nature of posttraumatic care, culminating in the transformation (not erasure) of the traumatic experience. As one survivor explains:

> When I first came into treatment, I thought okay I am going to work really hard on this and in a year's time it's going to be wrapped up in a package with a bow on top. And I can go on with life. And when it didn't, I fell into the pits of despair.[48]

But in a Christian context, rather than a secular therapeutic context, the term "healing" can be reclaimed as a present progressive participle if it is spoken in an eschatological key—that is, with an attention to the notion that the promise of comprehensive healing, which salvation entails, is not yet objectively complete anywhere. If, on the one hand, we abandon the notion of healing entirely on the grounds that "healing is not possible,"[49] we risk foreclosing the fertile, imaginative space to envision a fully redeemed human life. Furthermore, we risk an idolatrous vision of God, restricted by unnecessary limitation. If, on the other hand, we promote an unrealistic vision of healing, in which the process is linearly progressive and results in the erasure and apocalyptic destruction of pain, rather than its transformation, we risk disappointment, paralysis, and, paradoxically, a kind of truncated vision of the human person. Eschatological hope is capable of the sober recognition of human life for what it is—damaged by sin and yet able to be healed in cooperation with God.

Conclusion
A Theology of Healing

One afternoon, when my oldest son was about one and a half years old, and I was cleaning up a mess in the living room, he toddled in from another room with a crucifix in hand. It was the crucifix which had been placed on top of my grandmother's casket at her funeral and was then given to me—the family member most interested in religious objects—when the casket was interred in her stone niche.

I had tried many times to hang the crucifix on a wall in my home office, but it kept falling off at inopportune times. It must have fallen again, and now my son had it in his hands and was playing with it as if it were a toy sword.

Interrupting my (obviously futile) cleaning efforts, he swung the cross in the air and asked me, "What is this for?"

I was struck by the profundity of the question. I had already begun working on the research that would later become this book, so I was painfully aware of some unhelpful ways to answer. I did not want to tell him, as I had learned, "that's a crucifix and it reminds us that Jesus died in order to save us from our sins." But what could I say to my son, in language that he could understand? Furthermore, putting the problem of kid-friendly language aside, what would I say to him about Jesus's suffering as he grew up? I stood there, feeling the weight of my responsibility as his primary spiritual formator, partly in awe of the opportunity to guide another human person to faith, but mostly inadequate.

I tried to think carefully about a clear answer to give my son—one that would lift up all that was good in the Christian tradition about God's refusal to allow suffering to have the final word in Jesus's life and one that would clearly avoid anything that sanctified human suffering.

But my son mistook my ponderous pause for a refusal to tell him something important. He began to scream repeatedly, "What is it for?" while using the cross to stab the torso of a baby doll that also happened to be on the floor nearby.

"Not that!" I yelled. And then, clearly still in my own head, I added, "Well, sometimes it has been used that way . . ." Then, trying to recover, I stammered, "But we don't believe in that!"

He stopped stabbing the doll and looked at me with even more confusion. So much for clear spiritual formation.

Ten years later, I have another toddler. If he asks me that same question, I will tell him that crucifixes are for reminding us of the middle part of Jesus's story: Jesus announced the kingdom of God by healing people and eating with them; Jesus suffered and died; Jesus was raised from the dead. When we suffer, that is only the middle part of our story. We hope for the day when God will defeat suffering and evil for us as he did with Jesus. Just as God has resurrected Jesus, God has also promised us healing and restoration.

Eventually, I will explain to my children how the memory of Jesus's cross has often been used to hurt people. I hope that will be a historical lesson, rather than a corrective to something they have internalized as part of their own Christian heritage. But realistically, I know that in most Christian communities, it is nearly impossible to avoid the idea that human suffering is a vehicle for God's saving grace. I hope that this book can contribute something to the process of saving our broken ways of talking about God's grace in the Christian tradition, by discarding that which fosters violence, and unearthing the liberating resources buried within it.

Christian Suffering

In each of the previous chapters I have returned, in different ways, to the idea that God does not desire human suffering. This refrain is a response to the common Christian tendency to rationalize suffering. Sociologist Nancy Nason-Clark argues that, in response to sexual violence, Christians tend to offer two types of rationalizations: individual-centered or God-centered.

In the first approach, Christians assume (either implicitly or explicitly) that grave suffering is a consequence of bad personal choices. If one makes good choices and lives a good life, it is believed that one will be free from major suffering. Admittedly, good people might suffer from inconveniences or small-scale experiences of suffering (for example, the suffering of unrequited love, the suffering of limited professional failures, the suffering of waiting in line, etc.) but those who hold this position assume that good behavior protects one from the most significant forms of suffering, such as interpersonal violence or early death.[1]

As a fellow church member related to me several years ago, "When I spent a year volunteering abroad before college, I thought that I would be protected from political violence because I was doing holy work."[2] It was only as an older adult that she realized this notion (among other flaws) assumed that those who lived with the daily threat of political violence—such as those she was "serving"—had not lived holy lives.

When these assumptions about suffering are interpreted in the context of sexual violence, survivors can deduce that their experience of rape is evidence that they had (somewhere in their lives prior to their abuse) made bad choices and that this rape was the natural (or perhaps even cosmic) consequence of those choices.

Nason-Clark illustrates the "individual-centered explanation"[3] of suffering with the case study of rape survivor, "Gertrude."[4] She writes, "Gertrude, like some of the other abused Christian women interviewed, understands her suffering to be a result of her own actions, particularly her choices that, she feels, took her away from what God would have wanted for her or were contrary to 'God's will.'"[5] This interpretation of rape may give the victim a sense of comfort to the degree that it can suggest that she is capable of controlling what happens to her (namely, if she makes the right choices, this will not happen to her again). But ultimately, it carries more risks than benefits: it communicates that rape is the victim's fault, it obfuscates the culpability of the perpetrator (even, perhaps, deifying him as an agent of God's justice), and it hides the social and structural factors that make sexual violence a common experience. Furthermore, it is simply not true that good personal, moral choices ensure that individuals will be protected from sexual violence, and to suggest this to a victim struggling to survive may set her up for failure, catastrophic disappointment, and retraumatization.

An alternative (though often related) and common Christian interpretation of suffering is a "God-centered rationalization;"[6] suffering is allowed by God for reasons that are temporarily hidden to the sufferer but is ultimately at the service of some greater good. Jesus's death on the cross, willed by God so that human beings might be able to experience forgiveness for their sins, is often offered as a paradigm for this kind of suffering, desired by God for reasons that are (temporarily) mysterious. Many who offer "God-centered rationalizations" will suggest that "everything happens for a reason" although we may not know what those reasons are.

When this kind of interpretation of suffering is applied in a posttraumatic context, it might feel comforting for some of the same reasons that individual-centered explanations are; it suggests that however chaotic and unjust a violent attack may feel, someone is, in fact, in control.[7] Yet, the risks in this kind of approach, again, outweigh any potential comfort that this may bring to victims. It portrays God as one who desires the suffering of human beings, it acculturates vulnerable people to accept abuse,[8] it fails to create sufficient space to condemn interpersonal and social-political harm as sinful, and it minimizes victims' genuine pain. As Joanne Carlson Brown and Rebecca Parker have argued, the image of Christ as suffering in obedience to the Father's will is one in which "Divine child abuse is paraded as salvific and the child who suffers 'without even raising a voice' is lauded as the hope of the world."[9] When Jesus's death is portrayed as both authentically excruciating and somehow *for* a meaningful end, those who have suffered abuse find it difficult to understand their own suffering as worthy of protest, and may think that whatever pain they bear pales in comparison to the virtuous pain endured by Jesus.[10]

This understanding of suffering as fuel for growth—or worse, as the content of salvation itself—can be deadly for those suffering from sexual violence. Sexual violence does not produce any good in victims. It is "senseless suffering" that has "no structural place in the divine plan."[11] Rape does not have any hidden benefit for victims. There is no divine reason for rape. There is no ultimate meaning in rape. It is human sin. It is tragedy in an ultimate sense.[12]

Salvation: An Incarnational Approach

In Chapter 1, I framed Christian salvation as mystical-political healing from sexual violence, and I argued that a theological account of healing must be both incarnational and eschatological. Sexual violence wounds the whole human person—materially, psychologically, interpersonally, spiritually, and politically. Healing from sexual violence, then, has a comprehensive range. Healing involves restoring one's relationship with God, with oneself, and with others. Ultimately, the fullness of posttraumatic healing that is required must draw from reserves that are deeper than that which can be articulated by the secular field of psychology alone. Healing requires eschatological hope—that is, hope that is grounded in the genuine expectation of God's creative transformation of human life and our free, creative, and courageous cooperation with God in bringing this transformation about.

The healing that we require is deeply incarnational. Sexual violence harms our bodies. Bodies are personal (that is, my body is myself), yet bodies are also interpersonal, social, and political. The context(s) in which I am located shapes my body, namely, the ways that I care for and cultivate my body, the way that I (and others) interpret and make meaning with my body, and what happens to my body that is outside of my control.

Bodies are never wholly individual or corporate, they are always both. The traumatic wounds of sexual violence—particularly insofar as they affect every area of human *being*—personal, interpersonal, social-political, physical, psychological, spiritual, etc.—are "bodily" in this fullest sense. Salvation, if it is to have anything to do with posttraumatic recovery, must involve the restoration of our bodies.

In the Christian tradition, salvation involves bodies in all their spiritual, material, individual, and social fullness. In Chapters 5 and 6, I argued that salvation—"being whole," as Edward Schillebeeckx reminds us[13]—can never separate one aspect of human *being* from the others. The "height and breadth and depth of human salvation"[14] cannot be reduced to one dimension. In Chapter 5, I offered Schillebeeckx's argument that there are (at least) six dimensions to human eschatological wholeness, as represented in his discussion of the seven anthropological constants (namely, corporeality, interpersonality, sociality and institutionality, historicity, a "mutual relation of theory and practice," and spirituality). Even though we await the fullness of salvation with the eschatological consummation of creation, many Christian mystics have experienced foretastes of this wholeness during earthly life.

One of these mystics, Teresa of Avila, describes the fullness of union with God as the fullness of bodily-spiritual integration, poised for communion with others in the world. In Chapter 2, I introduced the reader to Teresa, highlighting her historical context in order to understand the political impact of her mystical ideas about the human person. In Chapters 3 and 4, I detailed Teresa's idea that encounter with God, who resides in the center of ourselves, reveals to us who we really are: deeply marked by our material afflictions, yet also more than that which has afflicted us. If, following Bernard McGinn, "mysticism" can be thought of as the process of direct consciousness of the presence of God,[15] then the writings of Teresa of Avila can be said to provide us with a kind of *incarnational* mysticism: a mysticism that particularly emphasizes the role of the body in consciousness of the presence of God. This kind of mysticism is not, in an ultimate sense, an experience of withdrawal from materiality into an experience that is spiritual alone—since, for Teresa, the spiritual is also material. This kind of mystical experience is also never an experience for the individual alone—since mystical union generates interpersonal and social-political actions of love. Incarnational mysticism is at the heart of the Christian tradition—a tradition that insists that God has become flesh and embedded Godself in our social and political histories.

If salvation in a posttraumatic context involves the healing of human beings in all of their dimensions, then salvation can never only involve the restoration of the individual's personal psychological health (or even simply a restoration of her personal relationship with God). Salvation in a posttraumatic context must extend to a restoration of interpersonal relationships and a transformation of rape culture. Indeed, for those who have suffered from sexual violence, it is impossible to separate personal psychological health or a personal relationship with God from interpersonal relationships with human others or one's sociopolitical context, because of the relational nature of the originary violence.

Sexual violence is committed by a relational other and targets the victim's sexuality—a central component of relationality to present and future others. Sexual violence aims to transform the victim's body from a means through which to feel and express love for others, into a weapon to be used against itself to enforce shame and isolation. Restoration of the mystical relationship with God is an inherently political act, as it resists cultures of rape which weaponize intimate relationality, isolating and shaming individuals.

The costs of truncating the deeply incarnational mysticism of the Christian tradition are idolatry (i.e., worship of a false, hemmed in God) and political impotence (i.e., material and social-institutional agency is stripped away).[16] Human bodies (material, interpersonal, and social-political) have important roles to play in discerning the nature of human eschatological good, especially insofar as we take the role of "experience" in Christian revelation seriously. When we suffer, we have an experience of "negative contrast." This experience is wholly negative. But in its negativity it reveals something to us—the good that is absent.

When we suffer sexual violence, we experience many kinds of pain. Survivors often experience *physical and psychological* maladies such as recurrent intrusive memories, a lifetime of elevated cortisol levels, corresponding diseases related to increased inflammation (e.g., cancers, diabetes, autoimmune diseases, obesity, allergies, etc.),[17] and self-destructive behaviors (e.g., drug use, self-mutilation, risky sexual behavior, and even suicide).[18] Survivors experience *interpersonal* pain in the form of decreased trust in others, social isolation and shame, as well as anxious and inappropriate attachment to others.[19] Survivors often experience *spiritual* pain, feeling abandoned by God or perhaps that God has desired that which has happened to them. This is amplified when religious language and imagery plays a role in the violent acts, as is often the case in instances of sexual violence committed by clergy against minors, or in cases of domestic violence in religious households.[20] Survivors experience the *social-political* pain of feeling that any violence they have already suffered was a consequence of a failure to curtail their bodies sufficiently.[21] And survivors often experience the pain of continuing to expect that their sexual, racial, or gender identity makes them forever vulnerable to further sexual violence.

CONCLUSION: A THEOLOGY OF HEALING

In Chapter 5, I argued that these sites of pain reveal to us what "should not be," and are supported by a deeper, intuitive sense of what 'should be' instead. Undergirding the natural feeling of contrast in a negative experience is an "incipient" and "vague" sense of "what should be here and now," a natural inclination toward "hope-filled promise and initiative which helps to shape the future."[22]

One need not have a specifically religious or theological interpretation of experience in order to have a negative contrast experience. An experience of negative contrast is a "worldly prophecy,"[23] a part of the secular experience of the whole of life—"our total experience of reality."[24] In other words, negative contrast experiences are natural human experiences. Jean Monroe (a pseudonym) writes about her relationship with her sexually abusive father in an essay titled "California Girl/1950." She describes wanting to alleviate his guilt:

> The strange look on his face makes me want to assure him that it's okay. Don't be afraid, daddy, it's okay with me.

But also, a deep sense of dread and dis-ease with his actions:

> I pray to Jesus that soon he'll tell me that I can go. I wish I were playing with the children.[25]

Although the prevalence of sexual violence in our culture can gradually desensitize us over time, the pain is still present. Even when there is an incomplete sense of what a healthy relationship looks like, survivors can often feel that their experience falls short of human wholeness. Even in the most abject of circumstances, human beings possess some dim kind of protest, a faint "no." As Jean Monroe narrates:

> I go to the garage to get my bike and he is there, working in his lighted corner. I know I am trapped.
> "Honey, come back here a minute."
> I slide between him and the car fender and when he asks I lift my T-shirt. He touches them and I smile when he looks at my face. I must show him it is all right with me. But I don't like it. . . . But it's not hurting me, and if I object, it will hurt him. He would see then that I know it is wrong. I couldn't bear for him to think that. Poor daddy. It's all right.[26]

This faint "no" reveals a hidden, but nevertheless powerful, "yes." Some hope, some expectation of what a healthier parental relationship might be like—one of protection and care, rather than exploitation and objectification. Eventually, Jean tells her mother what is going on. Her mother excuses her father's behavior saying, "he couldn't help it" and suggesting that Jean's body would sexually overwhelm any male. But she also tells her:

> I want you to tell me if he ever does it again. I'm sure that he never will, but if he does, will you tell me?

Jean writes:

> I feel greatly relieved and happy because I know that I'll never have the problem again. Mama will take care of it.²⁷

Therapeutic treatment for sexual violence can often take the form of re-narrating the survivor's experience of violence so as to emphasize the victim's creative resistance to that which happened to her in the moment—to make her small or hidden "no" more visible. For example, Judith Herman relates the case of "Stephanie," a college student who experienced a brutal gang rape at a fraternity party. Stephanie felt a great amount of shame at the fact that, in response to pressure from her rapists, she told them that "it was the best sex she ever had." As part of her healing process, her therapist helped her to re-narrate that part of her story to herself and recognize that this statement was a strategic decision in order to comply and bring an end to the two-hour long violent attack.²⁸

Bodily Experience as an Authentic Source of Revelation

The spontaneous reaction of the sufferer to her experience functions as a source of revelation. The "body"—i.e., that which is personal-material, relational, social, and political—provides an entry point into our ultimate destiny in God. The body reacts to excessive evil in history as negative experiences of contrast from which it can intuit what *ought to be*, providing an indirect vision of human good. Shirley, a childhood survivor of sexual abuse, writes in her poem titled "Allow for the Possibility" about her bodily, spontaneous reactions to violence.

> I was different from the other kids.
>
> I even ate differently!
> Cereal—no milk.
> French fries—no ketchup.
> Hamburgers—plain.
> Food had to be dry.
> Raw potatoes enticed me.
> "No one's looking!" Grab one—sneak it to the bedroom,
> Take a few bites and hide it in the closet.
> I couldn't eat school lunches.

CONCLUSION: A THEOLOGY OF HEALING

> A teacher forced me to drink milk once.
> I threw up on her shoes.
> Six years of peanut butter sandwiches,
> No jelly and no butter—food had to be dry.
> My bed was a different story—it was wet.
>
> I wet the bed for years.
> [. . .]
>
> The neighbors all thought Daddy was great.
> They didn't know he liked to hurt little girls.[29]

A recognition of experiences of negative contrast as spontaneous, bodily reactions locates the movement of revelatory grace (at least partially) with*in* the victim and preserves a sense of co-participation with God in bringing about healing; helping to preserve the agency of the individual in a description of posttraumatic healing. This is significant not only because psychologists identify agency as integral to healing, but also because it supports a rich theology of freedom that is necessary for an accounting of why these kinds of violent acts can occur at all. If human freedom is not understood as genuine and deep, we have no language to describe how it is possible that humans are able to commit these kinds of crimes against each other. Nor do we have language to insist that humans are accountable for these crimes when they do occur.

A robustly Christian understanding of union with God must be an incarnational mysticism. That is, it must involve bodies—both personal-material and social-political. Union with God in a posttraumatic context involves self-care, (re)construction of interpersonal relationships, and transformation of rape culture: actions which are beyond that which is typically understood to be "spiritual"—e.g., spiritual direction, prayer, fasting, etc. If trauma clinicians within the last thirty years have begun to recognize the great cost of dissociating mind from body,[30] Christian theologians need (even more) to (and have already begun to) recognize the great costs of separating the soul from the body: most importantly, a loss of the incarnational principles upon which Christian revelation depends.[31] The Christian doctrine of the incarnation does not refer only to the "act" of the Word assuming human nature, but also to the "abiding state" of humanity and human embodiment as a "fitting locus [of] God's revelation."[32]

God's Revelation in Bodies

A posttraumatic incarnational mysticism must therefore be conscious of God's revelation in bodies—emphasizing that bodily wellness is a critical component of the spiritual life. Yet it must also be able to create space to imagine that bodily wounds do not present the ultimate barriers to union with God. In Chapters 3 and 4, I discussed Teresa's description of the incarnational nature of the mystical relationship with God, and how she is able to make these connections between the material and spiritual without overdetermining the limitations of the traumatically wounded. While simultaneously emphasizing the responsibility of the practitioner of prayer to prepare herself for the reception of God's healing grace, and affirming that the limitations of sickness and injury do not pose insurmountable barriers to God, Teresa is able to encourage the cultivation of personal agency which is so integral to the trauma victim's healing process, without foreclosing the possibility that God's healing grace may exceed our capabilities to effect healing on our own.

Transformative Action for the Common Good

The life of prayer involves care for one's body as well as transformative (material) action in the world. Indeed, the life of prayer can generate the courage needed to persist in both care for oneself and care for others. The result of full awareness of God's presence within the wounded body, found in the center of the soul, is action on behalf of the common good. This action can only be propelled by an unbounded trust in what God can accomplish in and through the material. In the sixteenth century, Teresa of Avila's own conviction was that any efforts made on behalf of the common good here and now will be transformed by God eschatologically. Similarly, in the twentieth century, Schillebeeckx argued that as we strive for comprehensive human good (even when we fumble our way through), we cooperate with God in bringing about the fullness of salvation. Although human efforts always fall short of the eschatological promise of salvation—whether because of our finitude or our sin—our efforts are transformed by God and granted eternal significance. As Teresa told her sisters, "let us offer the Lord interiorly and exteriorly the sacrifice we can. His Majesty will join it with that which He offered on the cross to the Father for us. Thus, even though our works are small they will have the value our love for Him would have merited had they been great."[33] Even the cross (to which Teresa imagined our own shortcomings are united) was itself (originally) evidence of failure and defeat. It is in light of the apparent failure of Jesus's life, ending with the defeat of the cross, that Schillebeeckx argues, "our action in helping people, healing them and bringing them political liberation, fragmentary though it may seem, has definitive value in and of itself, even when it fails. It is precisely to this that the living God will grant an ever greater future. 'He gives a new face to darkness and light, to all that we did.'"[34]

In Chapter 6, I posited that comprehensive human good is not just some utopian fantasy: it is the very content of Christian salvation revealed in the life, death, and resurrection of Jesus Christ. The transformed future that we long for "is not a mere accumulation of vague wishful thinking but something that was promised in Jesus Christ and becomes real, through grace, in history, and so possible for man."[35] God has established the validity of the promise of human well-being and foreshadowed the full transformation of all earthly life in the resurrection of Jesus Christ. The resurrection affirms the message and life of Jesus, ensuring that it did not ultimately end in failure. And the resurrection extends Jesus's own proclamation and praxis of the kingdom of God beyond his death. This protects Jesus's (yet unfinished) work from the interruption of the crucifixion, guaranteeing that suffering and death do not have the last word. This reveals that God's cause is the human cause. Despite the partial nature of the work of Jesus's life, and even his apparent failures, God confirms Jesus's efforts and demonstrates God's concern for human good and desire (and, moreover, God's promise) to bring all finite and failing humanity to completion.[36]

In Chapter 7, I argued that Jesus's own actions, particularly in the face of death, can serve as a model of courage for survivors of sexual violence. He does not have control over what is done to him and he cannot envision how God will redeem the violence that he will suffer, yet he trusts that (despite his lack of clear vision) somehow God will vindicate him and continue the work that he is not able to finish himself.[37]

In Chapter 8, I reasoned that the Christian language of eschatological hope can hold a realistic assessment of what humans can accomplish in tension with an imaginative vision of a future in which rape is unthinkable. A Christian eschatological imagination allows us to reclaim the idea of posttraumatic healing—not as a "cured" state that the survivor achieves if she works hard enough, but rather as "healing"—a *process* in which we cooperate with God to restore wholeness, within and without. One which is not yet complete anywhere until rape culture has been thoroughly eradicated.

A Theology of Healing in an Eschatological Key

As Rebecca Ann Parker and Rita Nakashima Brock argue, "When the victims of violence are made singular, solitary, unprecedented in their pain, the power of violence remains,"[38] but posttraumatic healing is the restoration of relationships. Because the Christian story is the story of the persistence of relationships in the face of violence, the Christian tradition contains rich resources to animate (etymologically, "to instill with Spirit") posttraumatic healing. As Mary

Magdalene and the other women came upon the tomb of Jesus and found it emptied, they came to understand that the grave was not the place to encounter Jesus. "Come, see the place where he lay," (Mt 28: 6) the angel told the women. "He is not here." (Mt 28:6; Lk 24:5) Instead, they encounter Jesus when they are engaged in his mission of announcing the in-breaking kingdom of God[39] or in the practice of sharing food.[40] In the context of Jesus's life and ministry, these two activities—proclaiming the kingdom of God and the sharing of food—were tightly interrelated and, in the later tradition, the joy and freedom experienced at table with Jesus was remembered as a foretaste of the establishment of the kingdom of God on Earth. During his lifetime, Jesus's table fellowship with those who were normally considered beyond God's hospitality and nurturing care—gentiles, sex workers, those working in collaboration with Roman imperial authorities to oppress the Jews, etc.—symbolized God's own openness to friendship with all of humanity. In the way that Jesus organized his life and ministry, he recalled Jewish portrayals of God's own work as Sophia (i.e., Divine Wisdom), calling all to feast with her and commissioning all who love her to imitate her hospitality and generosity (Prov 1:20–33; Prov 3; Sirach 4).[41] The gathering of friends around a table, then, is not simply an icon of the kingdom of God. It is not meant merely as a pointer to some other, greater reality. Instead, it is a real symbol of the kingdom of God—a sign that actually brings about that which it signifies.[42]

It is the table, where personal, interpersonal, and social bodies are nourished, that is the authentic place of meaningful encounter with Jesus after his death.[43] In contrast, the tomb is emptied. It functions only as a negative symbol, representing divine absence and revealing divine presence somewhere else.[44] "Why do you look for the living among the dead?" (Lk 24:5). "He is not here" (Mt 28:6, Lk 24:5). Both on the road to Emmaus and on the shore, Jesus's disciples recognize him only after he has acted as host. In Luke, he blesses bread and breaks it, acting as host even in another's house, and they recognize him as the one who died and was risen (Lk 24:30–35).[45] In John, on the shore of the Sea of Tiberias, Jesus prepares a breakfast feast of fish and bread to share with the disciples (Jn 21:9–14). The table is the place where individuals are fortified, friendships are birthed and sustained, and the community is restored.

Biblical resurrection narratives—not meant, primarily, to explain what happened to Jesus after his death, since they do not narrate the event of resurrection itself,[46] but rather to explain what happened to his followers after his death[47]— illustrate the central significance of the persistence of community in the face of violence, especially in the continued practice of friendship around the table. In the gospels, "Jesus arises in the midst of the community."[48] The community reveals the risen Jesus, especially as they practice inclusive table fellowship.[49] In these accounts, Jesus's table fellowship combines two ancient meal practices—the symposium, a formal eating event limited to free males that centered on intellectual conversation or artistic performance, and the hospitality meal, a less formal sharing of food with guests and inclusive of women and children—and opens up the table to all, regardless of age, gender, or social status.[50]

The inclusive Christian practice of table fellowship is understood as the gathering of friends (friends of God and friends of each other) into a new family, animated by Christ's new life. With the resurrection of Jesus, a "collective—ecclesial—experience" is given birth in the face of violence.[51] This community has, as John narrates, the power to hold its members in loving embrace—whomever they "hold" is "held fast"[52]—mediating the support and steady hold of Godself.[53]

For survivors of sexual trauma, the embrace of Christian community can be profoundly healing if it is the embrace of true friendship—free, non-possessive, and egalitarian.[54] This embrace needs to enflesh Judith Herman's two requirements for the posttraumatic restoration of individual-community relationships; recognition and restitution.[55] This embrace needs to contain a recognition of survivors as both sinned against and yet capacious of God. And it needs to provide restitution for the specific harm that was endured, as well as the broader debilitating consequences of rape culture. The community has the capacity to mediate God's healing grace for the traumatized individual and traumatized culture. That Christian communities have frequently failed to do this is heartbreaking in light of both this power and responsibility.

Survivors of sexual trauma need communal, ecclesial support to restore the relationships which sexual trauma has threatened. This support is embodied in acts of loving friendship and mediates the friendship God desires to have with us. Concretely, this friendship might take many forms, depending on the circumstances of violence endured and the individuals involved. One survivor, a woman who was raped in her apartment, was able to reclaim her home with the help of her community of faith. On the anniversary of her attack, she kept vigil all night in prayer and her friends committed to staying awake with her in their own homes. In the morning, they gathered together for mass.[56]

Public rituals of lament and repentance can also function as healing for survivors and mediate the love of a community in which Jesus arises. For example, Anabaptist Mennonite Biblical Seminary in Elkhart, Indiana condemned former professor John Howard Yoder's sexual abuse of women, and their institutional failure to intervene in his abusive actions, as "evil." Yoder sexually abused anywhere from fifty to more than one hundred women (many of whom were students) from the mid-1970s to the early 1990s.[57] In a Service of Lament, Confession, and Hope in March of 2015, Yoder's abusive behavior was clearly named as "evil," the institution apologized for supporting it, and the seminary committed to making itself "a safe place for everyone."[58] The seminary developed sexual misconduct policies and procedures that prioritize the agency of survivors in determining how disciplinary actions play out, and has committed to "listen[ing] carefully to those who speak up about things that are wrong or incomplete in AMBS's policies or their implementation."[59] Notably, the accountability process for Yoder and the seminary was empowered by survivors' discovery of their shared experiences with Yoder through networks of female friendship and support.[60] In the same way that consciousness-raising groups in the 1970s spurred feminist structural advocacy in American life,[61] this philial support animated decades of advocacy in both the Mennonite church and broader Christian academic circles, demanding community sanctions against Yoder.

The fullness of posttraumatic healing—personal, interpersonal, and social-political—spans the full breadth of Christian salvation. Christians have traditionally gestured toward this breadth of restoration with two interlocking images: the resurrection of the body (representing personal-material well-being) and the kingdom of God (representing interpersonal and social-political well-being). These images work together to indicate the holistically mystical-political shape of Christian salvation.[62] The tradition holds these images together, remembering Jesus as one who announced and initiated both. The resurrection of Jesus's own body and the promise that it contains for our own bodies is recognized in the community of collected friends who gather to re-member Jesus after the violent dismemberment of his body and the intended dismemberment of his group through political tactics of terror by public execution. The communal activity of re-membering Jesus embodies—politically and religiously—a conviction that death is not the end and a hope in the resurrection. In a Christian context, animated by Jesus's practice of table fellowship and the memory of Jesus arising in the midst of the community gathered at table, posttraumatic restoration of relationships consists in the gathering of friends to recognize a "body broken" and to strive to re-member this body.

The body broken encompasses the individual survivor's damaged body—including a damaged psyche, damaged capacity for interrelationships, and damaged spirituality—as well as the social body, broken by betrayal. One broken body cannot be healed apart from the other. Without the social-political transformation of rape culture, sexually traumatized individuals know that they can never secure full safety (the first step of trauma recovery). And, without a healed and whole individual (i.e., one who has received recognition and restitution), any degree of social "wholeness" is an illusion, frequently weaponized against those who threaten to expose violence within the community.[63] The work of recognizing and re-membering the body broken by sexual violence is a long and arduous mystical-political practice, necessitating both courage and hope. Because God is "for us" and desires our wholeness, this is God's own eschatological saving work. Yet we don't do nothing for our salvation. God animates us for creative and courageous cooperation in the transformation of ourselves and our communities.

Acknowledgments

I give thanks, first, to my mother who sacrificed so much to introduce me to the Christian tradition, and to Fr. Gerard Marable, whose friendship and guidance supported her. I am grateful to Mary Catherine Hilkert, the best doctoral advisor anyone could ever ask for, who helped me to imagine myself as a "real theologian." Her passion for God, who never wills suffering, is infectious. Many thanks to Donna Freitas, who read and gave feedback on multiple drafts of this book, always encouraging me to lean deeper into my own voice. Sincere thanks to the colleagues who provided feedback on parts of my argument—especially Janna Hunter-Bowman, Jessica Coblentz, Elizabeth Antus, Megan McCabe, and Brianne Jacobs. Your insights have been gifts to me. Thanks to John Garza at Fordham University Press for believing in this project and making it possible.

I am appreciative of the warm support I received for this project from my colleagues in the Department of Theology at Creighton University, especially Julia Fleming, Christina McRorie, Susan Calef, Joseph Lenow, and Jay Carney. My writing accountability group colleagues—Surbhi Malik, Britta McEwen, and Elizabeth Elliot-Meisel—have been my constant cheerleaders. And the friendship, dedication, and creativity of colleagues Heather Fryer and Rebecca Murray have carried me through many moments, faced with human evil, when I otherwise might have given up. I am especially thankful for a Summer Faculty Research Grant from Creighton's Center for Undergraduate Research and Scholarship and for the hard work of Kayli Branan Blalock and Jessica Mizaur—my dedicated research assistants. Your thoughtfulness made this project so much richer.

I am grateful for the many years of support from the Center for the Study of Spirituality at Saint Mary's College. Previous directors Keith Egan and Kathleen Dolphin both helped to shape my research on Teresa of Avila and Edward Schillebeeckx, respectively. And, since I was a "new voice" in theology, Elizabeth Groppe, Michelle Egan, Arlene Montevecchio, and Daniel Horan have each, in turn, given me opportunities to present different components of this project.

Many thanks to my "Schillebeeckx for a New Generation" colleagues, especially Stephan van Erp, Mary Ann Hinsdale, Kathleen McManus, Daniel Minch, Christopher Cimorelli, and Beth Pyne. Your enthusiasm gives me hope. I am thankful for the encouragement of Lawrence Cunningham—who first inspired me to write about Teresa of Avila, and Anthony Godzieba—who taught me that Schillebeeckx and Teresa are both deeply incarnational thinkers. I am grateful for the unfailing support of mentors Gerald McKenny and Mary Rose D'Angelo. And I am continually thankful for Jennifer Beste's wisdom, friendship, and righteous anger.

There have been many spiritual communities and companions who have strengthened me and my family during the process of writing this book: Saint Augustine Parish (South Bend, IN); Kern Road Mennonite Church (South Bend, IN); Holy Family Catholic Church (Omaha, NE); Trinity Episcopal Cathedral (Omaha, NE); Brs. James Dowd and Jerry Thompson and The Benedictine Way (Omaha, NE); Ignatian Associates (Omaha, NE); Cana Community (South Bend, IN); Restoration Farm (Mishawaka, IN); Fr. Greg Carlson; and Matthew Insley and Jennifer Betz. Many thanks to Connie and Byron, who have provided countless hours of childcare, meals, and other nourishment.

Most of all, thank you to Shaun, who makes life beautiful, and to our children, who make life good.

Notes

Introduction: Saving Grace

1. Edward Schillebeeckx, *Christ: The Experience of Jesus as Lord*, trans. John Bowden, CW 7 (London: Bloomsbury/T&T Clark, 2014), 717–23 [724–30].
2. "Fast Facts: Preventing Sexual Violence," Centers for Disease Control, https://www.cdc.gov/violenceprevention/sexualviolence/fastfact.html.
3. *Omaha World-Herald*, https://omaha.com/news/crime/accusers-of-ex-creighton-prep-priest-describe-haunting-secrets-he-asks-for-proof/article_106375cf-f815-5d25-88e3-fbf62f96080b.html; https://omaha.com/news/crime/breaking-faith-growing-allegations-about-ex-creighton-prep-priest-cite-misconduct-in-confession/article_3d813bec-b157-5523-9128-314492c6ad18.html.
4. *Omaha World-Herald*, https://omaha.com/news/crime/accusers-of-ex-creighton-prep-priest-describe-haunting-secrets-he-asks-for-proof/article_106375cf-f815-5d25-88e3-fbf62f96080b.html.
5. Psychiatrist Judith Herman notes, "In 1980, when post-traumatic stress disorder was first included in the diagnostic manual, the American Psychiatric Association described traumatic events as, 'outside the range of usual human experience.' Sadly, this definition has proved to be inaccurate. Rape, battery, and other forms of sexual and domestic violence are so common a part of women's [and children's] lives that they can hardly be described as outside of the range of ordinary experience." Judith Lewis Herman, *Trauma and Recovery* (New York: Basic Books, 1992), 33.

1. Salvation as Mystical-Political Healing

1. Bessel van der Kolk, "The Body Keeps the Score," in *Traumatic Stress: The Effects of Overwhelming Experience on Mind, Body, and Society*, eds. Bessel A. van der Kolk, Alexander C. McFarlane, and Lars Weisaeth (New York: Guilford Press, 1996), 222, and Bessel van der Kolk and Alexander McFarlane, "The Black Hole of

Trauma," in *Traumatic Stress: The Effects of Overwhelming Experience on Mind, Body, and Society*, eds. Bessel A. van der Kolk, Alexander C. McFarlane, and Lars Weisaeth (New York: Guilford Press, 1996), 4, 10, 14.

2. Alexander McFarlane and Bessel van der Kolk, "Trauma and Its Challenge to Society," in *Traumatic Stress: The Effects of Overwhelming Experience on Mind, Body, and Society*, eds. Bessel A. van der Kolk, Alexander C. McFarlane, and Lars Weisaeth (New York: Guilford Press, 1996), 26.

3. Trauma researchers refer to this posttraumatic process of sensory overwhelming as the alternation between intrusion (as the victim relives the original traumatic event as triggered by new sensory input) and numbing (as the victim shuts down as a means of coping). These extreme states can present themselves so frequently that their alternation can be mistaken as a permanent and central feature of the victim's personality. Herman calls this a "costly error" because it can suggest that these symptoms cannot be ameliorated with treatment. Judith Lewis Herman, *Trauma and Recovery* (New York: Basic Books, 1992), 47, 49.

4. Herman, *Trauma and Recovery*, 52–66.

5. Christopher Houck, et al., "Sexual Abuse and Sexual Risk Behavior: Beyond the Impact of Psychiatric Problems," *Journal of Pediatric Psychology* 35, no. 5 (2010): 474.

6. Bronwyn Watson and W. Kim Halford, "Classes of Childhood Sexual Abuse and Women's Adult Couple Relationships." *Violence and Victims* 25, no. 4 (2010): 518.

7. Herman, *Trauma and Recovery*, 53.

8. Elaine Scarry, *The Body in Pain: The Making and Unmaking of the World* (New York: Oxford University Press, 1985), 41.

9. The Rape, Abuse & Incest National Network (RAINN) reports: "More than 50% of all rape/sexual assault incidents were reported by victims to have occurred within 1 mile of their home or at their home. 4 in 10 take place at the victim's home. 2 in 10 take place at the home of a friend, neighbor, or relative." http://www.rainn.org/get-information/statistics/sexual-assault-offenders.

10. Scarry, *The Body in Pain*, 45.

11. Herman, *Trauma and Recovery*, 61.

12. Herman, *Trauma and Recovery*, 33.

13. Menachem Ben-Ezra, et al., "Losing My Religion: A Preliminary Study of Changes in Belief Pattern After Sexual Assault," *Traumatology* 16, no. 2 (2010): 7–13.

14. Catherine Cameron, *Resolving Childhood Trauma: A Long-Term Study of Abuse Survivors* (London: Sage Publications, 2000), 276–77.

15. For example, more extensive adult couple relationship problems have been correlated with increased severity of sexual abuse, yet there is a lack of consensus about which characteristics best define severity. Some possible candidates include more intense physical intrusion, intimacy of relation to perpetrator, or length of exposure to abuse. Watson and Halford, "Classes," 519.

16. Watson and Halford explain, "While all classes of CSA [childhood sexual abuse] were associated with negative outcomes, family CSA was associated with the

most adult couple relationship problems." Watson and Halford, "Classes," 532. This may be because family CSA is likely to involve repeated exposure over a long period of time. Kate Walsh, Michelle A. Fortier, and David DiLillo, "Adult Coping with Childhood Sexual Abuse: A Theoretical and Empirical Review," *Aggression and Violent Behavior* 15 (2010): 1–13; Kristine Peace, Stephen Porter, and Leanne ten Brinke, "Are Memories for Sexually Traumatic Events 'Special'? A Within-Subjects Investigation of Trauma and Memory in a Clinical Sample," *Memory* 16, no. 1 (2008): 18; and Watson and Halford, "Classes," 520.

17. For example, exposure to violence at earlier ages is associated with the highest degrees of risk. Women tend to experience violence at younger ages than men do and, consequently, they are at greater risk for PTSD overall. Vivia McCutcheon et al., "Age at Trauma Exposure and PTSD Risk in Young Adult Women," *Journal of Traumatic Stress* 23, no. 6 (2010): 811.

18. Strong emotional attachments forged *prior* to the traumatic violence can guard against development of PTSD. Bessel van der Kolk, Alexander McFarlane, and Onno van der Hart, "A General Approach to Treatment of Posttraumatic Stress Disorder," *Traumatic Stress: The Effects of Overwhelming Experience on Mind, Body, and Society*, eds. Bessel van der Kolk, Alexander C. McFarlane, and Lars Weisaeth (New York: Guilford Press, 1996), 432–433. *After* the traumatic event has occurred, positive responses to the disclosure of the trauma greatly improve one's chances of recovery. Walsh, Fourtier, and Delillo, "Adult Coping," 8, 9.

19. Rachel Yehuda, *Risk Factors for Posttraumatic Stress Disorder* (Washington, D.C.: American Psychiatric Press, 1999), xv.

20. Maria Root, "Reconstructing the Impact of Trauma on Personality," in *Personality and Psychopathology: Feminist Reappraisals*, eds. L.S. Brown and M. Ballou (New York: The Guilford Press, 1992), 236.

21. Maria Root, "Reconstructing," 236, 237, and Theresa W. Tobin, "Religious Faith in the Unjust Meantime: The Spiritual Violence of Clergy Sexual Abuse," *Feminist Philosophy Quarterly* 5, no. 2 (2019): 6.

22. Root, "Reconstructing," 240.

23. Tobin, "Religious Faith," 7–8.

24. Root, "Reconstructing," 240.

25. Susan Brownmiller, *Against Our Will: Men, Women, and Rape* (New York: Simon & Schuster, 1975), 5, *original emphasis*.

26. Rebecca Stotzer, "Violence Against Transgender People: A Review of United States Data," *Aggression and Violent Behavior* 14, no. 3 (2009): 170–79.

27. Andrea Ritchie, "How Some Cops Use the Badge to Commit Sex Crimes," *Washington Post* (January 12, 2018).

28. Nichole M. Flores, "Trinity and Justice: A Theological Response to the Sexual Assault of Migrant Women," *Journal of Religion and Society*, Supplement 16 (2018): 39–51.

29. Audrey Savage, *Twice Raped* (Indianapolis: Book Weaver, 1990), 186–87.

30. Ann Cahill, *Rethinking Rape* (Ithaca: Cornell University Press, 2001), 121.

31. In 2017, Natalie Gontcharova wrote a popular article on the fashion and news website *Refinery 29*, titled "The Infuriating Reason A Lot of Women Wear Fake Engagement Rings at Work," detailing the efforts that women put into making it seem as if they are married to protect themselves from workplace sexual harassment. https://www.refinery29.com/2017/07/162357/wearing-fake-engagement-ring-at-work. Yet many have found that wearing a ring—either as a false or real indicator of married status—is another "protective spell" that offers little real protection. See, for example, Lauren Rodrigue's biting 2015 essay, "I Thought My Engagement Ring Would Act as a Shield Against Men. Nope." https://itheedread.jezebel.com/i-thought-my-engagement-ring-would-act-as-a-shield-agai-1711972606.

32. It is worth noting the work of German photographer Marianne Wex, who documented gender differences in bodily comportment through an extensive series of candid street photos. Philosopher Sandra Lee Bartky summarizes Wex's findings: "Women sit waiting for trains with arms close to the body, hands folded together in their laps, toes pointing straight ahead or turned inward, and legs pressed together. The women in these photographs make themselves small and narrow, harmless; they seem tense; they take up little space. Men, on the other hand, expand into the available space; they sit with legs far apart and arms flung out at some distance from the body. Most common in these sitting male figures is what Wex calls the 'proffering position': the men sit with legs thrown wide apart, crotch visible, feet pointing outward, often with an arm and a casually dangling hand resting comfortably on an open spread thigh. Cahill, *Rethinking Rape*, 159, citing Bartky's, "Foucault, Femininity, and the Modernization of Patriarchal Power" in *Feminism, and Foucault*, eds. Irene Diamond and Lee Quinby (Boston: Northeastern University Press, 1988), 67.

33. Shanita Hubbard, "Russell Simmons, R. Kelly, and Why Black Women Can't Say #MeToo," *The New York Times*, December 15, 2017.

34. Cahill, *Rethinking Rape*, 121.

35. Cahill, *Rethinking Rape*, 126.

36. As theological ethicist Mary Pellauer writes, "All women live with the knowledge and fear of rape as a component of our knowledge of and feelings about the world. Still, there is a qualitative difference between the worlds of those who have experienced rape and those who merely factor it in among the possible risks. The compromises, the risks, the timidity, and the occasional brashness with which women confront a world in which our violation may happen at any time render our worlds fragile. The victim's world, however, is shattered." Mary Pellauer, *Sexual Assault and Abuse* (San Francisco: Harper & Row, 1987), 87.

37. Cahill, *Rethinking Rape*, 130.

38. Cahill, *Rethinking Rape*, 133.

39. Cathy Winkler, "Rape as Social Murder," *Anthropology Today* 7, no. 3 (June 1991): 13.

40. Leonard Shengold, *Soul Murder* (New York: Ballantine, 1989), 2.

41. Cahill, *Rethinking Rape*, 143.

42. Cahill, *Rethinking Rape*, 143.

43. Cahill, *Rethinking Rape*, 157.
44. Cahill, *Rethinking Rape*, 160.
45. Cahill, *Rethinking Rape*, 157.
46. As Ann Cahill explains, "For a woman, the travelable world is a small place. Entire portions of each twenty-four-hour day are deemed unsafe, and unless accompanied by a man (or, alternatively, many women), a woman should spend these hours in the safety of her own home. Geographical areas that may be considered completely accessible to men are, for women, sites of possible (even likely) harassment, molestation, or rape." According to Cahill the threats around which women organize their lives are not generalized. They are specifically sexual in nature. Cahill, *Rethinking Rape*, 159.
47. Winkler, "Rape as Social Murder," 13.
48. Winkler, "Rape as Social Murder," 12.
49. Winkler, "Rape as Social Murder," 13.
50. Winkler, "Rape as Social Murder," 13.
51. Marie M. Fortune, *Sexual Violence: The Unmentionable Sin* (New York: Pilgrim Press, 1983), 19.
52. Fortune, *Sexual Violence*, 119.
53. Fortune, *Sexual Violence*, 37.
54. Fortune, *Sexual Violence*, 101.
55. Although others have advanced their own schemas of the recovery process, most are similar to the basic movement of Herman's classic. See for example, S. M. Sgroi, ed., *Vulnerable Population, Volume 2: Sexual Abuse Treatment for Children, Adult Survivors, Offenders, and Persons with Mental Retardation* (New York: Free Press, 1989), and Van der Kolk, McFarlane, and van der Hart, "A General Approach," 417–440. For the purposes of a theological appropriation of contemporary psychological literature on trauma, the differences between these approaches are not significant. In this work I will use Herman's articulation of the recovery process as key to my own understanding.
56. Van der Kolk and McFarlane, "The Black Hole of Trauma," 18. Van der Kolk, McFarlane, and van der Hart, "A General Approach," 420.
57. Herman, *Trauma and Recovery*, 137.
58. Herman, *Trauma and Recovery*, 137–38, 143.
59. Herman, *Trauma and Recovery*, 175.
60. Herman, *Trauma and Recovery*, 176. Later, I will connect this insight from Herman about the intense degree of endurance required for progress in the healing process with Teresa's description of the purgative stage in the life of prayer.
61. Herman, *Trauma and Recovery*, 178.
62. Herman, *Trauma and Recovery*, 188. *Emphasis added.*
63. Herman explains, "Because an injustice has been done to her, the survivor naturally feels entitled to some form of compensation. . . . [Yet, m]ourning is the only way to give due honor to loss; there is no adequate compensation." Herman, *Trauma and Recovery*, 190.

64. Expression of traumatic pain makes a claim on the other. Veena Das, *Life and Words: Violence and the Descent into the Ordinary* (Berkley: University of California Press, 2007), 40. I use both Das and Herman in this section to emphasize the relational and social nature of traumatic healing and, relatedly, the ethical imperatives that follow from traumatic violence. Yet the reader should be aware that Das and Herman do have some significant theoretical differences, but to do a full analysis of these differences would take more space than I am allowed here.

65. Herman, *Trauma and Recovery*, 70.

66. Das, *Life and Words*, 48.

67. As Das notes, mourning consists in "the complex relation between speaking and hearing, between building a world that the living can inhabit with their loss and building a world in which the dead can find a home." Das, *Life and Words*, 58.

68. Herman, *Trauma and Recovery*, 70.

69. See, for example, the work of Chicago housekeepers to advocate for "panic" buttons to request help in protecting themselves from sexual assault. Benjamin Mueller, "For Hotel Workers, Weinstein Allegations Put a Spotlight on Harassment," *The New York Times*, December 17, 2017.

70. Jennifer Beste, *College Hookup Culture and Christian Ethics: The Lives and Longings of Emerging Adults* (New York: Oxford University Press, 2018), 292–295.

71. See, for example, United States Conference of Catholic Bishops, "Charter for the Protection of Children and Young People," 2018. https://www.usccb.org/test/upload/Charter-for-the-Protection-of-Children-and-Young-People-2018-final(1).pdf, as an example of a zero-tolerance standard for sexual assault of minors, though inadequate policies are in place to respond to sexual assault of adults.

72. See, for example, Boy Scouts of America, "Youth Protection and Adult Leadership Policies," accessed January 23, 2022, https://www.scouting.org/health-and-safety/gss/gss01/.

73. Herman, *Trauma and Recovery*, 72.

74. Catherine MacKinnon, "Feminism, Marxism, Method, and the State: An Agenda for Theory," *Signs* 7, no. 3 (1982): 651, qtd. by Herman, *Trauma and Recovery*, 72.

75. Herman, *Trauma and Recovery*, 195.

76. Herman, *Trauma and Recovery*, 197.

77. Herman, *Trauma and Recovery*, 197. See also Stephen Prior, *Object Relations in Severe Trauma* (London: Jason Aronson, Inc., 1996), 135 ff. Later, it will be interesting to compare this psychological observation with Teresa of Avila's personal narration of the value of encountering danger in prayer and the conquest of devils as a result of prayerful combat.

78. Herman, *Trauma and Recovery*, 199.

79. Herman, *Trauma and Recovery*, 202.

80. Herman, *Trauma and Recovery*, 206.

81. Herman, *Trauma and Recovery*, 214. Group processes at different stages in recovery look different. In the first stage it is most helpful to be in a present-focused

group to avoid overwhelming the individual. In the second stage it is helpful to have a trauma-focused group. In the third stage of recovery there are more options depending on the goals of the recovering individual. Helpful options include a trauma-focused group or interpersonal group, or even a self-defense class. Group processes in all stages of recovery are helpful, but in this last stage of healing, in particular, the connections between the value of therapeutic group work and non-therapeutic interpersonal and social relationships can be most clear. Herman, *Trauma and Recovery*, 220, 221–33, 233 ff, 234–35.

82. See also Prior, who argues that finding a safe place in another and within oneself can help to bring significant change. Prior, *Object Relations*, 167 ff.

83. Herman, *Trauma and Recovery*, 207, 208.

84. Herman, *Trauma and Recovery*, 210.

85. Herman writes, "Although giving to others is the essence of the survivor mission, those who practice it recognize that they do so for their own healing" Herman, *Trauma and Recovery*, 209.

86. Herman, *Trauma and Recovery*, 153. *Emphasis in original.*

87. Herman, *Trauma and Recovery*, 133.

88. McFarlane and Van der Kolk, "Trauma and Its Challenge to Society," 25.

89. Catherine Cameron, *Resolving Childhood Trauma*, 291.

90. Cameron, *Resolving Childhood Trauma*, 293. *Emphasis added.*

91. Kim Anderson and Catherine Hiersteiner, "Recovering from Childhood Sexual Abuse: Is a 'Storybook Ending' Possible?" *The American Journal of Family Therapy* 36, no. 5 (2008): 417.

92. Herman, *Trauma and Recovery*, 72.

93. Herman, *Trauma and Recovery*, 73.

94. Edward Schillebeeckx, *God the Future of Man*, trans. Norman Smith (New York: Sheed and Ward, 1968), 76–77.

95. Edward Schillebeeckx, *Christ: The Experience of Jesus as Lord*, trans. John Bowden (New York: Crossroad, 1980), 792.

96. Susan Brison, "Outliving Oneself: Trauma, Memory and Personal Identity," *Feminists Rethink the Self* (Boulder, Westview Press, 1996), 19.

97. Brison, "Outliving Oneself," 19.

98. Brison, "Outliving Oneself," 31.

99. Brison, "Outliving Oneself," 18.

100. Cahill, *Rethinking Rape*, 131.

101. Sandra Schneiders, "Touching the Risen Jesus: Mary Magdalene and Thomas the Twin in John 20," *Proceedings of the Catholic Theological Society of America* 60 (2013): 14, and Anthony Godzieba, "Bodies and Persons, Resurrected and Postmodern: Towards a Relational Eschatology," in *Theology and Conversation: Towards a Relational Theology*, eds. Jacques Haers and Peter De Mey (Leuven: Leuven University Press, 2003).

102. Sandra Schneiders, *Jesus Risen in Our Midst: Essays on the Resurrection of Jesus* (Collegeville: Liturgical Press, 1989), 22.

103. Schneiders, *Jesus Risen*, 95.

104. Jürgen Moltmann, "To Believe with All Your Senses: The Resurrection of the Body," CTSA proceedings, 60 (2005): 5.

105. Anthony Godzieba, "Resurrection—Interruption—Transformation: Incarnation as Hermeneutical Strategy," *Theological Studies* 67 (2006): 786, citing Raymond E. Brown, "The Problem of the Bodily Resurrection of Jesus," in *The Virginal Conception and Bodily Resurrection of Jesus* (New York: Paulist Press, 1973), 69–129 at 128–129.

106. Brown, "The Problem," 128–129, quoted by Godzieba, "Resurrection," 786.

107. Godzieba, "Resurrection," 788.

108. Schillebeeckx, *Christ*, 723 [730], 722 [729].

109. Relatedly, Flora Keshgegian argues that the early Christians, while affirming the full humanity of Jesus Christ in the abstract, struggled to incorporate the full humanity of Jesus into their theological frameworks in any complete way: "They affirmed that Jesus Christ was human and divine, but they did not affirm his life. Their Jesus Christ had no life history. For them, what was necessary for salvation was the event and reality of incarnation. Jesus' incarnated life, the story of his birth and life, his ministry and relationships, his teaching and healing, his loves, and values, dropped out of the picture in a way. In other words, they were not able to imagine the divine in human terms—vulnerable to suffering, subject to change, involved in relationships, being affected by people and events. Though they attested to the union of divine and human, there was still a world of difference between the life of divinity and that of humanity." Flora Keshgegian, *Redeeming Memories: A Theology of Healing and Transformation* (Nashville: Abingdon Press, 2000), 183.

110. Pellauer, *Sexual Assault and Abuse*, 98–100.

111. Jennifer Beste, *God and the Victim*, AAR Academy Series (New York: Oxford University Press, 2007), 116 f.

112. Herman, *Trauma and Recovery*, 155–74. Serene Jones is also clear about the salience of agency and creativity in the healed human person. Serene Jones, *Trauma and Grace: Theology in a Ruptured World* (Louisville: Westminster John Knox Press, 2009), 101–25, especially 116–19.

113. While Shelly Rambo addresses the ongoing quality of posttraumatic healing as a challenge to some Christian ideas of resurrection most directly, others advance related claims. For example, Beste suggests that trauma survivors challenge Christians triumphalist visions of "happy endings" (Beste, *God and the Victim*, 126) and Annie Selak argues that trauma disrupts a linear model of time and memory. Annie Selak, "The Power of Memory and Witnessing: A Trauma-Informed Analysis of *Anamnesis* in the Roman Catholic Mass," *Liturgy and Power*, vol. 62, College Theology Society (Maryknoll: Orbis, 2016), 22–33. Similarly, reflecting on the scars on Christ's resurrected body attested to in the Gospel of John, Keshgegian is careful to insist that the resurrection does not erase the suffering of his death. In light of the ongoing nature of traumatic wounds and the ways that these challenge linear descriptions of redemption, many trauma theologians are wary of Christian language that rushes too quickly to "talk of forgiveness" since this can function in such a way as to suggest that victims should "get over" their injuries as quickly as

possible and this can threaten proper remembering and mourning. Keshgegian, *Redeeming Memories*, 175, 195, see also Fortune, *Sexual Violence*, 208–11.

114. Shelly Rambo, *Spirit and Trauma: A Theology of Remaining* (Louisville: Westminster John Knox Press, 2010), 140. See also Shelly Rambo, *Resurrecting Wounds: Living in the Afterlife of Trauma* (Waco: Baylor University Press, 2017).

115. Herman, *Trauma and Recovery*, 211.

116. As Karen Bray suggests, building on Rambo's argument, "a resurrection may not be needed, wanted, or coming." Karen Bray, *Grave Attending: A Political Theology for the Unredeemed* (New York: Fordham University Press, 2019). While I appreciate the impulse not to rush to resurrection, since rushing risks failing to reverence the gravity of the harm inflicted, to suggest that a resurrection may not be needed also risks failing to acknowledge the depth of harm. I argue that healing is not only needed, but also promised by God—if only eschatologically. Indeed, a Christian eschatological framework of salvation is particularly well-poised to articulate the ways in which comprehensive posttraumatic healing is both needed and beyond our imaginative grasp.

117. Rambo, *Spirit and Trauma*, 10, 74–80, 124–25, 133.

118. Jane M. Grovijahn, "Theology as an Irruption into Embodiment: Our Need for God," *Theology and Sexuality* 9 (1998): 29–35. Tertullian, *De resurrectione carnis*, 8–9.

119. Edward Schillebeeckx, "Erfahrung und Glaube," in *Christerlicher Glaube in moderner Gesellschaft*, Volume 25, eds. F. Böckle, F.-X. Kaufmann, K. Rahner, and B. Welte (Frieburg: Herder, 1980), 99 f. and Schillebeeckx, *Jesus*, 141.

120. Victims of sexual abuse—especially those who experience abuse within their families, religious communities, or educational settings—often risk dissolving the very bonds upon which they depend if they resist abuse.

121. I phrase it in this way, i.e., with a double negative, in order to reflect the paradoxical nature of this Christian teaching as well as to mirror the language of the Council of Trent on Justification. The decree reads, "while God touches the heart of man by the illumination of the Holy Ghost, neither is man himself utterly without doing anything while he receives that inspiration." *The Council of Trent: The Canons and Decrees of the Sacred and Oecumenical Council of Trent*, trans. J. Waterworth (London: Dolman, 1848), 33.

2. Teresa of Avila: A Saint for Survivors

1. In a new afterword, added five years after the publication of the first edition of her classic *Trauma and Recovery*, Judith Herman notably changed her own position on disassociation from "merciful protection" to a "respite from terror . . . purchased at far too high a price." Judith Lewis Herman, *Trauma and Recovery* (New York: Basic Books, 1992), 239.

2. Teresa of Avila, *The Book of Her Life*, trans. Kieran Kavanaugh and Otilio Rodriguez, The Collected Works of St. Teresa of Avila, Volume 1 (Washington: Institute of Carmelite Studies, 1976), 252.

3. Teresa of Avila, *The Book of Her Life*, 252.

4. In response to French psychoanalyst Jacques Lacan's (in)famous commentary on female sexuality—that appropriated Teresa as a primary source—"You have only to go and look at Bernini's statue in Rome to understand immediately that she's coming [qu'elle jouit], there's no doubt about it." French philosopher and cultural theorist Luce Irigary sharply and perceptively retorted, "In Rome? So far away? To look? At a statue? Of a saint? Sculpted by a man? What pleasure are we talking about? Whose pleasure? For where the pleasure of the Theresa in question is concerned, her own writings are perhaps more telling." Carole Slade, *St. Teresa of Avila: Author of a Heroic Life* (Berkeley: University of California Press, 1995), 134.

5. Cathleen Medwick, *Teresa of Avila: The Progress of a Soul* (New York: Alfred A. Knopf, 1999), viii.

6. Herman, *Trauma and Recovery*, 11. Jean-Martin de Charcot controversially claimed to have found existence of hysteria in some men, though admittedly only in poor and socially marginalized men. Cristina Mazzoni, *Saint Hysteria: Neurosis, Mysticism, and Gender in European Culture* (Ithaca: Cornell University Press, 1996), 5.

7. Herman, *Trauma and Recovery*, 15–16. Medwick, *Teresa of Avila*, xv. Charcot terms this kind of analysis "retrospective medicine". Cristina Mazzoni argues that this work was Charcot's attempt to illustrate that "the visibility of hysteria fills in, for the artist seeking a model, the empty space of the invisible God or demon." Mazzoni, *Saint Hysteria*, 20–23, 22, 24.

8. Mazzoni, *Saint Hysteria*, 19.

9. Herman, *Trauma and Recovery*, 10–11.

10. Herman, *Trauma and Recovery*, 14. Herman notes that not all nineteenth-century physicians repudiated the connection between traumatic violence and hysteria, but those who did not—such as Pierre Janet—ended up marginalized in the psychological canon. Therefore, Herman argues that Freud's recantation is not an isolated sin, but rather reflective of a broader social refusal to support psychological investigation of sexual violence. Herman, *Trauma and Recovery* 18.

11. Herman, *Trauma and Recovery*, 14.

12. As Herman explains, "The solution of the mystery of hysteria was intended to demonstrate the triumph of secular enlightenment over reactionary superstition, as well as the moral superiority of a secular worldview." Herman, *Trauma and Recovery*, 16.

13. Herman, *Trauma and Recovery*, 16. In some sense, this was an understandable conclusion. Burning at the stake had been a real threat for women who exhibited the symptoms now classified as "hysterical" and medical diagnosis was, in some instances, an improvement in safety. Mazzoni argues that under a Christian medieval framework, those who exhibited symptoms of hysteria (or, what we might think of today as symptoms of trauma) were understood to be possessed by the devil. Turn-of-the-century physicians argued that these women were not possessed, but rather that they were undiagnosed hysterics "suffering from a bodily disease like all

other medical conditions." Yet, medical diagnosis frequently failed to liberate women from active modes of discrediting their own interpretations of their experience and functioning as pawns in the larger ideological battles of men over their bodies. As Mazzoni argues, "The bodies of the possessed" are the "battlefield of the conflict between religion and science." Mazzoni, *Saint Hysteria*, 8, 9, 14.

14. As Herman notes, it is not an accident, therefore, that the "same men who advocated an enlightened view of hysteria often strongly opposed the admission of women into higher education or the professions and adamantly opposed female suffrage." Herman, *Trauma and Recovery* 16.

15. Mazzoni, *Saint Hysteria*, 21, 26. The link between hysteria and mysticism has proved durable, since as Mazzoni argues, "it is still today a cliché to represent mystical experiences as inherently neurotic." Mazzoni, *Saint Hysteria*, ix.

16. Herman, *Trauma and Recovery*, 13, qting J. Breuer and S. Freud, "Studies on Hysteria [1893–95]," in *Standard Edition*, Volume 2, trans. J. Strachey (London: Hogarth Press, 1955), 35.

17. Herman, *Trauma and Recovery* 12–13, 19–20. Marion Kaplan, "Pappenheim, Bertha," in *The Oxford Encyclopedia of Women in World History*, ed. Bonnie G. Smith (Oxford: Oxford University Press, 2008).

18. Mazzoni, *Saint Hysteria*, 42.

19. As Mazzoni argues, "the body is not in her text the inarticulate and inarticulatable receptacle of the darts of unconscious and traumatic reminiscences" but rather "Saint Teresa rejoices as she directs the hermeneutic value of her own metaphors." Mazzoni, *Saint Hysteria*, 194.

20. Slade, *St. Teresa of Avila*, 2.

21. Grace Jantzen argues persuasively that the tendency to categorize mysticism as other-worldly experience is an intentional move to depoliticize spirituality and, in particular, to silence women's voices. As Jantzen explains, "[if] women are 'naturally' more spiritual than men, then only a small step is necessary to confine both the 'feminine' and the 'spiritual' to a context in which they are rendered thoroughly ineffectual." Grace Jantzen, "Feminists, Philosophers, and Mystics," *Hypatia* 9, no. 4 (1994): 200. I suggest that both Bernini and the founders of psychoanalysis may be motivated by this agenda. For this reason, among others, the continuity of the mystical life with the normal life of faith is of primary concern for contemporary Christian theologians, especially in the field of spirituality. See Sandra M. Schneiders, "Spirituality in the Academy," *Theological Studies* 50 (1989): 686–87 and Edward Schillebeeckx, *Church: The Human Story of God*, trans. John Bowden, The Collected Works of Edward Schillebeeckx, Volume 10 (London: Bloomsbury/T&T Clark, 2014), 67 [069]. See also Karl Rahner, "Mystical Experience and Mystical Theology," in *Theological Investigations* (New York: Crossroad, 1974), 17, 90–99.

22 Jodi Bilinkoff, *The Avila of Saint Teresa: Religious Reform in a Sixteenth-Century City* (Ithaca: Cornell University Press, 1989), 114.

23. Teresa of Avila, *The Book of Her Life*, 177–78.

24. Teresa of Avila, *The Book of Her Life*, 177–78.
25. Teresa of Avila, *The Book of Her Life*, 361, 118.
26. Bilinkoff, *The Avila of Saint Teresa*, 109.
27. Bilinkoff, *The Avila of Saint Teresa*, 109. Marcelin Defourneaux, *Daily Life in Spain in the Golden Age*, trans. Newton Branch (Stanford: Stanford University Press, 1970),125. Barbara Mujica, *Teresa de Avila: Lettered Woman* (Nashville: Vanderbilt University Press, 2009), 19.
28. Alison Weber, *Teresa of Avila and the Rhetoric of Femininity* (Princeton: Princeton University Press, 1990), 8. Medwick, *Teresa of Avila*, 11.
29. Defourneaux, *Daily Life in Spain*, 127.
30. Lisa Fullam, "Teresa of Avila's Liberative Humility," *Journal of Moral Theology* 3, no. 1 (2014): 177.
31. Bilinkoff, *The Avila of Saint Teresa*, 13.
32. Bilinkoff, *The Avila of Saint Teresa*, 13.
33. Bilinkoff, *The Avila of Saint Teresa*, 13. Mary Elizabeth Perry, *Gender and Disorder in Early Modern Seville* (Princeton: Princeton University Press, 1990), 4.
34. Bilinkoff, *The Avila of Saint Teresa*, 14.
35. Bilinkoff, *The Avila of Saint Teresa*, 10.
36. Bilinkoff, *The Avila of Saint Teresa*, 110, 17. Medwick, *Teresa of Avila*, 12.
37. In 1519, Teresa's father and three uncles refused to pay taxes in order to provoke litigation, knowing that the case would be judged by an ally—a relative to the brothers by marriage. The case was settled by 1522 in their favor, officially making them gentlemen. Bilinkoff, *The Avila of Saint Teresa*, 65–67.
38. Bilinkoff, *The Avila of Saint Teresa*, 18–21.
39. See Rowan Williams, *Teresa of Avila* (Harrisburg: Morehouse Publishing, 1991), 34, for the position that she was aware of her Jewish heritage.
40. Bilinkoff, *The Avila of Saint Teresa*, 53.
41. See Barbara Mujica who argues that Teresa learned from her father and grandfather how to defend herself skillfully, especially through defensive writing. Mujica writes, "*Conversos* like Alonso de Cepeda did not defend themselves with the sword from the onslaught of persecutions wrought by the crown, the church, and society at large; they defended themselves with the pen." In imitation, "[Teresa] used the post to influence the decisions of the hierarchy and to spur her lieutenants to action. She was like a general strategizing, maneuvering, and striking from a distance." Mujica, *Teresa de Avila*, 25, 68.
42. Bilinkoff, *The Avila of Saint Teresa*, 109.
43. Audrey Savage, *Twice Raped* (Indianapolis: Book Weaver, 1990), 122.
44. Savage, *Twice Raped*, 140.
45. Savage, *Twice Raped*, 266.
46. Bilinkoff, *The Avila of Saint Teresa*, 54.
47. Bilinkoff, *The Avila of Saint Teresa*, 56–57, 60–62.
48. Kieran Kavanaugh, "The Book of Her Life: Introduction," in *The Book of Her Life*, trans. Kieran Kavanaugh and Otilio Rodriguez, The Collected Works of St. Teresa of Avila, Volume 1 (Washington: Institute of Carmelite Studies, 1976), 15.

49. Bilinkoff, *The Avila of Saint Teresa*, 58.
50. Bilinkoff, *The Avila of Saint Teresa*, 58.
51. Bilinkoff, *The Avila of Saint Teresa*, 36.
52. Bilinkoff, *The Avila of Saint Teresa*, 39.
53. Bilinkoff argues that in Avila "religious patronage served as a means for women to express economic and spiritual independence." Bilinkoff, *The Avila of Saint Teresa*, 39.
54. Maya Angelou, "From I Know Why the Caged Bird Sings" in *I Never Told Anyone: Writings by Women Survivors of Child Sexual Abuse*, eds. Ellen Bass and Louise Thornton (New York: Harper Perennial, 1983), 127.
55. Kavanaugh, "The Book of Her Life: Introduction," 19.
56. Teresa of Avila, *The Book of Her Life*, 61–62.
57. Though she explains that she had always had poor health, she experienced acute symptoms at this time including high fevers and fainting spells. Teresa of Avila, *The Book of Her Life*, 63.
58. Kavanaugh, "The Book of Her Life: Introduction," 18.
59. Shannon Sullivan, *The Physiology of Sexist and Racist Oppression* (Oxford: Oxford University Press, 2015), 86.
60. Sullivan, *The Physiology*, 86.
61. Teresa of Avila, *The Book of Her Life*, 62.
62. Kavanaugh, "The Book of Her Life: Introduction," 19.
63. Bilinkoff, *The Avila of Saint Teresa*, 50–52.
64. It is no coincidence then, as Bilinkoff describes it, that "Eventually a nun who had begged on her knees for the soul of Bernardo Robles would develop a new vision of the religious based upon voluntary poverty and interior, *mental*, prayer. Saint Teresa's reform represented a daring alternative to the fundamentally aristocratic style of spirituality articulated in Avila during the first decades of the sixteenth century." Bilinkoff, *The Avila of Saint Teresa*, 52.
65. Kavanaugh, "The Book of Her Life: Introduction," 18.
66. Bilinkoff, *The Avila of Saint Teresa*, 115.
67. Bilinkoff, *The Avila of Saint Teresa*, 112–113. This kind of personal wealth within religious orders was made possible with Pope Eugenius IV's 1432 *Bull of Mitigation*, loosening the commitments of poverty, chastity, and obedience, to allow nuns to retain their wealth upon entering the convent and even to receive income from personal property holdings.
68. Gillian T.W. Ahlgren, *Teresa of Avila and the Politics of Sanctity* (Ithaca: Cornell University Press, 1996), 35.
69. Bilinkoff, *The Avila of Saint Teresa*, 114.
70. Since la Encarnación was significantly less restrictive than the convent school she attended as a teenager, Teresa's choice to join la Encarnación, in particular, was reflective of her ultimate unwillingness to renounce wealth as a young person. Bilinkoff, *The Avila of Saint Teresa*, 112–13.
71. E. W. Trueman Dicken, *The Crucible of Love: A Study of the Mysticism of St. Teresa of Jesus and St. John of the Cross* (New York: Sheed and Ward, 1963), 12.

72. Bilinkoff, *The Avila of Saint Teresa*, 113.

73. Bilinkoff, *The Avila of Saint Teresa*, 115.

74. Teresa herself describes la Encarnación as filled with "so many who serve the Lord authentically and with great perfection that His Majesty, being so good, cannot keep from favoring them . . . in it is observed a truly religious way of life." (Teresa of Avila, *The Book of Her Life*, 84). Teresa continues to speak highly of la Encarnación, even as she reforms the traditions there, in order to avoid conflict with Carmelite authorities. Yet, tellingly, she establishes San José as in the jurisdiction of the local bishop—Bishop Mendoza—an eventual ally, rather than under the Carmelite order's authority structure. Bilinkoff, *The Avila of Saint Teresa*, 148.

75. Teresa of Avila, *The Book of Her Life*, 66.

76. Medwick, *Teresa of Avila*, 26.

77. Teresa of Avila, *The Book of Her Life*, 66. Bilinkoff, *The Avila of Saint Teresa*, 116–17.

78. Teresa of Avila, *The Way of Perfection*, trans. Kieran Kavanaugh and Otilio Rodriguez, The Collected Works of St. Teresa of Avila, Volume 2 (Washington: Institute of Carmelite Studies, 1980), 141.

79. Teresa of Avila, *The Book of Her Life*, 96.

80. Teresa of Avila, *The Book of Her Life*, 74.

81. Teresa of Avila, *The Book of Her Life*, 74.

82. Karl Rahner, *Mary: Mother of the Lord* (New York: Herder and Herder, 1963).

83. Teresa of Avila, *The Book of Her Life*, 77.

84. Teresa of Avila, *The Book of Her Life*, 75.

85. Teresa of Avila, *The Book of Her Life*, 76.

86. Cathy Winkler, "Rape as Social Murder," *Anthropology Today* 7, no. 3 (1991): 12–14.

87. Susan Brison, "Outliving Oneself: Trauma, Memory and Personal Identity," *Feminists Rethink the Self* (Boulder: Westview Press, 1996), 19.

88. Shelly Rambo, *Spirit and Trauma: A Theology of Remaining* (Louisville: Westminster John Knox Press, 2010), 25. See also Rambo's *Resurrecting Wounds* where she argues, "life is not a departure from death but, instead, a different relationship to death and life . . . resurrecting is not so much about life overcoming death as it is about *life resurrecting amid the ongoingness of death.*" Shelly Rambo, *Resurrecting Wounds: Living in the Afterlife of Trauma* (Waco: Baylor University Press, 2017), 7, *emphasis in original.*

89. Teresa of Avila, *The Book of Her Life*, 88.

90. Kavanaugh, "The Book of Her Life: Introduction," 20.

91. Sullivan, *The Physiology*.

92. Teresa of Avila, *The Book of Her Life*, 77–78.

93. Teresa of Avila, *The Book of Her Life*, 82.

94. Teresa of Avila, *The Book of Her Life*, 90–91, 98.

95. Teresa of Avila, *The Book of Her Life*, 98.

96. Teresa of Avila, *The Book of Her Life*, 100–1. Slade, *St. Teresa of Avila*, 5–6.

97. Teresa of Avila, *The Book of Her Life*, 103.
98. Teresa of Avila, *The Book of Her Life*, 103–5.
99. Bilinkoff, *The Avila of Saint Teresa*, 118.
100. Bilinkoff, *The Avila of Saint Teresa*, 85–86.
101. Williams, *Teresa of Avila*.
102. Bilinkoff, *The Avila of Saint Teresa*, 119.
103. Bilinkoff, *The Avila of Saint Teresa*, 119 f.
104. Bilinkoff, *The Avila of Saint Teresa*, 120.
105. Bilinkoff, *The Avila of Saint Teresa*, 120–21.
106. Bilinkoff, *The Avila of Saint Teresa*, 121.
107. Facing, as Medgwick describes it, "a virtual army of skeptics," her confessors and their colleagues subjected Teresa to intense scrutiny "as if she were Martin Luther himself" (Medwick, *Teresa of Avila*, 52) in order to protect themselves from Inquisitional punishment as much as anything else. As moral theologian Lisa Fullam notes, "what is striking about Teresa is not the opposition she faced, but the fact that she continually resisted, working within a corrupt ecclesial context to try to reform it and defying social norms for women in her time. She did so with great prudence, to be sure: for example, she sought out sound theological advice before her works were circulated. But what is important is that she *did* continue in her mission of reform to write and publish her work. Too many subsequent scholars have been cowed by less dire threats than those Teresa endured." Fullam, "Teresa of Avila's Liberative Humility," 196, *emphasis in original*.
108. Weber, *Teresa of Avila*. Fullam, "Teresa of Avila's Liberative Humility," 195–96. Ahlgren, *Teresa of Avila*, 169. The reader should note that some scholars argue that Teresa's self-denigration in her writings is less about presenting herself as a properly feminine woman and more as an attempt to follow (non-specifically gendered) ancient writing tropes that stress the unsuitability of the author as a way to begin any significant intellectual work. See Benedicta Ward, "Introduction," in *The Life of Teresa of Jesus*, trans. E. Allison Peers (New York: Doubleday, 1991), 54–55.
109. Jill Morgan, "It Began for Me," in *I Never Told Anyone: Writings by Women Survivors of Child Sexual Abuse*, eds. Ellen Bass and Louise Thornton (New York: Harper Perennial, 1983), 109.
110. Bilinkoff, *The Avila of Saint Teresa*, 121.
111. Teresa of Avila, *The Book of Her Life*, 276.
112. Teresa of Avila, *The Book of Her Life*, 276.
113. Medwick, *Teresa of Avila*, 64–65.
114. Historically, this meant to reject the loosening of the rule that Eugenius IV had permitted in 1432 with the *Bull of Mitigation*. Teresa of Avila, *The Book of Her Life*, 279–280.
115. Teresa did not join the monastery at San José right away at the obedience of her prioress at la Encarnación but joins them later in February of 1563. Slade, *St. Teresa of Avila*, 110. Medwick, *Teresa of Avila*, 85–87.

116. Bilinkoff, *The Avila of Saint Teresa*, 108.

117. Bilinkoff, *The Avila of Saint Teresa*, 123. This was a radical proposition for the time since, as Medwick puts it, "If a convent were founded in poverty and a nun from an impoverished family were equal in stature to one from the aristocracy, then what *doña* in her right mind would take up the religious life? What family with *honra* would permit her to do so? The symbiotic relationship of religious institutions and the social elite would come to an end. Clearly the idea of a poor convent was not only romantic; it was revolutionary." Medwick, *Teresa of Avila*, 80.

118. Bilinkoff, *The Avila of Saint Teresa*, 126, 162. One should note that this was not an easy decision for Teresa to stick to, but a vision of Peter of Alcántara after his death in 1562 strengthened her resolve. (Teresa of Avila, *The Book of Her Life*, 318–319.) She was influenced—through a deep friendship with Franciscan reformer and frequent visitor to Avila, Peter of Alcántara—by the Franciscan ideals of asceticism and voluntary poverty. She was also shaped, through close relationships with Jesuit confessors, by Ignatian ideals of religious autonomy from benefactors and private interests. Bilinkoff, *The Avila of Saint Teresa*, 124–26, 89–92.

119. Teresa of Avila, *The Way of Perfection*, 45.

120. Bilinkoff, *The Avila of Saint Teresa*, 127–28.

121. Bilinkoff, *The Avila of Saint Teresa*, 130–31.

122. Bilinkoff, *The Avila of Saint Teresa*, 128.

123. Bilinkoff, *The Avila of Saint Teresa*, 128. Jantzen, "Feminists, Philosophers, and Mystics," 191–92. Ahlgren, *Teresa of Avila*. Carole Slade, "St. Teresa as a Social Reformer," in *Mysticism and Social Activism* (Syracuse: Syracuse University Press, 2001), 91–103. As Bilinkoff explains, for Teresa, "Genuine honor resided in a person's moral virtues and willingness to serve God. This included, of course, those whom the world considered 'lowly' or 'tainted,' such as the descendants of Jews." Bilinkoff, *The Avila of Saint Teresa*, 129.

124. Teresa of Avila, *The Book of Her Foundations*, trans. Kieran Kavanaugh and Otilio Rodriguez, The Collected Works of St. Teresa of Avila, Volume 3 (Washington: Institute of Carmelite Studies, 1985), 198.

125. Teresa of Avila, *The Book of Her Foundations*, 237.

126. Teresa of Avila, *The Book of Her Foundations*, 238.

127. Slade, "St. Teresa as Social Reformer," 102.

128. Bilinkoff, *The Avila of Saint Teresa*, 116.

129. Kavanaugh, "The Book of Her Life: Introduction," 36–37.

130. Medwick, *Teresa of Avila*, 87.

131. Medwick, *Teresa of Avila*, 98–100.

132. Bilinkoff, *The Avila of Saint Teresa*, 139.

133. Medwick, *Teresa of Avila*, 87.

134. As Bilinkoff explains, "Avila's principales in short, possessed a vested interest in perpetuating the socio-religious system that Teresa of Jesus had come to reject. Elites undoubtedly realized that if upper-class women accepted the discalced reform,

they might see their daughters starve or, perhaps even worse in their eyes, sever the bonds of family and honor essential to the ordering of life as they knew it. The twice-yearly payments they made to a convent guaranteed its continued association with, even dependence on, the world—that is, on *them*." Bilinkoff, *The Avila of Saint Teresa*, 140.

135. Bilinkoff, *The Avila of Saint Teresa*, 141–42.
136. Biilinkoff, *The Avila of Saint Teresa*, 143.
137. Bilinkoff, *The Avila of Saint Teresa*, 144.
138. Bilinkoff, *The Avila of Saint Teresa*, 145, 147.
139. She began the process of expanding her vision at the direction of Giovanni Battista Rubeo, the General of the Carmelite Order, who in 1567, asked her to establish "as many houses under the Discalced Rule as she had hairs on her head." Dicken, *The Crucible of Love*, 15.
140. Teresa established seven rural houses with rentas and nine urban houses in poverty. Bilinkoff, *The Avila of Saint Teresa*, 164.
141. In contrast, the unreformed Carmelites adopted measures in 1566 prohibiting entrance to Muslim and Jewish descendants. Bilinkoff, *The Avila of Saint Teresa*, 146–147.
142. Bilinkoff, *The Avila of Saint Teresa*, 147.
143. Slade, "St. Teresa as Social Reformer," 100.
144. Slade, "St. Teresa as Social Reformer," 100.
145. Bilinkoff, *The Avila of Saint Teresa*, 165.
146. Kavanaugh, "The Book of Her Life: Introduction," 46–47.
147. Kavanaugh, "The Book of Her Life: Introduction," 47. Ahlgren, *Teresa of Avila*, 50–51.
148. Ahlgren, *Teresa of Avila*, 54–60.
149. Kieran Kavanaugh, "Meditations on the Song of Songs: Introduction" in *Meditations on the Song of Songs*, trans. Kieran Kavanaugh and Otilio Rodriguez, The Collected Works of St. Teresa of Avila, Volume 2 (Washington: Institute of Carmelite Studies, 1980), 213.
150. Kieran Kavanaugh, "Interior Castle: Introduction," in *Interior Castle*, trans. Kieran Kavanaugh and Otilio Rodriguez, The Collected Works of St. Teresa of Avila, Volume 2 (Washington: Institute of Carmelite Studies, 1980), 264.
151. Kieran Kavanaugh, "Interior Castle: Introduction," 265 f.
152. Kieran Kavanaugh, "Interior Castle: Introduction," 265 f.
153. Ahlgren, *Teresa of Avila*, 63.
154. Dicken, *The Crucible of Love*, 15. Williams, *Teresa of Avila*, 7.
155. Teresa of Avila, *The Way of Perfection*, 265.
156. Francisco de Osuna, *Norte de Estados* (Seville, 1531), qtd in Kieran Kavanaugh, "The Way of Perfection," 23.
157. Ahlgren, *Teresa of Avila*, 143, 148.
158. Ward, "Introduction," 53.

159. Ward, "Introduction," 53.
160. Bilinkoff, *The Avila of Saint Teresa*, 200–201.

3. Teresa's Embodied Anthropology

1. Susan J. Brison, *Aftermath: Violence and the Remaking of a Self* (Princeton: Princeton University Press, 2002), 44.
2. E. W. Trueman Dicken, *The Crucible of Love: A Study of the Mysticism of St. Teresa of Jesus and St. John of the Cross* (New York: Sheed and Ward, 1963), 5–6.
3. Jane M. Grovijahn, "Theology as an Irruption into Embodiment: Our Need for God," *Theology and Sexuality* 9 (1998): 31.
4. Cristina Mazzoni, *Saint Hysteria: Neurosis, Mysticism, and Gender in European Culture* (Ithaca: Cornell University Press, 1996), 195.
5. Teresa of Avila, *The Book of Her Life*, trans. Kieran Kavanaugh and Otilio Rodriguez, The Collected Works of St. Teresa of Avila, Volume 1 (Washington: Institute of Carmelite Studies, 1976), 195.
6. Peter Tyler, "Teresa of Avila's Transformative Strategies of Embodiment in Meditations on the Song of Songs," in *Sources of Transformation: Revitalizing Christian Spirituality*, eds. Edward Howells and Peter Tyler (London: Continuum, 2010), 137–38.
7. Grovijahn, "Theology," 30.
8. Grovijahn, "Theology," 31.
9. Grovijahn, "Theology," 30.
10. Teresa of Avila, *The Book of Her Life*, 55.
11. Teresa of Avila, *The Book of Her Life*, 55.
12. Teresa of Avila, *The Book of Her Life*, 55.
13. Teresa of Avila, *The Book of Her Life*, 54.
14. Teresa of Avila, *The Book of Her Life*, 70.
15. Teresa of Avila, *The Book of Her Life*, 71.
16. See Lisa Fullam, "Teresa of Avila's Liberative Humility," *Journal of Moral Theology* 3, no. 1 (2014): 195.
17. Serene Jones, *Trauma and Grace: Theology in a Ruptured World* (Louisville: Westminster John Knox Press, 2009), 143–50.
18. Teresa of Avila, *The Book of Her Life*, 88.
19. Teresa of Avila, *The Book of Her Life*, 88.
20. Teresa of Avila, *The Book of Her Life*, 99.
21. Teresa of Avila, *The Book of Her Life*, 112.
22. See Chapter 1 of this book, particularly the first stage of Judith Herman's recovery process— "establishment of safety"—for a discussion of the importance of restoration of personal agency.
23. Teresa of Avila, *The Book of Her Life*, 118.
24. Teresa of Avila, *The Book of Her Life*, 124.
25. Teresa of Avila, *The Book of Her Life*, 118. *Emphasis added.*

26. Teresa of Avila, *Interior Castle*, trans. Kieran Kavanaugh and Otilio Rodriguez, The Collected Works of St. Teresa of Avila, Volume 2 (Washington: Institute of Carmelite Studies, 1980), 312.

27. Teresa of Avila, *Interior Castle*, 333.

28. Teresa of Avila, *Interior Castle*, 334.

29. In her study of Teresa's epistolary writings, *Teresa de Ávila: Lettered Woman*, Bárbara Mujica names four key correspondents to whom nearly half of all her letters were addressed: Jerónimo Gracián, María de San José, María Bautista, and Lorenzo de Cepeda. Barbara Mujica, *Teresa de Avila: Lettered Woman* (Nashville: Vanderbilt University Press, 2009), 103–39.

30. See Mujica, *Teresa de Ávila*, 108, citing Teresa of Avila, *The Collected Letters of St. Teresa of Avila, Volume 1*, trans. Kieran Kavanaugh (Washington, D.C.: Institute of Carmelite Studies, 2001) Oct. 1577: 1, and Teresa of Avila, *The Collected Letters of St. Teresa of Avila, Volume 2*, trans. Kieran Kavanaugh (Washington, D.C.: Institute of Carmelite Studies, 2007), 4 Oct. 1579: 2.

31. Mujica, *Teresa de Ávila*, 117, citing Teresa of Avila, *The Collected Letters of St. Teresa of Avila* Volume I, 11 July 1576: 6.

32. Mujica, *Teresa de Ávila*, 124.

33. Teresa of Avila, *The Collected Letters of St. Teresa of Avila* I, 17 Jan 1577: 13–14.

34. Teresa of Avila, *The Collected Letters of St. Teresa of Avila* I, 10 Feb 1577: 7.

35. Teresa of Avila, *The Collected Letters of St. Teresa of Avila* I, 27–28 Feb 1577: 6.

36. Laura Delaplain, *Cutting a New Path: Helping Survivors of Childhood Domestic Trauma* (Cleveland: United Church Press, 1997), 5. Certainly, however, anything is capable of triggering traumatic memories. See, for example, Serene Jones's account of "Leah" who experienced overwhelming disorientation at a communion service as she remembered the traumatic violence of her childhood. Jones, *Trauma and Grace*, 3–5.

37. Teresa of Avila, *The Collected Letters of St. Teresa of Avila* I, 27–28 Feb 1577: 3.

38. Teresa of Avila, *The Collected Letters of St. Teresa of Avila* I, 7 Dec 1577: 10.

39. Teresa of Avila, *The Book of Her Life*, 361.

40. Teresa of Avila, *The Book of Her Life*, 361.

41. Teresa of Avila, *The Letters of Saint Teresa*, trans. John Dalton (London: Thomas Baker, 1893), 16.

42. Jones, *Trauma and Grace*, 7.

43. Teresa of Avila, *The Book of Her Life*, 112.

44. Teresa of Avila, *The Book of Her Life*, 119.

45. Teresa of Avila, *The Book of Her Life*, 114.

46. Marilyn McCord Adams, "Praying Angry and Surviving Abuse," *Reverberations: New Directions in the Study of Prayer*, October 22, 2013. http://forums.ssrc.org/ndsp/2013/10/22/praying-angry-and-surviving-abuse/

47. Teresa of Avila, *The Book of Her Life*, 115.

48. Teresa of Avila, *The Book of Her Life*, 153.

49. Teresa of Avila, *The Book of Her Life*, 153–54.

50. Teresa of Avila, *The Book of Her Life*, 154.
51. Teresa of Avila, *Interior Castle*, 334.
52. Teresa of Avila, *The Book of Her Life*, 156.
53. Herman, *Trauma and Recovery*, 228.
54. Teresa of Avila, *The Book of Her Life*, 155.
55. Teresa of Avila, *The Book of Her Life*, 157.
56. Teresa of Avila, *The Book of Her Life*, 232.
57. Teresa of Avila, *The Book of Her Life*, 161.
58. Teresa of Avila, *The Book of Her Life*, 252.
59. Teresa of Avila, *Interior Castle*, 384.
60. Teresa of Avila, *Interior Castle*, 379.
61. Herman, *Trauma and Recovery*, 176.
62. Yarrow Morgan, "From Remember," in *I Never Told Anyone: Writings by Women Survivors of Child Sexual Abuse*, eds. Ellen Bass and Louise Thornton (New York: Harper Perennial, 1983), 89.
63. Mike Domitrz, *Voices of Courage: Inspiration from Survivors of Sexual Assault* (Greenfield: Awareness Publications, 2005), 93.
64. Edward Howells, *John of the Cross and Teresa of Avila: Mystical Knowing and Selfhood* (New York: Crossroad Publishing, 2002), 84–85.
65. Teresa of Avila, *Interior Castle*, 428.
66. Teresa of Avila, *Interior Castle*, 433.
67. Teresa of Avila, *Interior Castle*, 299.
68. Fullam, "Teresa of Avila's Liberative Humility," 195.
69. Teresa of Avila, *Interior Castle*, 438.
70. As Rowan Williams explains, "Teresa's concern is that the moral life should be lived without the deep corruptions of self-consciousness: the devil's work is to make us *interested* in our spiritual state in an obsessive way, whether this takes the form of self-satisfaction or of false humility, paralyzing anxiety about one's condition . . . Proper self-awareness is, for Teresa, the opposite of self-consciousness, not fascination with oneself but familiarity with oneself, candour about strengths and weaknesses, alertness to dangers." Rowan Williams, *Teresa of Avila* (Harrisburg: Morehouse Publishing, 1991), 100–1. *Emphasis in original.*
71. Teresa of Avila, *Interior Castle*, 439.
72. Herman, *Trauma and Recovery*, 207–11.
73. Ellen Bass, "Introduction: In the Truth Itself, There is Healing" in *I Never Told Anyone: Writings by Women Survivors of Child Sexual Abuse*, eds. Ellen Bass and Louise Thornton (New York: Harper Perennial, 1983), 53.
74. Teresa of Avila, *Interior Castle*, 442.
75. One should note that the peace felt here remains partial in at least two ways: first, this is always a provisional form of stability compared to that experienced after death; second, one feels at peace and in union with God *most* of the time while in this stage. Yet, this is not the truest form of peace, the most final peace, since there is always the danger of falling away from God as long as life goes on: "For, in the

end, people must always live with fear until You give them true peace and bring them there where that peace will be unending. I say 'true peace,' not because this peace is not true but because the first war could return if we were to withdraw from God." This is the state of the soul most of the time once it has reached this stage, but not strictly all of the time. Teresa of Avila, *Interior Castle*, 443–444.

76. Williams, *Teresa of Avila*, 138.
77. Teresa of Avila, *Interior Castle*, 448.
78. Teresa of Avila, *Interior Castle*, 435.
79. Teresa of Avila, *Interior Castle*, 446.
80. Teresa of Avila, *The Book of Her Life*, 154.
81. Tyler, "Teresa of Avila's Transformative Strategies," 142. *Emphasis added.* See also Howells who argues that this is an anthropological development between the *Vida* and the *Interior Castle* to involve the body and "worldly activity" in final union. Howells, *John of the Cross*, 79 ff.
82. Teresa of Avila, *The Book of Her Life*, 118.
83. Tyler, "Teresa of Avila's Transformative Strategies," 142.
84. The union of the full human person—interiorly and exteriorly—symbolized by the union of Martha and Mary, is patterned both after the union of human nature and divine nature in the person of Christ and after the union of three persons in the one God. For Teresa, the full union of the human person within herself and with God is possible because she has been created in the image of God. Howells, *John of the Cross*, 70, 96.
85. Teresa of Avila, *Interior Castle*, 448.
86. Teresa of Avila, *Interior Castle*, 450.
87. Howells, *John of the Cross*.

4. The Survivor as *Imago Dei*: Created for Friendship

1. Teresa of Avila, *The Book of Her Life*, trans. Kieran Kavanaugh and Otilio Rodriguez, The Collected Works of St. Teresa of Avila, Volume 1 (Washington: Institute of Carmelite Studies, 1976), 113.
2. Teresa of Avila, *The Book of Her Life*, 112.
3. Teresa of Avila, *The Book of Her Life*, 114, 119.
4. Teresa of Avila, *Interior Castle*, trans. Kieran Kavanaugh and Otilio Rodriguez, The Collected Works of St. Teresa of Avila, Volume 2 (Washington: Institute of Carmelite Studies, 1980), 291.
5. Teresa of Avila, *Interior Castle*, 293.
6. Teresa of Avila, *Interior Castle*, 291.
7. Teresa of Avila, *Interior Castle*, 284.
8. Teresa of Avila, *Interior Castle*, 283.
9. Teresa of Avila, *Interior Castle*, 291.
10. Pamela Cooper-White, *The Cry of Tamar: Violence against Women and the Church's Response*, second edition (Minneapolis: Fortress Press, 2012), 55.

11. Teresa of Avila, *Interior Castle*, 289.
12. Teresa of Avila, *Interior Castle*, 288.
13. Teresa of Avila, *Interior Castle*, 288–29.
14. Teresa of Avila, *Interior Castle*, 285–86.
15. Teresa of Avila, *Interior Castle*, 284.
16. Stephanie Krehbiel et al., "David Haas Report," *Into Account*, 4. https://intoaccount.org/wp-content/uploads/2020/12/Haas-Report-Narrative.pdf.
17. Krehbiel et al, "David Haas Report," 13.
18. Judith Lewis Herman, *Trauma and Recovery* (New York: Basic Books, 1992), 105.
19. Teresa of Avila, *Interior Castle*, 294.
20. Teresa of Avila, *Interior Castle*, 294.
21. Joan Miller, "Remain Here with Me," *America Magazine*, October 13, 2014.
22. Teresa of Avila, *Interior Castle*, 286.
23. Teresa of Avila, *Interior Castle*, 286.
24. Teresa of Avila, *Interior Castle*, 292.
25. Teresa of Avila, *Interior Castle*, 292.
26. Teresa of Avila, *Interior Castle*, 283.
27. Hilary Jerome Scarsella et al., "The Lord's Supper: A Ritual of Harm or Healing?" *Leader* (Summer 2016): 35.
28. Teresa of Avila, *Interior Castle*, 291.
29. Teresa of Avila, *Interior Castle*, 289.
30. As Teresa describes, using a fount of clear water as a metaphor for God, "in the case of a soul that through its own fault withdraws from this fount and plants itself in a place where the water is black and foul-smelling, everything that flows from it is equally wretched and filthy." Teresa of Avila, *Interior Castle*, 289.
31. The authors of Genesis etymologically relate humanity—'adham—to ground—'adhamah—or humus (soil). See *The New Oxford Annotated Bible of Apocrypha*, Revised Standard Version (1973): Genesis 2:7.
32. Fullam elaborates, Teresa's humility "bears no resemblance to the self-abasing servility so often lauded in the Christian tradition." Lisa Fullam, "Teresa of Avila's Liberative Humility," *Journal of Moral Theology* 3, no. 1 (2014): 195.
33. Teresa of Avila, *Interior Castle*, 283.
34. Fullam, "Teresa of Avila's Liberative Humility," 196.
35. Teresa of Avila, *The Book of Her Life*, 96, 106.
36. Scarsella et al., "The Lord's Supper," 35. For this reason, Scarsella elaborates that sin language and especially liturgical confessions of sin should not be limited to sin as self-prioritizing behavior. As I will argue, Teresa helpfully broadens sin language beyond self-prioritization to excessive self-abnegation, but she fails to explicitly acknowledge the effects of being sinned-against.
37. Teresa of Avila, *Interior Castle*, 293.
38. Teresa was convinced that the forces of evil can work against the individual in the process of achieving true humility by giving her a desire to overindulge in penance. Because Teresa understood one's health as an important tool for observing the rule and for expressing love for and service to one another, she is nervous that

sisters might practice such a penitential life that they might endanger their health. Teresa of Avila, *Interior Castle*, 312.

39. Teresa of Avila, *The Book of Her Life*, 124.
40. Teresa of Avila, *The Book of Her Life*, 166.
41. Teresa of Avila, *The Book of Her Life*, 170.
42. Michael Domitrz, ed., *Voices of Courage: Inspiration from Survivors of Sexual Assault* (Greenfield: Awareness Publications, 2005), 36–37.
43. Jane M. Grovijahn, "Theology as an Irruption into Embodiment: Our Need for God," *Theology and Sexuality* 9 (1998): 29.
44. Rita Nakashima Brock and Rebecca Ann Parker, *Proverbs of Ashes: Violence, Redemptive Suffering, and the Search for What Saves Us* (Boston: Beacon Press, 2001), 21.
45. Teresa of Avila, *The Book of Her Life*, 122.
46. Teresa of Avila, *The Book of Her Life*, 124.
47. Teresa of Avila, *The Book of Her Life*, 124.
48. See Herman, *Trauma and Recovery*, 51–56, 92–93, 137–38 and Craig Steven Titus, *Resilience and the Virtue of Fortitude* (Washington, D.C.: Catholic University Press, 2006), 207–208 for contemporary confirmations of Teresa's instincts on this point.
49. Herman, *Trauma and Recovery*, 93.
50. Teresa of Avila, *The Book of Her Life*, 130.
51. Rowan Williams, *Teresa of Avila* (Harrisburg: Morehouse Publishing, 1991), 115. See also Gillian Ahlgren who highlights that Teresa was more afraid of sloth (and its fruits, including despair) rather than pride. Gillian Ahlgren, *Teresa of Avila and the Politics of Sanctity* (Ithaca: Cornell University Press, 1996), 95
52. Williams, *Teresa of Avila*, 115.
53. Williams, *Teresa of Avila*, 116.
54. Edward Howells, *John of the Cross and Teresa of Avila: Mystical Knowing and Selfhood* (New York: Crossroad Publishing, 2002), 97.
55. Teresa of Avila, *Interior Castle*, 302.
56. Susan Shooter, *How Survivors of Abuse Relate to God: The Authentic Spirituality of the Annihilated Soul* (Burlington: Ashgate, 2012), 101.
57. Teresa of Avila, *Interior Castle*, 452.
58. Roxane Gay, *Hunger: A Memoir of (My) Body* (New York: HarperCollins, 2017), 20–21.
59. Donna Freitas, *Consent: A Memoir of Unwanted Attention* (New York: Little, Brown and Company, 2019), 288–89.
60. Teresa of Avila, *Interior Castle*, 289.
61. Grovijahn, "Theology as an Irruption," 31.
62. Teresa of Avila, *Interior Castle*, 289.
63. Kevin P. Considine, *Salvation for the Sinned-Against* (Eugene: Pickwick, 2015).
64. Kieran Kavanaugh, "The Way of Perfection: Introduction" in *The Way of Perfection*, trans. Kieran Kavanaugh and Otilio Rodriguez, The Collected Works

of St. Teresa of Avila, Volume 2 (Washington: Institute of Carmelite Studies, 1980), 20; Ahlgren, *Teresa of Avila*, 36; Barbara Mujica, *Teresa de Avila: Lettered Woman* (Nashville: Vanderbilt University Press, 2009), 9; and Williams, *Teresa of Avila*, 33–34.

65. She also, notably, was not convinced that violent force should be used to combat heresy. Williams, *Teresa of Avila*, 26.

66. Tara Soughers, "Friendship with Teresa of Avila: Spiritual Companionship Across Time and Space," *Spiritus* 14, no. 2 (Fall 2014): 172.

67. We are also oriented toward friendship with other species, though those relationships are not at the center of either Teresa's thought or this project. See, for example, Marcus Baynes-Rock, "In the Minds of Others," in *The Evolution of Human Wisdom* (Lanham: Lexington Books, 2017), 47–67 and Ben Campbell, "Growing Wisdom" in *The Evolution of Human Wisdom* (Lanham: Lexington Books, 2017), 71–84, for a fuller treatment of human beings in relationship to biotic and abiotic, non-human others.

68. Williams, *Teresa of Avila*, 103–4.

69. Teresa of Avila, *The Book of Her Life*, 98.

70. Teresa of Avila, *The Book of Her Life*, 96–97.

71. Williams, *Teresa of Avila*, 26.

72. One might object that, in advancing the image of friendship with oneself, I contradict a previous statement that friendship is a relationship between two *distinct* equals. But, here, just as Teresa bends our conception of who can be made equal in friendship (viz., the human person and God), Teresa can bend our sense of self and other. The human person is not strictly one thing, but contains a multitude of intersecting identities, as her "many dwelling places" might signify. This resonates with contemporary trauma theorists' understanding of subjectivity as "multiple and fluid." Cooper-White, *The Cry of Tamar*, 13.

73. Cathy Winkler, *One Night: Realities of Rape* (Walnut Creek: AltaMira Press, 2002), 13.

74. Herman, *Trauma and Recovery*, 83, 104–5, 192–93.

75. Williams, *Teresa of Avila*, 22.

76. Williams, *Teresa of Avila*, 22.

77. Williams, *Teresa of Avila*, 22.

78. Teresa of Avila, *The Way of Perfection*, trans. Kieran Kavanaugh and Otilio Rodriguez, The Collected Works of St. Teresa of Avila, Volume 2 (Washington: Institute of Carmelite Studies, 1980), 55.

79. Williams, *Teresa of Avila*, 103.

80. Williams, *Teresa of Avila*, 109.

81. Soughers, "Friendship with Teresa of Avila," 175.

82. See Lisa Fullam who argues that Teresa's presentation of humility draws sharp distinctions between the kind of humility that is needed in relationship with God and the kind that is needed in relationships with others—namely, "interpersonal humility is subject to limitation, humility before God is unmitigated" Fullam writes,

"It is this difference and interrelationship between interhuman humility and humility before God that marks Teresa's contribution to rehabilitating the suspect virtue of humility." Fullam, "Teresa of Avila's Liberative Humility," 182, 194.

83. Susan J. Brison, *Aftermath: Violence and the Remaking of a Self* (Princeton: Princeton University Press, 2002), 29. For this reason, Brison ultimately argues against a citadel model of the self in favor of a childbearing model of the self, yet Teresa's imagery does not fit the profile of a closed citadel that Brison imagines, since Teresa's castle is inherently relational.

84. Teresa of Avila, *The Book of Her Life*, 206.

85. Williams, *Teresa of Avila*. See, for example, Teresa of Avila, *The Book of Her Life*, 206–7.

86. Teresa of Avila, *The Book of Her Life*, 220.

87. Teresa of Avila, *The Book of Her Life*, 220.

88. Teresa of Avila, *The Book of Her Life*, 222.

89. Teresa of Avila, *The Book of Her Life*, 222.

90. Teresa of Avila, *Interior Castle*, 287.

91. Herman, *Trauma and Recovery* 137–38, 143, 197 ff.

92. Herman, *Trauma and Recovery*, 205.

93. Williams, *Teresa of Avila*, 92.

5. Edward Schillebeeckx's Theology of Suffering

1. See for example James Hal Cone, *A Black Theology of Liberation* (Philadelphia: Lippincott, 1970) and Delores Williams, *Sisters in the Wilderness: The Challenge of Womanist God-Talk* (Maryknoll: Orbis Books, 1993).

2. Gustavo Gutiérrez, *A Theology of Liberation: History, Politics, and Salvation* (Maryknoll: Orbis, 1973).

3. Elizabeth Bettenhausen, "Foreword" in *Christianity, Patriarchy, and Abuse: A Feminist Critique* (New York: Pilgrim Press, 1989), xii.

4. Bettenhausen, "Foreword," xii.

5. Scott Schieman, "Socioeconomic Status and Beliefs about God's Influence in Everyday Life," *Sociology of Religion* 71, no. 1 (2010): 25–51.

6. See, for example, Joanne Carlson Brown and Rebecca Parker who argue that traditional Christianity glorifies child abuse as salvific and acculturates women into accepting suffering as redemptive. Joanne C. Brown and Rebecca Ann Parker, "For God So Loved the World?" in *Christianity, Patriarchy, and Abuse: A Feminist Critique*, eds. Joanne Brown and Carole Bohn (New York: Pilgrim Press, 1989), 1–30.

7. Edward Schillebeeckx, *Church: The Human Story of God*, trans. John Bowden, The Collected Works of Edward Schillebeeckx, Volume 10 (London: Bloomsbury/T&T Clark, 2014), 60 [62].

8. Schillebeeckx, *Church*, 83 [085].

9. Benjamin Mueller, "For Hotel Workers, Weinstein Allegations Put a Spotlight on Harassment," *The New York Times*, December 17, 2017.

10. Schillebeeckx, *Church*, 83 [085].
11. Schillebeeckx, *Church*, xxvii [xix].
12. Schillebeeckx, *Church*, 4 [004].
13. Schillebeeckx, *Church*, 32 [033].
14. See, for example, the papal endorsement of slavery in Africa, *Romanus Pontifex* in 1455, and *Sublimis Deus* in 1537, that forbade the enslavement of Indigenous Americans on the basis that they are rational persons with souls, though its issuer—Pope Paul II—did not oppose the transatlantic slave trade from Africa on the same grounds.
15. Augustine, *De Trinitate* XII. See also *Inter Insignores* (1976) for the argument by Pope Paul VI that men image Christ in ways that women cannot. Interestingly, Paul VI invokes the legacy of Teresa of Avila as evidence of the honor that the Roman Catholic Church bestows upon women (without allowing women's ordination) and promulgates this declaration on her feast day: October 15th.
16. *Persona Humana* (1975).
17. It is notoriously difficult to obtain comprehensive data on perpetrator rates, in part, because accurate data relies on perpetrators' transparency. But it seems, for example, that rates of Roman Catholic priests, who have been credibly accused of sexually abusing minors, is roughly parallel with rates of admitted perpetration in the general public. See http://www.bishop-accountability.org/AtAGlance/data_priests.htm., and Michele L. Ybarra and Kimberly J. Mitchell, "Prevalence Rates of Male and Female Sexual Violence Perpetrators in a National Sample of Adolescents," *JAMA Pediatrics* 167, no. 12 (December 1, 2013): 1125–34.
18. Theresa W. Tobin, "Religious Faith in the Unjust Meantime: The Spiritual Violence of Clergy Sexual Abuse," *Feminist Philosophy Quarterly* 5, no. 2 (2019): Article 5, especially Tobin's analysis of Kathleen Dwyer as a case study, pages 11–14.
19. Edward Schillebeeckx, *Christ. The Christian Experience in the Modern World*, trans. John Bowden, The Collected Works of Edward Schillebeeckx, Volume 7 (London: Bloomsbury/T&T Clark, 2014), 741 [746].
20. Schillebeeckx, *Christ*, 717–18 [724–25].
21. Schillebeeckx, *Christ*, 718 [725].
22. Schillebeeckx, *Christ*, 718 [725].
23. Schillebeeckx, *Christ*, 718 [726].
24. Schillebeeckx, *Christ*, 720 [727]. *Emphasis in original.*
25. Schillebeeckx argues that even though some scriptural texts support the idea that God both gives and destroys life, Israel came to reject that idea overtime. Schillebeeckx, *Christ*, 720 [727].
26. Sarah Michal Greathouse et al, *A Review of the Literature on Sexual Assault Perpetrator Characteristics and Behaviors* (Santa Monica: RAND Corporation, 2015), and Pamela Cooper-White, *The Cry of Tamar: Violence against Women and the Church's Response*, second edition (Minneapolis: Fortress Press, 2012), 189.
27. Schillebeeckx, *Christ*, 722 [729].
28. Schillebeeckx, *Christ*, 722 [729].

29. Edward Schillebeeckx, "Liberating Theology," in *Essays: Ongoing Theological Quests*, The Collected Works of Edward Schillebeeckx, Volume 11 (London: Bloomsbury/T&T Clark, 2014), 78.

30. Edward Schillebeeckx, *God the Future of Man*, trans. N.D. Smith, The Collected Works of Edward Schillebeeckx, Volume 3 (London: Bloomsbury/T&T Clark, 2014), 83 [136].

31. Schillebeeckx, *God the Future of Man*, 83, 84 [136, 137].

32. Michael Domitrz, ed., *Voices of Courage: Inspiration from Survivors of Sexual Assault* (Greenfield: Awareness Publications, 2005), 73–74.

33. Audrey Savage, *Twice Raped* (Indianapolis: Book Weaver, 1990), 169.

34. Schillebeeckx, *God the Future of Man*, 83 [136].

35. Schillebeeckx, *Church*, 5, 6 [005, 006].

36. Schillebeeckx, *God the Future of Man*, 83 [136].

37. Schillebeeckx, "Liberating Theology," 79.

38. Schillebeeckx, "Liberating Theology," 78.

39. One should note that Schillebeeckx does not seem to think that any persons' life—however horrific—is completely devoid of any of this sharpening positive experience. Some trauma scholars, especially upon witnessing the depths of harm that human beings are capable of inflicting upon others, feel uncomfortable about this kind of optimism. I, however, remain hopeful that all human lives contain some positive experiences, though, of course, I recognize that such universal proclamations are impossible to judge in the abstract and ultimate judgment of the quality of one's experiences must be left to each sufferer.

40. Schillebeeckx, *God the Future of Man*, 93 [154].

41. Edward Schillebeeckx, *Jesus: An Experiment in Christology*, trans. John Bowden, The Collected Works of Edward Schillebeeckx, Volume 6 (London: Bloomsbury/T&T Clark, 2014), 7 [24].

42. Susan Shooter, *How Survivors of Abuse Relate to God: The Authentic Spirituality of the Annihilated Soul* (Burlington: Ashgate, 2012), 58.

43. Schillebeeckx, *Jesus*, 582–83 [620–21].

44. Schillebeeckx, *Jesus*, 583–84 [622].

45. Schillebeeckx, *Jesus*, 584 [622].

46. Schillebeeckx, *God the Future of Man*, 92–93 [154–55], cf. 95–96 [158–59]. One should note that the second stage of reflection does not always go well, meaning one can act incorrectly or even unjustly on a good intuition upon further reflection. One can opt to act violently, taking out one's rage on others and making more victims of sin rather than to act creatively to dismantle structures of evil.

47. Schillebeeckx, *Christ*, 788 [792].

48. Schillebeeckx, *Christ*, 727–28 [733–34].

49. Edward Schillebeeckx, "Experience and Faith," in *Essays: Ongoing Theological Quests*, The Collected Works of Edward Schillebeeckx, Volume 11 (London: Bloomsbury/T&T Clark, 2014), 17.

50. Schillebeeckx, "Experience and Faith," 16.

51. Schillebeeckx, "Experience and Faith," 16–17.
52. Schillebeeckx, "Experience and Faith," 17.
53. Schillebeeckx, *Christ*, 733 [739].
54. Schillebeeckx, "Experience and Faith," 17.
55. Schillebeeckx, *Christ*, 734 [740].
56. Schillebeeckx, *Christ*, 735 [741].
57. Schillebeeckx, *Christ*, 735–36 [741].
58. Theresa W. Tobin, "Religious Faith," Article 5, and Marilyn McCord Adams, "Praying Angry and Surviving Abuse," *Reverberations: New Directions in the Study of Prayer*, October 22, 2013. http://forums.ssrc.org/ndsp/2013/10/22/praying-angry-and-surviving-abuse/
59. Schillebeeckx, *Christ*, 736 [741].
60. Schillebeeckx, *Christ*, 726 [732].
61. Schillebeeckx, *Christ*, 725 [731].
62. Schillebeeckx, *Christ*, 740 [745].
63. Shelly Rambo, *Spirit and Trauma: A Theology of Remaining* (Louisville: Westminster John Knox Press, 2010), 74–80.
64. I have referred here to the importance of the body primarily by appealing to Schillebeeckx's later works, especially his formulation of material well-being as integral to human salvation in his discussion of the anthropological constants. Schillebeeckx, *Christ*, 728–37 [734–43]. One should also note, however, the body has been integral to Schillebeeckx from the beginning of his career. See Edward Schillebeeckx, *Christ the Sacrament of the Encounter with God*, The Collected Works of Edward Schillebeeckx, Volume 1 (London: Bloomsbury/T&T Clark, 2014).
65. Edward Schillebeeckx, *On Christian Faith: The Spiritual, Ethical, and Political Dimensions* (New York: Crossroad, 1987), 55.
66. Schillebeeckx, *On Christian Faith*, 28.
67. Schillebeeckx, *On Christian Faith*, 31.

6. The Story of Jesus and the Mystical-Political Shape of Salvation

1. Edward Schillebeeckx, *Christ. The Christian Experience in the Modern World*, trans. John Bowden, The Collected Works of Edward Schillebeeckx, Volume 7 (London: Bloomsbury/T&T Clark, 2014), 722 [729].
2. Schillebeeckx, *Christ*, 722 [729].
3. Schillebeeckx, *Christ*, 722 [729].
4. Serene Jones, *Trauma and Grace: Theology in a Ruptured World* (Louisville: Westminster John Knox Press, 2009), 123, 82.
5. Jones, *Trauma and Grace*, 164.
6. Jones, *Trauma and Grace*, 72.
7. Jones, *Trauma and Grace*, 148.
8. Edward Schillebeeckx, *Church: The Human Story of God*, trans. John Bowden, The Collected Works of Edward Schillebeeckx, Volume 10 (London: Bloomsbury/T&T Clark, 2014), 7 [007].

9. Schillebeeckx, *Church*, 32 [33].

10. Schillebeeckx, *Church*, 85 [087].

11. Schillebeeckx, *Church*, 34 [034] and Edward Schillebeeckx, *God Among Us: The Gospel Proclaimed*, trans. John Bowden (New York: Crossroad, 1983), 127.

12. Edward Schillebeeckx, *Jesus: An Experiment in Christology*, trans. John Bowden, The Collected Works of Edward Schillebeeckx, Volume 6 (London: Bloomsbury/T&T Clark, 2014), 228 [257].

13. Schillebeeckx, *Jesus*, 230 [259]. For a different reading of "Abba" in an early Christian context see Mary Rose D'Angelo, "Abba and 'father': Imperial Theology and the Jesus Traditions," *Journal of Biblical Literature* 111, no. 4 (Winter 1992): 611–30. D'Angelo disputes the attribution of the term "Abba" to Jesus himself, as well as the suggestion that the term, by the early Church, indicates a relationship of intimacy. Instead, D'Angelo argues that the use of the term "Abba" by early Christians, including the Gospel writers, should be read in the context of imperial resistance. Therefore, though D'Angelo argues against Schillebeeckx's reading of the biblical literature, her conclusions are similar: the Christian experience of God as "for" humanity, especially in their struggles for liberation, has something to do with reference to God as "Abba."

14. One should note that use of the term "Abba" is not used as evidence of Jesus's unique relationship with God. It does not refer to a divine self-understanding, apart from his fellow human beings. Because the Christian community later takes up this practice of addressing God, we can assume that Jesus's teaching (and indeed, his personal conviction as well) was that humanity enjoys an intimate relationship with God as a child does to its parent. Schillebeeckx, *Jesus*, 230–32 [260–61].

15. Schillebeeckx, *Jesus*, 238 [268].

16. Note that this does not imply that the championing of the human cause apart from or over the cause of the rest of creation. If that were to be the case, it would represent some of the worst forms of environmental conquest (bad on its own) and inevitably lead to the oppression of the poorest members of humanity (even worse, and obviously contrary to Schillebeeckx's explicit intention). He is merely identifying God's cause as the cause of humanity in contrast to an image of God as indifferent to suffering or, even worse, requiring suffering in repayment for sin.

17. Schillebeeckx, *Jesus*, 239 [269].

18. Schillebeeckx, *Jesus*, 270 [302]. Some scholars refer to this enduring trust in God as "obedience"—see, for example, Kathleen McManus, *Unbroken Communion: The Place and Meaning of Suffering in the Theology of Edward Schillebeeckx* (Oxford: Rowman & Littlefield Publishers, Inc., 2003), 4—although I intentionally refrain from using "obedience" in the main body of this text because of the negative connotations it can carry for survivors of abuse at the hands of authority figures (especially parents and clergy). To properly capture McManus's sense of obedience as a relational term connoting "committed trust and unbroken communion" rather than a term connoting fear of retribution or disappointment, would require more nuance than space allows here.

19. Schillebeeckx, *Jesus*, 276 [308].
20. Edward Schillebeeckx, "God the Living One," *New Blackfriars* 62 (1981): 369.
21. Schillebeeckx, *Jesus*, 270 [302].
22. Schillebeeckx, *Jesus*, 237–38 [267].
23. Susan Shooter, *How Survivors of Abuse Relate to God: The Authentic Spirituality of the Annihilated Soul* (Burlington: Ashgate, 2012), 63.
24. Rita Nakashima Brock and Rebecca Ann Parker, *Proverbs of Ashes: Violence, Redemptive Suffering, and the Search for What Saves Us* (Boston: Beacon Press, 2001), 3.
25. Schillebeeckx, *Jesus*, 278 [311].
26. Helen Bergin, "The Death of Jesus and Its Impact on God—Jürgen Moltmann and Edward Schillebeeckx," *Irish Theological Quarterly* 52, no. 3 (1986): 195.
27. Schillebeeckx, *Christ*, 823–24 [828].
28. Michael Domitrz, ed., *Voices of Courage: Inspiration from Survivors of Sexual Assault* (Greenfield: Awareness Publications, 2005), 1–2.
29. Furthermore, he was known to have had a close relationship with John the Baptist, thus increasing his chances of getting in lethal trouble. Schillebeeckx, *Jesus*, 267–68 [299].
30. Schillebeeckx, *Jesus*, 274 [306].
31. Schillebeeckx, *Jesus*, 278 [311].
32. Schillebeeckx, *Christ*, 821 [825].
33. Schillebeeckx, *Christ*, 820–21 [825].
34. Schillebeeckx, *Church*, 7 [007].
35. Schillebeeckx, *God Among Us*, 133.
36. Schillebeeckx, *Church*, 87–88 [90].
37. Edward Schillebeeckx, "Theological Quests," in *Essays: Ongoing Theological Quests*, The Collected Works of Edward Schillebeeckx, Volume 11 (London: Bloomsbury/T&T Clark, 2014), 159. Bergin, "The Death of Jesus," 197.
38. Domitrz, *Voices of Courage*, 44–45.
39. Susan Estrich, *Real Rape: How the Legal System Victimizes Women Who Say No* (Cambridge: Harvard University Press, 1987), 3.
40. Edward Schillebeeckx, "The Mystery of Injustice and the Mystery of Mercy: Questions Concerning Human Suffering," in *Tijdschrift Voor Theologie*, ed. Michael Fitzpatrick, Volume 15 (1975), 19.
41. Bergin, "The Death of Jesus," 208.
42. Edward Schillebeeckx, *On Christian Faith: The Spiritual, Ethical, and Political Dimensions* (New York: Crossroad, 1987), 27, 19–20.
43. Schillebeeckx, "The Mystery of Injustice and the Mystery of Mercy," 24.
44. Schillebeeckx explains, "The resurrection is, therefore, also the eschatological beginning of the actual conquest of the history of suffering." The only kind of unreconciled suffering at the eschaton will be the refusal to love. Schillebeeckx, "The Mystery of Injustice and the Mystery of Mercy," 20.
45. Schillebeeckx, *Christ*, 722 [729].

46. Edward Schillebeeckx, *For the Sake of the Gospel*, trans. John Bowden (New York: Crossroad, 1990), 96.

47. Schillebeeckx, *On Christian Faith*, 7.

48. Janet O'Meara, "Salvation: Living Communion with God," *The Praxis of the Reign of God: An Introduction to the Theology of Edward Schillebeeckx*, second edition, eds. Mary Catherine Hilkert and Robert J. Schreiter (New York: Fordham University Press, 2002), 114.

49. Schillebeeckx, *Christ*, 816–17 [820–21].

50. Schillebeeckx, "The Mystery of Injustice and the Mystery of Mercy," 24. Schillebeeckx, *Christ*, 831–32 [836].

51. Theresa W. Tobin, "Religious Faith in the Unjust Meantime: The Spiritual Violence of Clergy Sexual Abuse," *Feminist Philosophy Quarterly* 5, no. 2, article 5 (2019): 13. See also Robert Orsi, "Praying Angry," *Reverberations: New Directions in the Study of Prayer*, August 27, 2013 (http://forums.ssrc.org/ndsp/2013/08/27/praying-angry/), and Marilyn McCord Adams, "Praying Angry and Surviving Abuse," *Reverberations: New Directions in the Study of Prayer*, October 22, 2013 (http://forums.ssrc.org/ndsp/2013/10/22/praying-angry-and-surviving-abuse/).

52. Brock and Parker, *Proverbs of Ashes*, 199.

53. Brock and Parker, *Proverbs of Ashes*, 215.

54. Edward Schillebeeckx, "Experience and Faith," in *Essays: Ongoing Theological Quests*, The Collected Works of Edward Schillebeeckx, Volume 11 (London: Bloomsbury/T&T Clark, 2014), 31.

55. Audrey Savage, *Twice Raped* (Indianapolis: Book Weaver, 1990), 170.

56. Julia Baird and Hayley Gleeson, "'Submit to Your Husbands': Women Told to Endure Domestic Violence in the Name of God," ABC News (Australian Broadcasting Corporation)," October 22, 2018, http://mobile.abc.net.au/news/2017-07-18/domestic-violence-church-submit-to-husbands/8652028.

57. John Sheveland, "Redeeming Trauma: An Agenda for Theology Fifteen Years On," in *American Catholicism in the 21st Century: Crossroads, Crisis, or Renewal?* eds. Nicholas Rademacher and Benjamin Peters (Maryknoll. Orbis Books, 2018), 137–48.

58. Edward Schillebeeckx, "Culture, Religion and Violence: Theology as a Component of Culture," in *Essays: Ongoing Theological Quests*, The Collected Works of Edward Schillebeeckx, Volume 11 (London: Bloomsbury/T&T Clark, 2014), 173–74.

59. Schillebeeckx, "Culture, Religion and Violence," 174.

60. Schillebeeckx, *Christ*, 9 [025].

61. Edward Schillebeeckx, "God, Society and Human Salvation," in *Faith and Society: Acta Congressus Internationalis Theologici Lovaniensis 1976*, ed. Marc Caudron (Paris: Duculot, 1978), 99.

62. As Schillebeeckx puts it, "Where human liberation is possible, it remains a universal human task in the name of the Creator God, the redeemer." Schillebeeckx, *Christ*, 763 [765].

63. Edward Schillebeeckx, "Liberating Theology," in *Essays: Ongoing Theological Quests*, The Collected Works of Edward Schillebeeckx, Volume 11 (London: Bloomsbury/T&T Clark, 2014), 83.

64. Schillebeeckx, "Liberating Theology," 83.

65. Edward Schillebeeckx, *God the Future of Man*, trans. N.D. Smith, The Collected Works of Edward Schillebeeckx, Volume 3 (London: Bloomsbury/T&T Clark, 2014), 115 [190].

66. Edward Schillebeeckx, "Towards a Rediscovery of the Christian Sacraments: Ritualising Religious Elements in Daily Life," in *Essays: Ongoing Theological Quests*, vol. 11, The Collected Works of Edward Schillebeeckx (London: Bloomsbury/T&T Clark, 2014) 187.

67. Schillebeeckx, "Towards a Rediscovery of the Christian Sacraments," 187.

68. Schillebeeckx, *Christ*, 741 [746].

69. For Schillebeeckx, Jesus is the revelation of the "supreme possibility of human life"—a whole, healthy, and happy human person. Thus, Jesus brings together God and humanity in one person embodying both the "'parable of [hu]man[ity]' (i.e., the person committed to God) and the 'parable of God' (i.e., the God committed to persons)." Edward Schillebeeckx, "Can Christology Be an Experiment?" *Proceedings of the Catholic Theological Society of America*, vol. 35 (1980): 13, 14. Bergin, "The Death of Jesus," 205.

70. Judith Lewis Herman, "Justice from the Victim's Perspective," *Violence Against Women* 11, no. 5 (May 2005): 585.

71. Herman, "Justice from the Victim's Perspective," 594–597.

72. Schillebeeckx, "God, Society and Human Salvation," 91.

73. Schillebeeckx, *On Christian Faith*, 19–20.

74. Schillebeeckx, *On Christian Faith*, 18, 20.

75. Schillebeeckx, *Jesus*, 151, 153, 244–51 [174, 177, 274–82].

76. Schillebeeckx, *Jesus*, 157 [179].

77. Schillebeeckx, *Jesus*, 175–81 [200–206].

78. Schillebeeckx, *Jesus*, 181 [206]. As Schillebeeckx explains, "Jesus' earthly career and ministry demonstrate the praxis of the kingdom of God, which he preached and implemented. In his earthly, historical life the eschatological praxis of the coming reign of God was already discernible in the dimension of human history here on earth . . . in this concrete Jesus phenomenon proclamation, praxis and person seem to be inseparable." Schillebeeckx, *Jesus*, 188 [213].

79. For example, Susan Calef notes that the hemorrhaging woman in Mark 5 spent all she had, seeking relief from physicians and was finally healed by Jesus who exacted no funds from her. Susan Calef, "Taking Up the Cross: Suffering and Discipleship in the Gospel of Mark," in *Suffering and the Christian Life*, ed. Richard W. Miller (Maryknoll: Orbis Books, 2013), 58–65.

80. John Dominic Crossan, *The Historical Jesus: The Life of a Mediterranean Jewish Peasant* (New York: HarperOne, 1991).

81. Edward Schillebeeckx, "Theological Interpretation of Faith in 1983," in *Essays: Ongoing Theological Quests*, The Collected Works of Edward Schillebeeckx, Volume 11 (London: Bloomsbury/T&T Clark, 2014), 55.

82. Schillebeeckx, *Jesus*, 192, 179, 132, 29–30 [218, 204, 152, 150]. Schillebeeckx, *On Christian Faith*, 20.

83. Schillebeeckx, "Experience and Faith," 19.

84. Schillebeeckx, "Experience and Faith," 19.

85. As psychiatrist Judith Herman argues, "if one set out intentionally to design a system for provoking symptoms of traumatic stress, it might look very much like a court of law." Herman, "Justice from the Victim's Perspective," 574.

86. Herman, "Justice from the Victim's Perspective," 581.

87. Catharine A. MacKinnon, *Toward a Feminist Theory of the State* (Cambridge: Harvard University Press, 1991).

88. Megan K. McCabe, "A Feminist Catholic Response to the Social Sin of Rape Culture," *Journal of Religious Ethics* 46, no. 4 (2018): 635–57.

89. Schillebeeckx, "Experience and Faith," 19.

90. McCabe, "A Feminist Catholic Response," 648.

91. Hilary Jerome Scarsella, "Victimization via Ritualization: Christian Communion and Systems of Sexualized Violence," in *Trauma and Lived Religion: Transcending the Ordinary*, eds. R. Ruard Ganzevoort and Srdjan Sremac (London: Palgrave MacMillan, 2019), 226. See also Theresa Tobin's case study of Ann Hagan Webb who was raped by a priest with a crucifix. Tobin argues that using a crucifix as an instrument of sexual abuse sets up the victim to see her own suffering as redemptive since it parallels Jesus's suffering which redeems the world. Tobin, "Religious Faith," 11, 20–21.

92. See, for example, Steven J. Cole, "Living with a Difficult Husband," *Flagstaff Christian Fellowship*, 1992, http://www.fcfonline.org/content/1/sermons/092092M.pdf.

93. This is from the account of "Maria" reported in *America Magazine*. Simcha Fisher, "How the Church Can Help (or Hurt) Women in Abusive Marriages," *America Magazine*, June 26, 2018, https://www.americamagazine.org/faith/2018/06/26/how-church-can-help-or-hurt-women-abusive-marriages.

94. Fisher, How the Church."

95. Schillebeeckx, *Christ*, 739 [744].

96. Schillebeeckx, *On Christian Faith*, 70. Emphasis added.

97. Schillebeeckx, *On Christian Faith*, 72.

98. Schillebeeckx, *On Christian Faith*, 71–72.

99. Schillebeeckx, *On Christian Faith*, 71.

100. Schillebeeckx, *On Christian Faith*, 72.

101. Schillebeeckx, *Church*, 67 [68–69]. Edward Schillebeeckx, "Foreword," *Poetry of Hadewijch*, Studies in Spirituality, Supplement 3 (Peeters, 1998): 1.

102. Schillebeeckx, *Church*, 67–68 [69–70].

103. Schillebeeckx, "The Mystery of Injustice and the Mystery of Mercy," 15.
104. Schillebeeckx, *Church*, 70 [072].
105. Schillebeeckx, *Church*, 75 [77].
106. Elisabeth Schussler Fiorenza identifies the roots of this competitive interpretation in Origen and Augustine and argues that a more contemporary version of this Martha-Mary competition tends to pit social activism and love of neighbor against love of God. Elisabeth Schussler Fiorenza, "A Feminist Critical Interpretation for Liberation: Martha and Mary: Luke 10:38–42," *Religion and Intellectual Life* 3, no. 2 (1986): 27.
107. See Peter Tyler, "Teresa of Avila's Transformative Strategies of Embodiment in Meditations on the Song of Songs" in *Sources of Transformation: Revitalizing Christian Spirituality*, eds. Edward Howells and Peter Tyler (London: Continuum, 2010), 142, and Teresa of Avila, *Interior Castle*, trans. Kieran Kavanaugh and Otilio Rodriguez, The Collected Works of St. Teresa of Avila, Volume 2 (Washington: Institute of Carmelite Studies, 1980), 448.
108. Shannon Sullivan, *The Physiology of Sexist and Racist Oppression* (Oxford: Oxford University Press, 2015).
109. Schillebeeckx, "Theological Quests," 142, 159.

7. Courage in the Work of Posttraumatic Healing

1. Edward Schillebeeckx, *Church: The Human Story of God*, trans. John Bowden, The Collected Works of Edward Schillebeeckx, Volume 10 (London: Bloomsbury/T&T Clark, 2014), 6 [006].
2. Jane M. Grovijahn, "Theology as an Irruption into Embodiment: Our Need for God," *Theology and Sexuality* 9 (1998): 33.
3. Flora Keshgegian, *Redeeming Memories: A Theology of Healing and Transformation* (Nashville: Abingdon, 2000), 45.
4. Even on the personal level, Flora Keshgegian argues, the healing process involves the personal development of a critical, social-political analysis: "Another step of healing comes when the survivor is able to move from blaming herself—for the abuse and idealizing the perpetrator and/or the family—to a different perspective on what happened. In order to claim her agency, she may well adopt a new understanding of family and society, beyond denial and toward a critical, political analysis. She may also develop insight into the ideological structures that supported the denial and self-blame, including religious systems." Keshgegian, *Redeeming Memories*, 54.
5. Judith Herman explains, "Political captivity is generally recognized, whereas the domestic captivity of women and children is often unseen. . . . In domestic captivity, physical barriers to escape are rare. In most homes, even the most oppressive, there are no bars on the windows, no barbed wire fences. Women and children are not ordinarily chained, though even this occurs more often than one might think. The barriers to escape are generally invisible. They are nonetheless

extremely powerful. Children are rendered captive by their condition of dependency. Women are rendered captive by economic, social, psychological, and legal subordination, as well as by physical force." Judith Lewis Herman, *Trauma and Recovery* (New York: Basic Books, 1992), 74.

6. Edward Schillebeeckx, *Christ. The Christian Experience in the Modern World*, trans. John Bowden, The Collected Works of Edward Schillebeeckx, Volume 7 (London: Bloomsbury/T&T Clark, 2014), 641 [651–52].

7. Herman, *Trauma and Recovery*, 211. *Emphasis added.*

8. Craig Steven Titus, *Resilience and the Virtue of Fortitude* (Washington, D.C.: Catholic University Press, 2006), 207.

9. Pamela Cooper-White argues that sexual violence survivors' most common grievance with Christian religious leaders and counselors is the pressure to forgive those who have harmed them. Pamela Cooper-White, *The Cry of Tamar: Violence against Women and the Church's Response*, second edition (Minneapolis: Fortress Press, 2012), 251. ABC News of Australia reported, in 2017, that Australian Christians who approached their pastors about domestic violence were frequently advised to forgive their partners and submit sexually to them. Julia Baird and Hayley Gleeson, "'Submit to your husbands': Women told to endure domestic violence in the name of God," ABC News Australia. http://www.abc.net.au/news/2017-07-18/domestic-violence-church-submit-to-husbands/8652028 July 2017. This kind of advice directly opposes that which is best for the victim-survivor's healing. As Hilary Scarsella et al. argue, "when victims of sexual abuse understand forgiveness to mean letting go of their anger at the perpetrator or staying in relationship with him, her, or them, it functions as a major obstacle to a victim's ability to get out of the violent situation and find safety. It demolishes the victim's first line of defense—anger—and keeps the one being harmed in close enough physical and emotional proximity to the perpetrator that the abuse can continue." Hilary Jerome Scarsella and et al., "The Lord's Supper: A Ritual of Harm or Healing?" *Leader* (Summer 2016): 36.

10. Quality pastoral resources for sexually abused individuals tend to address questions about Jesus's teaching on forgiveness head on, deliberately signaling the importance of accountability and recognition of the harm suffered. For example, in a pastoral resource for abused women, Marie Fortune skillfully interprets Jesus's teachings on forgiveness, noting that the Gospel of Luke (17:1–4) describes Christian forgiveness as subsequent to both rebuke and repentance. Fortune explains, "To repent, in both the Old and New Testaments, means to turn away from, to change, never to repeat again. True repentance on the part of the abuser means that he never hits again and that he learns to relate to other people in ways that are not controlling, demanding, and dominating. [. . .] Only when you have seen true repentance (and over a period of time) can you consider forgiveness." She adds that some survivors may be able to forgive their perpetrators without the perpetrator's repentance, only if they have experienced some sense of accountability for the perpetrator's actions elsewhere—e.g., through the recognition of a supportive

church community who hears and believes the survivor's story, through justice delivered by the court system, or through some other system of community accountability. When, and if, forgiveness is granted by the victim-survivor, it is important to remember that it is for the victim-survivor's own benefit and her continued survival—not for healing the abuser. As Fortune writes, "Forgiveness means putting that experience in perspective, putting it behind you, and not allowing it to continue to victimize you. You can let go of it; you can remember it only when you need to. This is part of your healing of the pain of those experiences. Forgiveness is for you, not for the abuser. His repentance, not your forgiveness, is what will finally bring about his healing. Your forgiveness of him frees you from the memories of those experiences." Marie M. Fortune, *Sexual Violence: The Unmentionable Sin* (New York: Pilgrim Press, 1983), 47–50.

11. Nancy Nason-Clark argues that Christian women are especially vulnerable to taking on responsibility for the reform of family members who sexually violate them. She explains:

> across the contemporary Christian landscape (Protestant and Catholic alike) there is persistent and overwhelming nostalgia for 'the family' and a pining for a bygone era when families were believed to stick it out through 'thick and thin,' with death the only divide. One of the by-products of this fascination with family togetherness is the failure family members feel— wives and children in particular—when they participate in a family characterized by unhappiness, conflict, or abuse. Since women are expected to set the 'tone' that pervades the family home, they are particularly sensitive to failure and guilt when family life or their marital relationship is marked by tension, fear, and physical battery. While women not connected with religious communities also experience feelings of failure at the dissolution of marriage, the focus on the *sacredness of the family unit* serves to exacerbate this experience for religious women. As a result, women connected to churches, and especially conservative faith traditions, stay in abusive marriages longer and work harder at marriage repair.

Nancy Nason-Clark, *The Battered Wife: How Christians Confront Family Violence* (Louisville: Westminster John Knox Press, 1997), 109–10. *Emphasis in original.* There is evidence that Christian pastors are typically aware of women's "commitment to family stability," and the way that it functions to keep women in domestically abusive situations. Yet pastors tend to have a much harder time identifying the ways in which "economic and social pressures" make it difficult for women to leave. Nason-Clark interprets this to be "a reflection of conservative clergy's overemphasis on personal responsibility for life events, coupled with a reluctance to see the role of structural inequalities in the system that impact women's lives." Another factor that limits Christian pastors' effectiveness in ministering to those who are victims of sexual violence is that, while they are aware that domestic violence is a problem, they frequently assume that rates of violence are higher in communities other than that in which they are ministering. In other words, they tend to assume that domestic violence is a problem "out there," but not in their own church community. Nason-Clark, *The Battered Wife*, 59, 62–63

12. As ethicist Mary Pellauer warns, "'This is a cross you must learn to bear' or 'turn the other cheek' can be deadly dimensions of traditional Christian piety in this context." Mary D. Pellauer, Barbara Chester, and Jane Boyajian, eds., *Sexual Assault and Abuse: A Handbook for Clergy and Religious Professionals* (San Francisco: HarperSanFrancisco, 1991), 55.

13. Scarsella and et al, "The Lord's Supper," 38. *Emphasis added.*

14. Susan J. Brison, *Aftermath: Violence and the Remaking of a Self* (Princeton: Princeton University Press, 2002), 17.

15. Ann Cahill, *Rethinking Rape* (Ithaca: Cornell University Press, 2001), 130.

16. Pamela Cooper-White helpfully notes that the word that Jesus most commonly uses in his teachings on forgiveness, *aphiemi*, means "letting go" or even "divorce." She writes, "Viewed in this way, [. . .] forgiveness is not a gesture of sentimentality toward the offender, but a step toward wholeness for the survivor herself. It is a releasing of all the heavy burdens of rage and hatred and moving forward in life with a new lightness of breath and step." To say to my rapist, "I forgive you" is a way of saying, "I'm done with you. We are divorced." Furthermore, this release is not something that we bring about on our own, but rather is something that is given to us gratuitously. Cooper-White explains, "There is no word in the English language that adequately describes the experience of this spiritual gift. Rather than the transitive verb 'to forgive him,' which implies an active effort, we need a word like 'to be forgiven of him,' which conveys the sense of *having been* released from pain and bitterness." Cooper-White, *The Cry of Tamar*, 258–259.

17. Cooper-White, *The Cry of Tamar*, 251.

18. Scarsella et al make it clear that, "true reconciliation—by which we mean a restoration of right relationship—between victims and perpetrators of sexual abuse is most of the time impossible." Scarsella et al., "The Lord's Supper," 36. As a result, forgiveness "is not the goal, and not even necessarily the end point of the healing process." Pastors and others who wish to support those who have suffered from sexual violence need to make it clear that "[f]orgiveness is not required of a victim. If she dies before she experiences forgiveness, she will not be consigned to hell." Cooper-White, *The Cry of Tamar*, 257.

19. Thomas Aquinas, *Summa Theologica*, trans. The Fathers of the English Dominican Province (New York: Benziger Brothers, 1947) II-II, 123–124.

20. Aquinas, *Summa Theologica*, II-II. 123.

21. As philosophical ethicist Rebecca Konyndyk DeYoung explains, "Courage, or *fortitudo*—so named from the Latin *fortis* (strong)—is the virtue most directly concerned with power and vulnerability, strength, and weakness," thus, it is appropriate to consider "courage" and its subvirtue, "endurance," when discussing how one can act with strength and integrity in the face of powerlessness and apparent lack of agency. Rebecca Konyndyk DeYoung, "Power Made Perfect in

Weakness: Aquinas's Transformation of the Virtue of Courage," *Medieval Philosophy and Theology* 11, no. 2 (Fall 2003): 150.

22. Rita Nakashima Brock and Rebecca Ann Parker, *Proverbs of Ashes: Violence, Redemptive Suffering, and the Search for What Saves Us* (Boston: Beacon Press, 2001), 27.

23. Susan Calef, "Taking Up the Cross: Suffering and Discipleship in the Gospel of Mark," in *Suffering and the Christian Life*, ed. Richard W. Miller (Maryknoll: Orbis Books, 2013), 56.

24. Edward Schillebeeckx, *Jesus: An Experiment in Christology*, trans. John Bowden, The Collected Works of Edward Schillebeeckx, Volume 6 (London: Bloomsbury/T&T Clark, 2014), 270 [302].

25. This narrative of Jesus's resistive Holy Thursday action is influenced in part by the work of Mennonite Church USA, with significant direction from theologian and activist Hilary Jerome Scarsella to rewrite their communion liturgy in response to the experiences of victims of sexual abuse. The communion liturgy highlights Jesus's creative, resistive action of "choosing to entrust his body to those who loved him" as a way to "den[y . . .] crucifixion the ability to destroy him fully." Scarsella et al., "The Lord's Supper," 45.

26. Schillebeeckx, *Jesus*, 278 [311].

27. Schillebeeckx, *Jesus*, 278 [311].

28. Schillebeeckx, *Christ*, 821 [825].

29. Cathy Winkler, "Rape as Social Murder," *Anthropology Today* 7, no. 3 (1991): 14.

30. Winkler, "Rape as Social Murder," 14.

31. Andrea Ritchie, "How Some Cops Use the Badge to Commit Sex Crimes," *Washington Post*, January 12, 2018; Emily Kassie and Hari Sreenivasan, "While in ICE Custody, Thousands of Migrants Reported Sexual Abuse," *PBS News Hour*, July 22, 2018, https://www.pbs.org/newshour/show/while-in-ice-custody-thousands-of-migrants-reported-sexual-abuse.

32. Herman, *Trauma and Recovery*, 72–73.

33. Christine Rousselle, "New Allegations Against David Haas Prompt Top Music Publisher to Sever Ties With Hymn Composer," *Catholic News Agency*, August 4, 2021, https://www.catholicnewsagency.com/news/248588/new-allegations-against-david-haas-prompt-top-music-publisher-to-sever-ties-with-hymn-composer; ELCA Worship, "When Trust Is Broken: A Response to Allegations Against Musician David Haas," *Evangelical Lutheran Church in America* (blog), November 2, 2020, https://blogs.elca.org/worship/2979/; Voices Together, "Haas Songs Removed From Voices Together Hymnal: Changes Made after Accusations of Serial Sexual Misconduct," June 23, 2020, http://voicestogetherhymnal.org/2020/06/23/haas-songs-removed-from-voices-together-hymnal/.

34. Elaine Scarry, *The Body in Pain: The Making and Unmaking of the World* (New York: Oxford University Press, 1985), 41.

35. Herman states, "Protracted depression is the most common finding in virtually all clinical studies of chronically traumatized people." Herman, *Trauma and Recovery*, 94.

36. Shannon Sullivan, *The Physiology of Sexist and Racist Oppression* (Oxford: Oxford University Press, 2015), 66–98. Herman, *Trauma and Recovery*, 86.

37. Herman, *Trauma and Recovery*, 124, 166.

38. Cahill, *Rethinking Rape*, 14, 201–207. Brison, *Aftermath*, 65, 74, 76. Wendy Rouse, *Her Own Hero: The Origins of the Women's Self-Defense Movement* (New York: New York University Press, 2017), 151–88.

39. Brison, *Aftermath*, 46.

40. Donna Freitas, *Consent: A Memoir of Unwanted Attention* (New York: Little, Brown and Company, 2019), 151.

41. Notably, even the desire to end one's own life can be an attempt to seek autonomy in "extreme circumstances" of enduring captivity. Herman argues that suicidality can function as a "sign of resistance and pride" and "not inconsistent with a general determination to survive." Herman explains, "The stance of suicide is active; it preserves an inner sense of control. As in the case of the hunger strike, the captive asserts his defiance by his willingness to end his life.". But, as Herman elaborates, "Suicidality, which sometimes served as a form of resistance during imprisonment, may persist long after release, when it no longer serves any adaptive purpose. . . . Thus, former prisoners carry their captors' hatred with them even after release, and sometimes they continue to carry out their captors' destructive purposes with their own hands." Herman, *Trauma and Recovery*, 85, 95.

42. Michael Domitrz, ed., *Voices of Courage: Inspiration from Survivors of Sexual Assault* (Greenfield: Awareness Publications, 2005), 3.

43. Roxane Gay, *Hunger: A Memoir of (My) Body* (New York: HarperCollins, 2017), 13.

44. Gay, *Hunger*, 16.

45. Mary E. Hunt, *Fierce Tenderness: A Feminist Theology of Friendship* (Minneapolis: Fortress Press, 2009).

46. Joan Miller, "Remain Here with Me," *America Magazine*, October 13, 2014.

47. Audrey Savage, *Twice Raped* (Indianapolis: Book Weaver, 1990), 11–12.

48. Savage, *Twice Raped*, 49.

49. Winkler, "Rape as Social Murder," 13.

50. Keshgegian, *Redeeming Memories*, 123.

51. Mark's account makes the economic realities most clear since, as he narrates, she "had spent all that she had, and was no better but rather grew worse." (Mk 5:26) Although economic precarity would be true of any sick and socially isolated individual.

52. Calef, "Taking Up the Cross," 60.

53. Calef, "Taking Up the Cross," 61.

54. See Marie M. Fortune, *Keeping the Faith: Guidance for Christian Women Facing Abuse* (New York: HarperCollins, 1987), 43, who explicitly links recovery from sexual violence to the recovery of the hemorrhaging woman in Luke.

55. Calef, "Taking Up the Cross," 59.

56. Bella Moon, "Silence" in *I Never Told Anyone: Writings by Women Survivors of Child Sexual Abuse*, eds. Ellen Bass and Louise Thornton (New York: Harper Perennial, 1983),156.

57. Delores Williams, *Sisters in the Wilderness: The Challenge of Womanist God-Talk* (Maryknoll: Orbis Books, 1993), 532.

58. Williams, *Sisters in the Wilderness*, 5.

59. Williams, *Sisters in the Wilderness*, 160–61.

60. Aristotle, *Nicomachean Ethics in The Basic Works of Aristotle*, ed. Richard McKeon (New York: Random House, 1941), III.6–7.

61. Aquinas, *Summa Theologica*, II-II, 123.6.

62. Aquinas, *Summa Theologica*, II-II, 123.3.

63. Konyndyk DeYoung, "Power Made Perfect," 170.

64. Konyndyk DeYoung, "Power Made Perfect," 163–64. *Emphasis in original.*

65. Keshgegian, *Redeeming Memories*, 41.

66. As Meghan McCabe has noted in a response to this portion of my argument at the 2021 annual meeting of the CTSA, virtues are habits for Aquinas. Therefore, one can assume that courage is practiced in small ways in everyday life. See *Summa Theologica*, II-II, 123.9 where Aquinas, confirming McCabe's point, explains that although courage is chiefly displayed in response to sudden dangers, it is a virtuous habit sedimented ahead of the moment of crisis. Perhaps there can be room in Aquinas's thought for unshouted courage. But, in my view, Aquinas is not explicit enough.

67. Katie G. Cannon, *Black Womanist Ethics* (Eugene: Wipf and Stock, 1988), 144.

68. Cannon, *Black Womanist Ethics*, 144.

69. Teresa of Avila, *The Book of Her Life*, trans. Kieran Kavanaugh and Otilio Rodriguez, The Collected Works of St. Teresa of Avila, Volume 1 (Washington: Institute of Carmelite Studies, 1976), 55.

70. Teresa, *The Book of Her Life*, 55.

71. Here, she uses the word "*ánimo.*"

72. As Andrew Prevot argues, "it is necessary to recognize that there are horizons of human liberation that only doxology [i.e., "receiving, offering, and desiring the glory and word of God"] can reach and yearnings of the human spirit that only God can finally satisfy. These aspects of the blessed life are such that no merely secular theory or practice could ever hope to approximate them. Prayer discloses them as nothing else can. One might consider, for example, the hope in resurrection and justice for the dead, the confidence that one is definitively loved despite the hatred of the world, the promise that sins will be forgiven and that even the most horrifically damaged relationships will be mended, and the unshakable joy that comes from an ever-deepening friendship with God. In the absence of prayer, these goods begin to

seem illusory, and, as a result, the full scope of historical and eschatological goodness is left unacknowledged. Whatever conceptions of the good may arise in non-prayerful forms of ethical discourse (which may very well be compelling in their own right), the fact remains that still more will be required in order to overcome the world's radical propensity for evil and to experience the fullness of goodness as such." Andrew Prevot, *Thinking Prayer: Theology and Spirituality Amid the Crises of Modernity* (Notre Dame: University of Notre Dame Press, 2015), 27.

73. Teresa of Avila, *Interior Castle*, trans. Kieran Kavanaugh and Otilio Rodriguez, The Collected Works of St. Teresa of Avila, Volume 2 (Washington: Institute of Carmelite Studies, 1980), 448.

74. Rowan Williams, *Teresa of Avila* (Harrisburg: Morehouse Publishing, 1991), 57.

75. Teresa, *The Book of Her Life*, 112.

76. See Edward Schillebeeckx, *God Is New Each Moment: In Conversation with Huub Oosterhuis and Piet Hoogeveen*, trans. David Smith (New York: Seabury Press, 1983), 17. Interestingly, Schillebeeckx himself cites the Carmelite John of the Cross, greatly influenced by a personal relationship with Teresa of Avila, in his discussion of mysticism and negativity. Schillebeeckx, *Church*, 68 f [70 f].

77. See, for example, Teresa who talks about feeling as if her bones have been pulled apart after an encounter with God in prayer. *The Book of Her Life*, 177–79.

78. Herman, *Trauma and Recovery*, 198–99.

79. Teresa, *Interior Castle*, 294.

80. Teresa, *The Book of Her Life*, 222.

81. Teresa, *The Book of Her Life*, 217.

82. Teresa, *The Book of Her Life*, 222, 309.

83. Even with the fullness of healing, when we can look forward to the transformation of the structural elements of rape culture, memories of violence are likely to remain.

84. Cahill, *Rethinking Rape*, 203.

85. Brison, *Aftermath*, 65.

86. Cahill, *Rethinking Rape*, 202. See Rouse on the complex sexual and racial political history of the women's self-defense movement. Rouse, *Her Own Hero*.

87. Herman, *Trauma and Recovery*, 234, reporting an interview with M. Soalt, 1990. Recall, as Herman argues, that attacked individuals who use active strategies to defend themselves are less likely to suffer severe forms of PTSD than those who do not, even if their attempts at self-defense fail to protect them from physical harm. Herman, *Trauma and Recovery*, 59.

88. Teresa, *Interior Castle*, 447. Williams, *Teresa of Avila*, 138.

89. Teresa, *Interior Castle*, 447.

90. Teresa, *Interior Castle*, 446.

91. Teresa, *Interior Castle*, 447.

92. Brison, *Aftermath*, 66.

93. Teresa, *Interior Castle*, 450. See also, 447.

94. Herman, *Trauma and Recovery*, 210. Interview with S. Simone, 1991.

95. Herman, *Trauma and Recovery*, 89.
96. Herman, *Trauma and Recovery*, 87–88.
97. Herman, *Trauma and Recovery*, 207.
98. Herman, *Trauma and Recovery*, 207.
99. Herman, *Trauma and Recovery*, 207.
100. Herman, *Trauma and Recovery*, 209.

101. See, for example, the work of Rape, Abuse, & Incest National Network (RAINN) www.rainn.org/public-policy-action.

102. See, for example, Fostering Activism and Alternatives NOW! (FAAN Mail), a media literacy project based in Philadelphia supporting "talking back" to media and creating alternatives to racist and sexist media. www.faanmail.wordpress.com.

103. See, for example Survivors Network of those Abused by Priests (SNAP) www.snapnetwork.org or Bishop Accountability www.bishop-accountability.org.

104. Herman, *Trauma and Recovery*, 76–83.
105. Nason-Clark, *The Battered Wife*, 130.

106. Christians often engage in collective action on behalf of survivors out of their fidelity to Christ's passion for the reign of God on earth as it is in heaven. For example, Nason-Clark documents a churchwomen's support for transition houses—i.e., shelters for women and children fleeing domestic abuse—and collaboration with secular child welfare services through the state. (Nason-Clark, *The Battered Wife*, 127–30, 133–34, 144–46). Even when social services are not structured by an explicit call to Christian discipleship, Christians can recognize, in any action aimed at the common good, a concrete mediation of God's saving work in the world since, as Schillebeeckx argues, "being concerned with the world and practicing human solidarity, must therefore be, for the Christian *worship* of God, glorifying God's name." Edward Schillebeeckx, *God the Future of Man*, trans. N.D. Smith, The Collected Works of Edward Schillebeeckx, Volume 3 (London: Bloomsbury/T&T Clark, 2014), 59 [99]. *Emphasis in original.*

107. Hunt, *Fierce Tenderness*, 37.
108. Herman, *Trauma and Recovery*, 29–30.

109. Of course, the love of friendship and the love of eros are not necessarily mutually exclusive. Hunt, *Fierce Tenderness*.

110. Aristotle, *Nicomachean Ethics*, VIII.1, 1155a5-6.

111. Gilbert Meilaender, *Friendship: A Study in Theological Ethics* (Notre Dame: University of Notre Dame Press, 1985), 36–52.

112. As Mary Hunt writes, "friendship is available to everyone, from the tiny baby to the oldest, sickest member of the human community" Hunt, *Fierce Tenderness*, 106.

113. Elizabeth Johnson, *She Who Is: The Mystery of God in Feminist Theological Discourse* (New York: Crossroad, 1992). 217.

114. Meilaender, *Friendship*, 14–15.

115. Teresa, *The Book of Her Life*, 96. Relatedly, Johnson argues that friendship enhances and deepens personal differences rather than eliding over them. Johnson, *She Who Is*, 217.

116. Domitrz, *Voices of Courage*, 27–28.

117. Teresa, *Interior Castle*, 448.

118. Teresa, *Interior Castle*, 449.

119. Domitrz, *Voices of Courage*, 53–54.

120. Aristotle, *Nicomachean Ethics*, VIII.1, 1155a25-28.

121. Hunt, *Fierce Tenderness*, 8.

122. Hunt, *Fierce Tenderness*, 148.

123. Hunt, *Fierce Tenderness*, 29.

124. Cannon, *Black Womanist Ethics*, 22. As Hunt elaborates, "Justice involves making friends, lots of friends, many kinds of friends. Friendship in this sense is not a cheap effort to buy freedom with flattery or treachery, pretending to be friends for personal gain when in fact some structures and conditions make friendship impossible. Rather, justice is the fundamental relational goal that issues from communities of accountability where change takes place." Hunt, *Fierce Tenderness*, 21

125. Hunt, *Fierce Tenderness*, 141.

126. Serene Jones, *Trauma and Grace: Theology in a Ruptured World* (Louisville: Westminster John Knox Press, 2009), 160.

127. Hunt, *Fierce Tenderness*, 141, 147.

128. Shelly Rambo, *Spirit and Trauma: A Theology of Remaining* (Louisville: Westminster John Knox Press, 2010), 136–37.

129. Teresa, *Interior Castle*, 450.

130. Teresa, *Interior Castle*, 450.

131. Teresa, *Interior Castle*, 449.

132. Teresa, *Interior Castle*, 450.

133. It may be the case that the women in Nason-Clark's study have not done all they could to address sexual violence in their communities. But it also needs to be acknowledged clearly that, in addition to the reality that the breadth and depth of the problem of sexual violence is too much for any one group (however organized and well-intentioned) to solve, these women's agency and effectiveness is hampered from the start by the conditions of patriarchy. Nason-Clark explains that churchwomen, especially in communities that hold traditional "family values," tend to understand their role to be "tension managers" and take on family tranquility as their primary responsibility. This means that when tranquility is not present, they feel that they have failed in their role as women. Nason-Clark argues that these conditions set up religious women for failure, since they cannot possibly resolve all tension, especially when tension is generated by another's violence. Nason-Clark, *The Battered Wife*, 130–131.

134. Nason-Clark, *The Battered Wife*, 137. *Emphasis added.*

135. Teresa, *Interior Castle*, 450.

136. Edward Schillebeeckx, *On Christian Faith: The Spiritual, Ethical, and Political Dimensions* (New York: Crossroad, 1987), 27, 19–20.

137. Edward Schillebeeckx, "Liberating Theology," in *Essays: Ongoing Theological Quests*, The Collected Works of Edward Schillebeeckx, Volume 11 (London: Bloomsbury/T&T Clark, 2014), 83.

8. Recovery and Hope

1. Judith Lewis Herman, *Trauma and Recovery* (New York: Basic Books, 1992), 211.

2. Romanus Cessario, "The Theological Virtue of Hope," in *The Ethics of Aquinas*, ed. Stephen Pope (Washington, D.C.: Georgetown University Press, 2002), 232–33.

3. Mary Catherine Hilkert, "The Threatened *Humanum* as *Imago Dei*: Anthropology and Christian Ethics," in *Edward Schillebeeckx and Contemporary Theology*, eds. Lieven Boeve et al, (London: T&T Clark, 2010), 131.

4. Edward Schillebeeckx, *Jesus: An Experiment in Christology*, trans. John Bowden, The Collected Works of Edward Schillebeeckx, Volume 6 (London: Bloomsbury/T&T Clark, 2014), 584 [622].

5. Edward Schillebeeckx, *Church: The Human Story of God*, trans. John Bowden, The Collected Works of Edward Schillebeeckx, Volume 10 (London: Bloomsbury/T&T Clark, 2014), 6 [006].

6. Edward Schillebeeckx, *God the Future of Man*, trans. N.D. Smith, The Collected Works of Edward Schillebeeckx, Volume 3 (London: Bloomsbury/T&T Clark, 2014), 45 [74].

7. Schillebeeckx, *Church*, 6 [006].

8. Schillebeeckx, *Church*, 6 [006].

9. Schillebeeckx, *God the Future of Man*, 116–17 [191–92].

10. Schillebeeckx, *God the Future of Man*, 94 [156].

11. Edward Schillebeeckx, *Interim Report on the Books Jesus and Christ*, trans. John Bowden, The Collected Works of Edward Schillebeeckx, Volume 8 (London: Bloomsbury/T&T Clark, 2014), 101.

12. Rita Nakashima Brock and Rebecca Ann Parker, *Proverbs of Ashes: Violence, Redemptive Suffering, and the Search for What Saves Us* (Boston: Beacon Press, 2001), 210.

13. Brock and Parker, *Proverbs of Ashes*, 211.

14. Edward Schillebeeckx, *Christ. The Christian Experience in the Modern World*, trans. John Bowden, The Collected Works of Edward Schillebeeckx, Volume 7 (London: Bloomsbury/T&T Clark, 2014), 821 [825].

15. Schillebeeckx, *God the Future of Man*, 95 [158]. *Emphasis added.*

16. Anthony Godzieba, Lieven Boeve, and Michele Saracino, "Resurrection—Interruption—Transformation: Incarnation as Hermeneutical Strategy," *Theological Studies* 67 (2006): 777–815.

17. Edward Schillebeeckx, "The Mystery of Injustice and the Mystery of Mercy: Questions Concerning Human Suffering," in *Tijdschrift Voor Theologie*, ed. Michael Fitzpatrick, Volume 15 (1975), 18–20 and Edward Schillebeeckx, *Christ*, 787–788 [791].

18. Schillebeeckx, *God the Future of Man*, 118 [194].

19. Brock and Parker, *Proverbs of Ashes*, 115.

20. As Schillebeeckx writes, "[The Christian] knows that it [i.e., human flourishing] has been promised to him and to the whole of mankind as a gratuitous grace, a gift which faith has inwardly to *make its own* and which must therefore begin to become a reality in our human history. The Christian knows that he receives the future to make it—he does not simply receive it as a 'present' that is given to him, but receives it to 'make it' himself, to bring it about." *God the Future of Man*, 116 [191–92], see also 117–18 [193].

21. Serene Jones, *Trauma and Grace: Theology in a Ruptured World* (Louisville: Westminster John Knox Press, 2009), 19.

22. Jones, *Trauma and Grace*, 96.

23. Jones, *Trauma and Grace*, 22.

24. Pamela Cooper-White, *The Cry of Tamar: Violence against Women and the Church's Response*, second edition (Minneapolis: Fortress Press, 2012), 13, 15.

25. Steven Rodenborn, *Hope in Action: Subversive Eschatology in the Theology of Edward Schillebeeckx and Johann Baptist Metz* (Minneapolis: Fortress Press, 2014), 102.

26. Schillebeeckx, *God the Future of Man*, 95 [157].

27. As Catholic theologian Steven Rodenborn puts it, "It is not hope itself, then, that Christ's promise uniquely engenders but rather a hope with a uniquely inexhaustible range and reach" Rodenborn, *Hope in Action*, 191.

28. Schillebeeckx, *God the Future of Man*, 48 [78].

29. Schillebeeckx, *Christ*, 766–67 [769–70].

30. I phrase it in this way, i.e., with a double negative, in order to reflect the paradoxical nature of this Christian teaching as well as to mirror the language of the Council of Trent on Justification. The decree reads, "while God touches the heart of man by the illumination of the Holy Ghost, neither is man himself utterly without doing anything while he receives that inspiration." J. Waterworth, ed., *The Council of Trent: The Canons and Decrees of the Sacred and Oecumenical Council of Trent*, trans. J. Waterworth (London: Dolman, 1848), 33.

31. Schillebeeckx, *Christ*, 763 [765].

32. Schillebeeckx, *Christ*, 767 [769].

33. Rodenborn, *Hope in Action*, 106.

34. Schillebeeckx, *God the Future of Man*, 74 [77].

35. Schillebeeckx, *Christ*, 788 [791].

36. Schillebeeckx, *God the Future of Man*, 74 [77].

37. Schillebeeckx, *God the Future of Man*, 120–21 [197–98]. See also Schillebeeckx, *Christ*, 788 [792].

38. Herman, *Trauma and Recovery*, 7.
39. Herman, *Trauma and Recovery*, 7–8.
40. Herman, *Trauma and Recovery*, 9.
41. Herman, *Trauma and Recovery*, 9. As Herman argues, it is feminist political movements which have made the recognition of common activities such as violence possible and this designation is the condition for the possibility of legal forms of accountability. She writes, "Because subordination of women and children has been so deeply embedded in our culture, the use of force against women and children has only recently been recognized as a violation of basic human rights. Widespread patterns of coercive control such as battering, stalking, sexual harassment, and acquaintance rape were not even named, let alone understood to be crimes, until they were defined by the feminist movement." Herman, *Trauma and Recovery*, 244.
42. Agustin Fuentes, "Human Evolution, Niche Complexity, and the Emergence of a Distinctively Human Imagination," *Time and Mind* 7 (2014): 241–57.
43. As Herman notes, sexual trauma is largely "without formal recognition or restitution from the community. There is no public monument for rape survivors." Herman, *Trauma and Recovery* 73.
44. Craig Steven Titus, *Resilience and the Virtue of Fortitude* (Washington, D.C.: Catholic University Press, 2006), 207, 216, citing Martin Seligman, *Learned Optimism* (New York: Pocket Books, 1998) and Richard Lazarus and Bernice Lazarus, *Passion and Reason: Making Sense of Our Emotions* (Oxford: Oxford University Press, 1994).
45. Kim Anderson and Catherine Hiersteiner, "Recovering from Childhood Sexual Abuse: Is a 'Storybook Ending' Possible?" *The American Journal of Family Therapy* 36, no. 5 (2008): 413–24.
46. Anderson and Hiersteiner, "Recovering from Childhood Sexual Abuse," 415.
47. Anderson and Hiersteiner, "Recovering from Childhood Sexual Abuse," 418.
48. Anderson and Hiersteiner, "Recovering from Childhood Sexual Abuse," 418.
49. Anderson and Hiersteiner, "Recovering from Childhood Sexual Abuse," 417.

Conclusion: A Theology of Healing

1. This is a particularly strange position for a Christian to take, given that Jesus himself is reported in the gospels to have refused such an approach. See, for example, John 9:3 where Jesus heals a man who is blind and refuses to say that the man's blindness has resulted in his sin or the sins of his ancestors.
2. See, for example, the work of Kate Bowler who describes the prosperity gospel framework that assigns illness (and other maladies) as manifestations of unconfessed sins. Kate Bowler, *Blessed: A History of the American Prosperity Gospel* (Oxford: Oxford University Press, 2013) and *Everything Happens for a Reason (and Other Lies I've Loved)* (New York: Random House, 2018), especially 14–17, 114–15.
3. Nancy Nason-Clark, *The Battered Wife: How Christians Confront Family Violence* (Louisville: Westminster John Knox Press, 1997), 46.

4. One should note that "Gertrude" is not simply a pseudonym for a woman that Nason-Clark interviewed, but rather, she is a composite sketch of several women from Nason-Clark's study drawn together for the purpose of describing patterns and themes in abused women's experiences. Nason-Clark, *The Battered Wife*, 41–42.

5. Furthermore, this can portray God as one who desires suffering in retribution for disobedience. Of the people that Nancy Nason-Clark interviewed who were currently living in abusive relationships, she describes, "from their point of view, if they had listened to God, they wouldn't be in this mess in the first place. Not unlike abused women who do not adhere to a Christian worldview, these women blame themselves for their own suffering. What distinguishes this group from non-Christian women, however, lies in their tendency to relate their own suffering to the will of God. In other words, if one disobeys God, suffering will likely result." Nason-Clark, *The Battered Wife*, 46, 49..

6. Nason-Clark, *The Battered Wife*, 46.

7. Kate Bowler has an excellent exposition of this logic in her memoir. As she writes, "When someone is drowning, the only thing worse than failing to throw them a life preserver is handing them a reason." Bowler, *Everything Happens for a Reason*, 112–13, 170.

8. Joanne C. Brown and Rebecca Ann Parker, "For God So Loved the World?" in *Christianity, Patriarchy, and Abuse: A Feminist Critique*, eds. Joanne Brown and Carole Bohn (New York: Pilgrim Press, 1989), 1.

9. Brown and Parker, "For God So Loved the World?" 2.

10. Nason-Clark, *The Battered Wife*, 52. As Hilary Scarsella et al. explain, "When the stories of Jesus' execution that we tell in our communities of faith insinuate, first, that the Christian response to egregious personal harm is to love the perpetrator, and second, that love takes its most perfect shape in death on a cross, members of our communities who are being abused can easily come to feel that in the face of our own suffering our only option is to suffer quietly." Hilary Jerome Scarsella and et al., "'The Lord's Supper: A Ritual of Harm or Healing?" *Leader* (Summer 2016): 38.

11. Edward Schillebeeckx, *Christ. The Christian Experience in the Modern World*, trans. John Bowden, The Collected Works of Edward Schillebeeckx, Volume 7 (London: Bloomsbury/T&T Clark, 2014), 718 [725].

12. Brown and Parker, "For God So Loved the World?" 27.

13. Schillebeeckx, *Christ*, 741 [746].

14. Schillebeeckx, *Christ*, 725 [731].

15. Bernard McGinn, *The Foundations of Mysticism* (New York: Crossroad, 1991), xiii-xvi. Note that McGinn himself begins his reflection on the nature of "mysticism" with a quote from Teresa of Avila. In these three sentences, Teresa flags "consciousness of the presence of God" as "mystical theology." See Teresa of Avila, *The Book of Her Life*, trans. Kieran Kavanaugh and Otilio Rodriguez, The Collected Works of St. Teresa of Avila, Volume 1 (Washington: Institute of Carmelite Studies, 1976), 105.

16. Schillebeeckx, *Christ*, 788 [792].

17. Shannon Sullivan, *The Physiology of Sexist and Racist Oppression* (Oxford University Press, 2015).

18. Judith Lewis Herman, *Trauma and Recovery* (New York: Basic Books, 1992), 109–110 and Christopher Houck, "Sexual Abuse and Sexual Risk Behavior: Beyond the Impact of Psychiatric Problems," *Journal of Pediatric Psychology* 35, no. 5 (2010): 474.

19. See Herman, *Trauma and Recovery*, 51–73. Most saliently, Herman argues that "damage to relational life is not a secondary effect of trauma, as originally thought," but rather is a primary effect of trauma.

20. James Corkery, "Jesus and Children: Images of a Loving God" in *Safeguarding: Reflecting on Child Abuse, Theology and Care*, eds. Hans Zollner et al. (Leuven: Peeters, 2018), 13.

21. Ann Cahill, *Rethinking Rape* (Ithaca: Cornell University Press, 2001), 126–27, 154–64.

22. Edward Schillebeeckx, *God the Future of Man*, trans. N.D. Smith, The Collected Works of Edward Schillebeeckx, Volume 3 (London: Bloomsbury/T&T Clark, 2014), 83 [136].

23. Schillebeeckx, *God the Future of Man*, 92 [153].

24. Schillebeeckx, *God the Future of Man*, 90 [151].

25. Jean Monroe, "From California Girl" in *I Never Told Anyone: Writings by Women Survivors of Child Sexual Abuse*, eds. Ellen Bass and Louise Thornton, *I Never Told Anyone: Writings by Women Survivors of Child Sexual Abuse* (New York: Harper Perennial, 1983), 91.

26. Jean Monroe, "From California Girl," 93.

27. Jean Monroe, "From California Girl," 102.

28. Herman, *Trauma and Recovery*, 179.

29. Michael Domitrz, ed., *Voices of Courage: Inspiration from Survivors of Sexual Assault* (Greenfield: Awareness Publications, 2005), 9–10.

30. As Herman explains in the Afterword of her classic text, written five years after the text's original publication, "Previously, many clinicians, myself included, viewed the capacity to disconnect mind from body as a merciful protection, even as a creative and adaptive psychological defense against overwhelming terror. It appears now that this rather benign view of dissociation must be reconsidered. Though dissociation offers a means of mental escape at the moment when no other escape is possible, it may be that this respite from terror is purchased at far too high a price." Herman, *Trauma and Recovery*, 239.

31. Christians have long recognized the realities of dissociation as a coping mechanism for rape. Consider, for example, the early Christian retelling of Genesis 1–6 found at Nag Hammadi, *Hypostasis of the Archons* (dated between the mid-second to the fourth century). In this narrative, the world is ruled by oppressive authorities who rape Eve. When they capture Eve, her spirit flees to a tree, but she

leaves behind a "shadowy reflection of herself," i.e., her body, for them to rape. Bentley Layton, trans. "The Hypostasis of the Archons," *The Nag Hammadi Library in English* (New York: HarperOne, 1988), 164. This dissociation of spirit and body functions as a way, in the text, to dramatize resistance to unjust domination and ridicule; that the authorities who, in their "blindness" do not notice that she has escaped and that they are not as powerful as they think they are. Yet, the text ends with no resolution to this dissociation—Eve remains split into two entities: the "carnal woman" and the "Spiritual Woman". Karen L. King, "The Book of Norea, Daughter of Eve," in *Searching the Scriptures*, Volume 2, ed. Elisabeth Schussler Fiorenza (New York: Crossroad, 1994), 70–71. In her commentary on this ancient text, Karen King relates an imaginative retelling of the story titled "Re-Creation Story," composed by participants in the southwest Presbyterian Synod's Committee on Justice for Women. In this contemporary retelling, Sophia calls forth a circle of biblical women to assist Eve in leaving the tree and returning to her body again. The women support her in mourning, calling forth anger, and ridiculing those who have violated her, thus constructing a kind of justice to which Eve previously had no access. Then, they wash her body, perfume and oil her skin, braid her hair, dress her in beautiful clothing and sing a song of love to her, and to the beauty of their own bodies. This imaginative healing ritual recreates Eve as an embodied spiritual being and ends with Sophia's proclamation, "It is very good." King, "The Book of Norea," 66–85. As one reads the *Re-Creation Story*, it is hard not to be moved by the rich reflective experience of both the third-century Christians who composed the "Hypostasis of the Archons," the later Christians who preserved the text, and the twentieth-century Christians who, in a process of "participatory hermeneutics" re-narrate the narrative. All recognize the ways in which sexual violence fractures the self, as well as the potential of Christian spirituality to resist sexual violence. Yet contemporary Christians recognize, with a particular acuity, that a posttraumatic Christian theology must frame healing as a process of rich (re)embodiment, supported by a community of loving others.

    32. Anthony Godzieba, Lieven Boeve, Michele Saracino, "Resurrection—Interruption—Transformation: Incarnation as Hermeneutical Strategy," *Theological Studies* 67 (2006): 779, partially citing Wolfgang Beinert and Francis Schüssler Fiorenza, eds., *Handbook of Catholic Theology* (New York: Crossroad, 1995), s.v. "Incarnation" (Gerhard Ludwig Müller), 377.

    33. Teresa of Avila, *Interior Castle*, trans. Kieran Kavanaugh and Otilio Rodriguez, The Collected Works of St. Teresa of Avila, Volume 2 (Washington: Institute of Carmelite Studies, 1980), 450.

    34. Schillebeeckx, *Christ*, 9 [25].

    35. Schillebeeckx, *God the Future of Man*, 95 [158].

    36. Edward Schillebeeckx, "The Mystery of Injustice and the Mystery of Mercy: Questions Concerning Human Suffering," in *Tijdschrift Voor Theologie*, ed. Michael Fitzpatrick, Volume 15 (1975), 18–20. Schillebeeckx, *Christ*, 787–88 [791].

37. Edward Schillebeeckx, *Jesus: An Experiment in Christology*, trans. John Bowden, The Collected Works of Edward Schillebeeckx, Volume 6 (London: Bloomsbury/T&T Clark, 2014) 278 [311].

38. Rita Nakashima Brock and Rebecca Ann Parker, *Proverbs of Ashes: Violence, Redemptive Suffering, and the Search for What Saves Us* (Boston: Beacon Press, 2001), 249–50.

39. Matthew narrates the women encountering Jesus on the road, as they begin to faithfully carry out the directive to share the news of the resurrection with the disciples (Mt 28:9).

40. John's account is not quite as straightforward, but ultimately refers to the reality that the risen Jesus is encountered in the community of his friends. In John, Mary Magdalene recognizes Jesus as her Rabbi when he addresses her by name. (Jn, 20:16–18). But, as Sandra Schneiders notes, this is not a full recognition of Jesus as risen. She explains, "Mary recognizes him as her Teacher. But she is still struggling out of the darkness of her pre-paschal literalism into the light of Easter. Jesus forestalls her attempt to touch him, to encounter him in the flesh as his disciples could and did prior to his Glorification. . . . Jesus, glorified on the cross, has indeed gone to the Father, but in Mary's perception he has not yet ascended, for she has not yet integrated the fact that he has also been glorified into her realization that Jesus is risen. Jesus redirects her to the community of his brothers and sisters, which is, in a mysterious way, his glorified body." Sandra Schneiders, *Jesus Risen in Our Midst: Essays on the Resurrection of Jesus in the Fourth Gospel* (Collegeville: Liturgical Press, 2013), 87. Subsequent recognitions of Jesus in John follow a more straightforwardly similar structure to the one I am suggesting above.

41. Thus, as Elizabeth Johnson argues, "Jesus-Sophia is the incarnation of divine friendship, hosting meals of inclusive table community and being hospitable to people of all kinds, even responding to prodding to widen his circle of care, as in the case of the Canaanite woman whose daughter was ill (Mt 15:21–28). He calls the women and men of his circle not children, not servants, not even disciples, but friends (Jn 15:15)." Elizabeth Johnson, *She Who Is: The Mystery of God in Feminist Theological Discourse* (New York: Crossroad, 1992), 217.

42. As Schillebeeckx writes, "this table fellowship in itself, sharing a meal with Jesus, is an offer here and now of eschatological salvation." *Jesus*, 192 [218]. Consequently, "Jesus' call seems to be fundamentally connected with communion at table, eating and drinking together with Jesus," and an openness to this transformative food-sharing that is, itself, an instantiation of the kingdom of God where God delights in friendship with us and among us. *Jesus*, 179 [204].. Therefore, in one practice, "Jesus [both] proclaimed salvation to come, at the same time making it present by his conduct." *Jesus*, 132 [152].

43. I do not mean for "the table" to stand, today, exclusively for the celebration of the Eucharist in a religiously institutional setting. It may include that, but it may just as easily be exclusive of this, particularly as practices of the Eucharist embody sexualized forms of violence themselves. See Hilary Jerome Scarsella, "Victimization via Ritualization: Christian Communion and Systems of Sexualized Violence," in

Trauma and Lived Religion: Transcending the Ordinary, eds. R. Ruard Ganzevoort and Srdjan Sremac (London: Palgrave MacMillan, 2019), 225–52.

44. Schillebeeckx, *Jesus*, 305–6, 348–49 [336, 381].

45. Schillebeeckx, *Jesus*, 191 [216–17].

46. Schillebeeckx, *Jesus*, 300 [331].

47. Schneiders, *Jesus Risen in Our Midst*, 82.

48. Schneiders, *Jesus Risen in Our Midst*, 89.

49. Here, I do not mean to suggest that the hierarchical, institutional Church is the site of revelation of the risen Jesus today. Instead, I am arguing that it is Church as community that has the capacity to symbolically express the risen Jesus. See Schneiders, *Jesus Risen in Our Midst*, 90.

50. Eugene LaVerdiere, *Dining in the Kingdom of God: The Origins of the Eucharist According to Luke* (Chicago: Liturgy Training Publications, 1994), 18–20, 192.

51. Schillebeeckx, *Jesus*, 321 [352].

52. Schneiders, *Jesus Risen in Our Midst*, 91. John 20:23.

53. Serene Jones, *Trauma and Grace: Theology in a Ruptured World* (Louisville: Westminster John Knox Press, 2009), 159.

54. Johnson, *She Who Is*, 217.

55. Herman, *Trauma and Recovery*, 70.

56. Marie M. Fortune, *Sexual Violence: The Unmentionable Sin* (New York: Pilgrim Press, 1983), 222.

57. Rachel Waltner Goossen, "'Defanging the Beast': Mennonite Responses to John Howard Yoder's Sexual Abuse," *Mennonite Quarterly Review* 89 (January 2015): 10.

58. "AMBS Board Statement of Commitment. Service of Lament, Confession and Commitment, March 25, 2015" *Anabaptist Mennonite Biblical Seminary*, https://campussuite-storage.s3.amazonaws.com/prod/11168/c72da489-1ca3-11e6-b537-22000bd8490f/837505/4e72a8f5-ed6c-11e6-884f-22000bd8490f/file.

59. "Sexual Misconduct Policy and Procedures," *Anabaptist Mennonite Biblical Seminary*, https://ambs.edu/wp-content/uploads/2021/12/Sexual-Misconduct-Policy-and-Procedures-.pdf. "AMBS Board Statement of Commitment."

60. Goossen, "'Defanging the Beast,'" 30–31. Rachel Waltner Goossen, "Mennonite Bodies, Sexual Ethics: Women Challenge John Howard Yoder," *Journal of Mennonite Studies* 34 (2016): 251–53.

61. Herman, *Trauma and Recovery*, 29–30.

62. Edward Schillebeeckx, "Erfahrung und Glaube," in *Christerlicher Glaube in moderner Gesellschaft*, eds. F. Böckle, F.-X. Kaufmann, K. Rahner, and B. Welte, Volume 25 (Frieburg: Herder, 1980), 99 f. Schillebeeckx, *Jesus*, 121 [141].

63. Victims of sexual abuse—especially those who experience abuse within their families, religious communities, or educational settings—often risk dissolving the very bonds upon which they depend if they resist abuse. Herman, *Trauma and Recovery*, 62.

Index

agency, 14–15, 17, 24, 55, 70, 100–1, 108, 124, 126–39, 173–74
anger, 61–62, 111, 142
Ahlgren, Gillian, 37, 42, 43, 46–48, 79, 82

Beste, Jennifer, 16, 23–24
Bilinkoff, Jodi, 31–46,
Bowler, Kate, 167
Brison, Susan, 22–23, 39, 49, 85, 130, 132, 142, 143–45
Brock, Rita Nakashima, 106, 175
Brown, Raymond, 23
Brownmiller, Susan, 10

Cahill, Ann, 12–13, 22–23, 125, 142
Calef, Susan, 135
Cannon, Katie, 138–39
confession, sacrament of, 2
Cooper-White, Pamela, 71, 159, 217, 219
courage, 19, 40, 53, 55, 63–64, 77, 124–52; Jesus as model of, 127–29; Teresa of Avila as model of, 139
cross, 104, 151, 174

death of Jesus, 103–9, 127–29
divine judgement, 94, 95, 110, 121

eating together, 105–6, 109, 116–18, 128–29, 176–77. *See also* table fellowship

endurance, 40, 54, 63, 77, 124–51, 156, 161
eros, 65–66
eschatological healing, 3, 7, 19–22, 24–25, 98–101, 114–15, 149–50
eschatological hope, 21–22, 60–61, 67, 123–24, 144, 151, 152–63; Jesus and model of, 156; in contrast to optimism, 162–63
experience as trustworthy, 25, 29–30, 42, 96–98, 157, 172–73

forgiveness, 18, 84, 124–26
Fortune, Marie, 13–14, 217–18
freedom, 35. *See also* Teresa of Avila and holy freedom
Freitas, Donna, 81, 132
friendship 18, 43, 65, 133, 146–51, 176–77; political love and, 85, 147–51; with God, 38, 41, 48, 53, 62–68, 77, 80, 83–85, 116, 139–41, 148; with others, 38, 43–44, 78, 80, 83–84, 85–87, 140–41
Fullam, Lisa, 32, 42, 53, 65, 75, 85

Gay, Roxane, 81, 132–33
God as pure positivity, 93–98, 102, 108, 120
Godzieba, Anthony, 23, 173
Goossen, Rachel Waltner, 177–78
Grovijahn, Jane, 51, 52, 77, 82

Hagar, 136
"healing" language, critique of, 20, 162–63, 175
Hemorrhaging Woman, 135–36
Herman, Judith Lewis, 2, 8–9, 14–21, 25, 61–62, 63, 65, 78–79, 87, 123, 130–31, 145, 161, 172, 177
Hilkert, Mary Catherine, 154
Hubbard, Shanita, 11–12
humility, 74–77
Hunt, Mary, 147, 149
hysteria, 28–29

imagination, 61, 119, 135, 154, 159–62
incarnational healing, 3, 7, 22, 25, 49, 115, 157, 168–75
incarnational mysticism, 25, 50–68, 71, 101–2, 118–20, 169

Jones, Serene, 54, 104, 159

Keshgegian, Flora, 23–24, 134, 137
Kingdom of God, 116, 178
Konyndyk De Young, Rebecca, 137

Last Supper, 105–6, 128–29, 178
legal accountability, 16–17, 117, 126, 130–31
liturgy, 112–13, 125

MacKinnon, Catharine, 117
Martha and Mary, 67, 119–20, 148
martyrdom, 136–37, 140
Mazzoni, Cristina, 28–30
McCabe, Megan K., 117
McGinn, Bernard, 169
Medwick, Cathleen, 28, 32–33, 38, 42–45
Moltmann, Jürgen, 22–23
mourning, 15–19, 64, 80, 121, 133
Mujica, Barbara, 57, 82
mystical-political, 3, 26, 91–92, 117–22, 148, 178

Nason-Clark, Nancy, 146, 150–51, 218–19

Parker, Rebecca Ann, 77, 112–13, 155–56, 158, 168, 175
Pellauer, Mary, 12, 23, 125
political love, 118
prayer, 14, 54–68, 70, 73–74, 83–85, 87, 119, 156; as an embodied (or incarnational) practice, 28, 31, 49–68; and courage, 139–51; as exploration, 70–72; as irrigation, 34–35, 60, 70; as mystical flight, 27–28, 118; and pleasure, 52

Rambo, Shelly, 24–25, 39, 149
rape culture, 10–14, 22, 26, 117, 119, 123, 141, 144–46, 150, 159–60, 170, 178
restitution, 16–17, 18, 21, 26, 116, 130–31, 177–78
resurrection, 22–23, 25–26, 95, 109–11, 117, 155–57, 178; an eschatological (or transformative) model of the, 19–20, 22–25, 157

Savage, Audrey, 11, 34, 134
Scarry, Elaine, 8–9, 131
Scarsella, Hilary Jerome, 74, 75–76, 128–29, 217
Schillebeeckx, Edward: Abba experience and, 105–6, 108, 129, 156; anthropological constants and, 98–101; negative contrast experiences and, 95–98, 104–6, 122, 153–54, 171–72; senseless suffering and, 2, 4, 23, 54, 90–95, 103, 106–9, 168
Schneiders, Sandra, 175–77
Schüssler Fiorenza, Elisabeth, 119
self-care, 50, 55–60, 65, 73–74, 84
self-defense, 131–32, 142–43
self-hatred, 32, 50, 56–60
self-knowledge, 71–82, 84
shame, 2, 18, 32–35, 64–68, 72–74, 78, 81, 99, 133, 170, 172
Shengold, Leonard, 12–13
sin, 71, 74, 75–76, 81–82, 102
Slade, Carole, 28, 30, 40, 43–44, 46
Soalt, Melissa, 142–43
social action, 18, 43–44, 61, 65–67, 79, 85, 118–20, 143–51, 161–62, 174–75. See also survivor mission
social healing, 16–19, 43–44, 100, 116, 133, 141, 143–44
social murder, rape as, 12, 39
Soughers, Tara, 82–83
soul healing, 50–51, 115–16, 120, 122
soul murder, rape as, 12–13
suffering as God's will, 1, 53–54, 90, 106–9, 118, 166–68
Sullivan, Shannon, 36, 40
survivor mission, 18, 65–67, 109–10, 127, 144–46. See also social action

table fellowship, 105–6, 109, 116–18, 128–29, 176–77. *See also* eating together
Teresa of Avila: and "holy freedom," 35, 37, 41, 43–48; and illness, 31–32, 36, 52; and Jewish ancestry, 32–34, 43, 46, 48; as narrator of her own experience, 30–31, 33–34, 41–42

Tertullian, 52
Thomas Aquinas, 136–38
Tobin, Theresa, 10, 112

Weber, Alison, 42
Williams, Delores, 136
Williams, Rowan, 79, 83, 85, 88
Winkler, Cathy, 12, 39, 84–85, 130, 134

Julia Feder is the Assistant Director of the Center for the Study of Spirituality and Associate Professor of Religious Studies and Theology at Saint Mary's College in Notre Dame, Indiana. Her research focuses on theological anthropology, theologies of suffering, and human evolution. Her essays have been published in *Theological Studies, Horizons,* the *Journal of Moral Theology,* the *Journal of Religion and Society, Anthropology News,* and *Philosophy, Theology, and the Sciences.*

www.ingramcontent.com/pod-product-compliance
Lightning Source LLC
Chambersburg PA
CBHW020404080526
44584CB00014B/1161